KU-713-040

Contents at a Glance

Table of Contents

My Microsoft® Windows® 7 PC

Katherine Murray

QUE®

My Microsoft® Windows® 7 PC

Copyright © 2012 by Pearson Education, Inc.

ISBN-13: 978-0-7897-4895-9
ISBN-10: 0-7897-4895-9

Library of Congress Cataloging-in-Publication Data is on file.

Printed in the United States of America

First Printing: October 2011

Trademarks

All terms mentioned in this book that are known to be trademarks or service marks have been appropriately capitalized. Que Publishing cannot attest to the accuracy of this information. Use of a term in this book should not be regarded as affecting the validity of any trademark or service mark.

Warning and Disclaimer

Every effort has been made to make this book as complete and as accurate as possible, but no warranty or fitness is implied. The information provided is on an "as is" basis. The author and the publisher shall have neither liability nor responsibility to any person or entity with respect to any loss or damages arising from the information contained in this book.

Bulk Sales

Que Publishing offers excellent discounts on this book when ordered in quantity for bulk purchases or special sales. For more information, please contact

U.S. Corporate and Government Sales

1-800-382-3419

corpsales@pearsontechgroup.com

For sales outside of the U.S., please contact

International Sales

international@pearson.com

EDITOR-IN-CHIEF
Greg Wiegand

ACQUISITIONS EDITOR
Loretta Yates

MARKETING MANAGER
Dan Powell

DEVELOPMENT EDITOR
Todd Brakke

MANAGING EDITOR
Kristy Hart

SENIOR PROJECT EDITOR
Lori Lyons

COPY EDITOR
Chuck Hutchinson

INDEXER
Tim Wright

PROOFREADER
Sheri Cain

TECHNICAL EDITOR
Sharon Fields

PUBLISHING
COORDINATOR
Cindy Teeters

BOOK DESIGNER
Anne Jones

COMPOSITOR
Bronkella Publishing LLC

About the Author

Katherine Murray has been writing about technology since before Microsoft Windows—*any* Microsoft Windows—even existed. She's worked with every consumer version of Windows that has ever been made, marveling with the masses at Windows 3.1, swearing at Windows ME, enjoying Windows XP, and threatening to throw her computer off the roof, thanks to Windows Vista. Now with Windows 7, she feels we have arrived at a sleek, smart, reasonably lightweight operating system that does pretty much what most users need it to do. She started writing about technology 24 years ago and still enjoys it, specializing in Microsoft Office technologies and the fascinating ways in which we stay in touch with each other through cloud technology, blogging, social media, and more. You'll find Katherine's blog, BlogOffice, at www.murrayblogoffice.blogspot.com. In addition to writing books, she writes regularly for CNET's TechRepublic and Windows Secrets.

Dedication

This book is dedicated to the folks who just want their computers to work, simply and easily, so they can get on with the really fun things in life (like grandchildren!).

Acknowledgments

Most creative projects require the talents and know-how of a number of people, and this is certainly true in the world of book publishing. Many thanks to the whole crew at Que Publishing for their insight, encouragement, and great editing all the way through *My Microsoft Windows 7 PC*. Special thanks to Loretta Yates for thinking of me for this project and to Laura Norman, series editor, for her experience and good suggestions on practical preparations for this project. I also greatly appreciate the expertise of Todd Brakke, development editor; Lori Lyons, project editor; Chuck Hutchinson, copy editor; and Sharon Fields, technical editor, who helped ensure that everything you find in the book is accurate and easy to read.

It's been a real pleasure for me to come back to Que and write after all these years. My career in technical writing began at Que way back in 1987 (really!), when I wrote *Using PFS: First Publisher*. The world has changed since then, but it's great to see that Que's caring about quality has been a constant all the way along.

We Want to Hear from You!

As the reader of this book, *you* are our most important critic and commentator. We value your opinion and want to know what we're doing right, what we could do better, what areas you'd like to see us publish in, and any other words of wisdom you're willing to pass our way.

As Editor-in-Chief for Que Publishing, I welcome your comments. You can email or write me directly to let me know what you did or didn't like about this book—as well as what we can do to make our books better.

Please note that I cannot help you with technical problems related to the topic of this book. We do have a User Service group, however, where I will forward specific technical questions related to the book.

When you write, please be sure to include this book's title and author as well as your name, email address, and phone number. I will carefully review your comments and share them with the author and editors who worked on the book.

Email: feedback@quepublishing.com

Mail: Greg Wiegand
          Editor-in-Chief
          Que Publishing
          800 East 96th Street
          Indianapolis, IN 46240 USA

Reader Services

Visit our website and register this book at quepublishing.com/register for convenient access to any updates, downloads, or errata that might be available for this book.

Introduction

If you're new to computers (or even if you're not), you might not be too familiar with what your operating system can do for you. Many people purchase their computers with a specific set of tasks in mind. You want to check email, update your favorite social media sites, and browse and shop online. Or you plan to use your home computer to work on the files from work you're not quite finished with. Or maybe you're interested in organizing your photos, music, or videos in a way that makes them easy to find later.

In this book, you'll learn how to use Windows 7 to do all these things—and more—on your Windows 7 PC. We'll begin with a simple introduction to your machine, and soon you'll know how to connect various devices to your system and get Windows 7 talking to them. Throughout the rest of this book, you'll learn how to accomplish all the other basic tasks you'd like to master with Windows 7, including setting up security and privacy measures for your system, finding files, preparing media, working with pictures, networking your home computers, and much, much more.

Highlights of Windows 7

Windows 7 gives you a simple, streamlined way to work with the programs, files, and settings on your computer. As you'll learn in more detail in Chapter 1, the screen is easy to understand and navigate, and mouse and keyboard techniques are easy to learn. The familiar Start menu has been enhanced to give you easy access to programs and files of all sorts, and the taskbar, along the bottom of your window for starters, makes it simple to choose the file and program you want to work with.

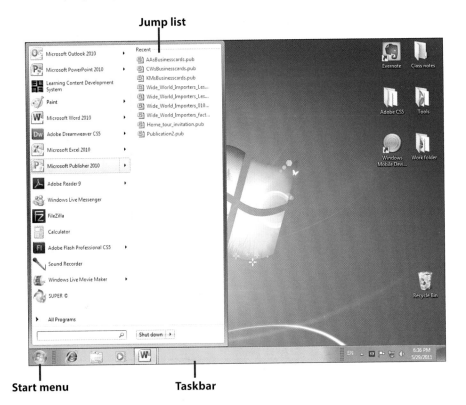

Jump list

Start menu   Taskbar

Windows 7 includes several features that make getting to the files and pro-grams you want—or enjoying music, movies, or pictures on your computer—easier than ever. These new features include

- Jump lists, which enable you to move directly to a file you want when you click a program icon—either in the Start menu or on the taskbar

- Taskbar previews, which show you a thumbnail image of the file when you hover the mouse pointer over the application icon on the taskbar

- Snap, Shake, and Peek, which make it simple for you to view and arrange open windows

- Homegroups, which give you a way to easily share files and printers on a home network

- Remote Media Streaming, which lets you listen to or watch the media on your home PC no matter where you are by connecting over the Internet

- Play To, which enables you to play music or movies on another computer or device in your home

- Touch capability, which lets you use the touch capability of your monitor to point to, open, select, and even paint images on the screen

You'll find these features covered throughout this book in the appropriate chapters. Note that to be able to take advantage of some of the features—such as Homegroups, Remote Media Streaming, or touch capability—you must have other computers connect to your Windows 7 PC or home network, or use a touch-capable device.

Versions of Windows 7

Windows 7 is available in several different editions, each of which offers capabilities related to what you want to accomplish with your PC:

- Windows 7 Starter is available on netbook computers. It is a lightweight version of Windows 7 that makes it easy to connect to wireless networks, add and set up devices, and work with the programs and files you need.

- Windows 7 Home Premium is designed to shine a spotlight on all your media, while giving you access to all the programs and files you need. You can easily set up a home network, watch and record Internet TV, and share music and media.

- Windows 7 Professional is geared toward the business user, offering a reliable and secure experience and making it easy to add devices and back up your files.

- Windows 7 Ultimate combines the features of Home Premium and Professional with enhanced security features such as BitLocker, which can protect your files against loss or theft.

Oranges to Oranges

If you want to compare the different versions of Windows 7 to see which edition works best for you, visit www.windows.microsoft.com.

What You'll Find in This Book

This book takes a practical and visual approach to showing you just the tasks you need to know to make the most of your Windows 7 PC. You'll find out how to set up, manage, and secure your hardware and software and discover ways to customize Windows 7 so that it works the way you do. Specifically, here's what you'll find:

- Chapter 1, "Getting Started with Windows 7," introduces you to Windows 7 and demonstrates how to use the Start menu and taskbar. You'll also learn how to use the mouse and keyboard, find out how windows operate, and find out how to get help.

- Chapter 2, "Preparing Your Windows 7 PC," shows you how to transfer your files and get everything set up and ready to roll in Windows 7. You'll also set up your printer, make sure you have Internet access, and learn about managing your PC's power.

- Chapter 3, "Getting and Staying Connected: Phones, Devices, and Tablets," shows you how to set up and manage devices with your Windows 7 PC.

- Chapter 4, "Securing Your Windows 7 PC," introduces you to the Action Center and shows you the ins and outs of setting passwords, creating user accounts, updating your security settings, turning on a firewall, backing up your files, and creating trusted contacts.

- Chapter 5, "Find What You're Looking For—Fast!" takes a close look at all the techniques you need for searching for specific files on your computer. You'll learn how to tailor your search to get accurate results and search on various file properties as needed.

- Chapter 6, "Exploring, Downloading, and Running Programs," begins by exploring the Windows 7 gadgets already installed on your Windows 7 PC. You'll also discover how to locate and launch a program, create a program shortcut, use the Task Manager, download a program from the Internet, and install and run programs.

- Chapter 7, "Organizing Files and Folders," starts off with coverage of the new Windows 7 libraries and then shows you how to add and remove folders in Windows Explorer. You'll also learn about changing file views, previewing files and folders, hiding folders, and sharing files in a variety of ways.

- Chapter 8, "Doing the Web Thing (Plus Email and Calendars, Too)," takes you online with Internet Explorer 8 and goes through the basics of secure browsing. You'll learn to work with multiple web pages, view Quick Tabs, add pages to your favorites list, and learn what web slices are all about.

- Chapter 9, "Ready, Set, Media!" introduces you to all things media on your Windows PC. You'll learn about Windows Media Player and Windows Media Center, find out how to sync media with your phone, discover how to create audio CDs, stream your media, change video display modes, record sound, make movies, and much more.

- Chapter 10, "Cataloging and Fine-Tuning Your Photos," helps you download your pictures to your PC and view them in your Pictures Library and in the Windows Photo Viewer. You'll find out how to create a Picture Slide Show; tag the photo files; and organize, share, and print your pictures.

- Chapter 11, "Personalizing Windows 7," shows you how you can tweak Windows 7 so that it fits the way you like to work and play. Choose a new theme, change your desktop, adjust the color scheme and font size, customize the way your mouse works, and add new alert sounds if you like.

- Chapter 12, "Connecting to a Network," explores how to create a new home network, add other PCs and a printer, and learn to share files among your computers. You also learn how to create a network connection, log on to available networks, and manage your network connections.

- Chapter 13, "Windows 7 Care, Feeding, and Troubleshooting," wraps up the book with information about how to upgrade your version of Windows 7, install and uninstall programs, and problem-solve any challenges you may be having with your PC. You'll also learn about the various diagnostic tools that are part of Windows 7 so that you can check your system regularly and keep things running smoothly.

The chapters are organized so that you can jump in and read about whatever interests you most, or you can choose to go through the book sequentially if you like. Along the way, you'll find tips, notes, and two kinds of sidebars: Go Further, which gives you additional information about getting more from the topic at hand, and It's Not All Good, which lists common pitfalls and trouble spots you can watch out for.

Let's Begin

If you have a new PC that you haven't yet set up, go ahead and unbox it and follow the instructions in the system to connect the system unit, monitor, keyboard, and mouse. You can also connect your printer if you have one. Have the disc that came with your computer handy. The first time you press the Power button, Windows 7 will start. The screen will likely walk you through a number of steps as your computer is configured for the first time. Follow along with the onscreen prompts and provide information as needed. When the desktop appears, with the Windows 7 Start button in the lower-left corner, you're ready to begin.

When you're ready, turn the page and let's get started exploring your Windows 7 PC!

With Windows 7, you can watch video clips,

find the files you need,

and work with your programs all on the same desktop.

In this chapter, you learn how to unbox your Windows 7 PC, start your computer, and begin working with Windows 7 with tasks such as

→ Starting Windows 7
→ Using the Start menu
→ Learning the taskbar
→ Navigation basics: Using the mouse and keyboard
→ Working with Windows
→ Getting the help you need

Getting Started with Windows 7

How exciting! Chances are, you have just purchased—or inherited—a new Windows 7 computer, and you are ready to learn how to get the operating system to do what you want it to do. Whether your new system arrived by UPS or you brought it home from the store yourself, your first major task involves unboxing the computer and getting everything set up. After everything is connected, you can push the Power button and begin to see Windows 7 do its stuff. This chapter is all about some of the basic tasks you'll want to do right off the bat when you begin using Windows 7.

>> Go Further

CHOOSE YOUR WINDOWS 7 EDITION

As you were doing your computer shopping, chances are you learned there are several versions of Windows 7 currently available. Depending on the type of computer you bought, your new system may have **Windows 7 Home Premium,** which gives you a great experience if you're interested in photos, videos, music, and more; **Windows 7 Professional**, which enables you to ramp up your productivity and secure your data; or **Windows 7 Ultimate**, which combines the media and entertainment talents of Home Premium with the business-class features of Windows 7 Professional.

If you have a netbook computer, **Windows 7 Starter** is likely the version of Windows 7 you have. Designed to be fast and easy to use, Windows 7 Starter includes flexible features that help you find what you need as quickly as possible, but it also has some limitations. You aren't able to customize your desktop image or change the color scheme, for example. But the trade-off is that you have a lightweight, fast operating system that works well on your small-imprint PC.

Starting and Stopping Windows 7

Depending on the type of new PC you have, setting up the system may be as simple as taking the computer out of the box, plugging in the power cord, and pressing the Power button. If you have a desktop computer, you need to use the cables to connect the system unit and monitor (as well as any other components you may have, such as speakers and a printer or scanner), but the process is simple (you just can't plug computer cables in the wrong spots on your system, no matter how hard you try).

When the hardware is ready, your next step is to find and press the Power button and watch your computer come to life. Windows 7 makes the whole process super easy for you. The first time your computer starts, it will likely walk you through a series of steps helping you personalize the program and set up your preferences.

Upgrading

If you haven't purchased a new Windows 7 PC but you are upgrading from
Windows Vista to Windows 7 or from one version of Windows 7 to another, you
can go to the Windows Anytime Upgrade site (http://windows.microsoft.com/
en-US/windows7/products/windows-anytime-upgrade) to get upgrade instructions, watch videos, and compare features among the different Windows 7
versions.

Starting Windows 7

One of the nice things about your operating system is that it is built to be
working the entire time your computer is turned on. That means powering
up your computer and starting Windows 7 are basically the same event. You
may have to take one or two additional steps, depending on how many users
are set up to work with your PC and whether you have assigned a password
to your account. (You learn how to add a password in Chapter 4, "Securing
Your Windows 7 PC.")

1. Press your computer's Power button.

2. Click your username to log on.

3. Enter your password if you assigned one and press Enter.

4. Review the various elements on the Windows 7 window.

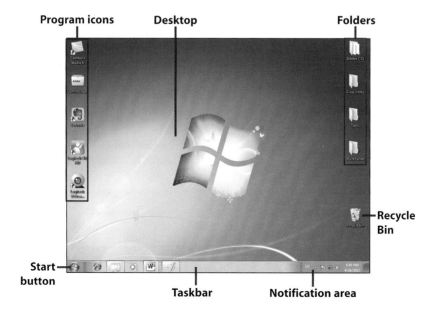

Program icons   **Desktop**   **Folders**

Recycle Bin

Start button   **Taskbar**   **Notification area**

Putting Your Windows 7 PC to Sleep

When you're going to be away from your computer for a period of time but you don't plan—quite yet—to turn everything off for the day, you can put your computer in Sleep mode to conserve energy and protect your files and programs while you're away.

1. Click the Start button on the far left side of the Windows 7 taskbar.

2. Click the arrow to the right of the Shut Down button.

3. Click Sleep.

Wake Up, Little Fella

One of the great things about Sleep mode is that it is designed to help your computer spring back to life quickly as soon as you're ready. So even though it's a little distressing to see everything fade to black so fast after you click Sleep, you'll be pleased to know that a wiggle of the mouse or the press of a key will reanimate your PC.

Learn More About Conserving PC Power

In Chapter 2, "Preparing Your Windows 7 PC," you learn how to set a number of preferences for the ways you want Windows 7 to operate. One of those options involves choosing how you want the program to conserve energy use. You can specify when you want the system to go to sleep, how long you want the display to be active if no one is using the computer, and so on.

Shutting Down Windows 7

When you're ready to power down your computer, you return to the Shut Down button at the bottom of the Start menu.

1. Click the Start button.

2. Click the Shut Down button. If you have any open, unsaved files, Windows 7 prompts you to save them before shutting down.

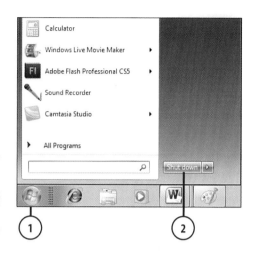

Using the Start Menu

Much of what you'll do in Windows 7 begins in the Start menu. Whether you want to launch a new program, find a specific file, install a new printer, or change the way you organize your media files, you'll find that the tools you need are just a click away.

Finding What You Need on the Start Menu

The Start menu gives you access to the programs on your computer and makes it easy for you to get to the programs you use most often. You can also get to your file libraries, view system information, install programs, and get help from the Start menu.

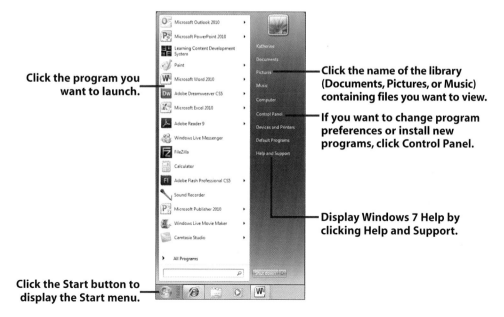

Click the program you want to launch.

Click the name of the library (Documents, Pictures, or Music) containing files you want to view.

If you want to change program preferences or install new programs, click Control Panel.

Display Windows 7 Help by clicking Help and Support.

Click the Start button to display the Start menu.

Find Your Favorite Files

You can display files saved in your My Documents folder by clicking your username at the top of the library list.

Locating the Program You're Looking For

Programs pinned to the Start menu

When you first begin using your computer, you may not have too many programs installed, so finding the program you want to use may not be much of a hassle. But over time, you will likely add programs, utilities, games, and more, and then finding a particular program may require a bit of scrolling. By default, Windows 7 displays the most recently used programs at the top of the Start menu, where they are easiest to find. The rest of the programs on your computer are stored in the All Programs folder at the bottom of the programs list.

1. Click Start to open the Start menu.

2. Click All Programs.

3. Scroll down and click the folder with the program you want to run.

4. Click the program name.

5. Click Back to return to the Start menu list.

Pinned for Good

After you pin a program to the Start menu, the program icon appears above the dividing line at the top of the Start menu list. Now you can find the program easily whenever you click Start.

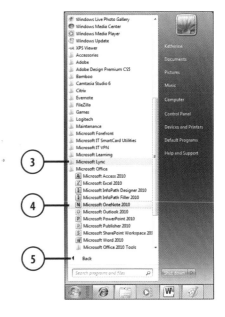

BIG ICONS, SMALL ICONS

Windows 7 knows that your comfort zone—when it comes to the way your desktop appears—has a lot to do with how much you enjoy working with your computer (or not). For that reason, Windows 7 enables you to make lots of custom changes so that you can control the way items appear onscreen.

When you first begin using the Start menu, you'll notice that the icons on the Start menu list are large and easy to see. When you click All Programs, the program icons are smaller and look like folders in a list. You can change the default way Windows 7 displays these program choices by making them smaller. To do this, click Start and then right-click the blank area of the Start menu above the Shut Down button. Click Properties and then click Customize; scroll down the list until you see Use Large Icons. Click the box to clear the check and click OK. Now the program icons in the Start menu appear smaller, like the icons in the All Programs list.

Pinning a Program to the Start Menu

You probably have a few programs you use regularly. Instead of searching for those programs by scrolling through the long list, you can simply pin the program icons to the top of the Start menu.

1. Click Start.

2. Right-click the program you want to pin to the Start menu.

3. Click Pin to Start Menu.

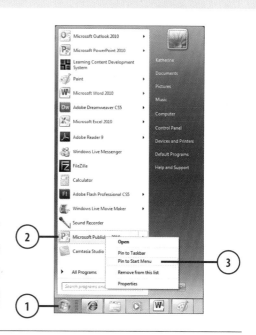

Unpinning Your Unfavorites

If you're finished working with a particular program—or you simply found one you like better—and want to remove the program from its pinned place on the Start menu, click Start, right-click the program icon, and click Unpin from Start Menu. The program returns to its position, alphabetized in the All Programs list, where you can find it easily the next time you need it.

It's Not All Good

But You're All My Favorites!

Whoever first said, "You can get too much of a good thing" was on to something. Sure, pinning programs to the Start menu is a nice timesaving feature. But if you pin everything you use to the Start menu—and increase the number of items displayed there so you can get them all in—you create that same I-can't-find-what-I-need experience for yourself that you can get from the All Programs menu.

If you find that you're scrolling through the list when you should just be able to point and click, remove the programs you don't use often and streamline the content displayed in the Start menu. It will make getting into your favorite programs a much cleaner experience.

Using Jump Lists

You'll notice that some of the programs on your Start menu display arrows on the right side of the program name. These handy little pointers mean there is a *jump list* available for that program which will display the files you've most recently viewed, edited, or created using that program.

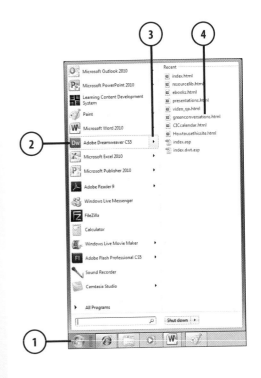

1. Click Start to open the Start menu.

2. Locate the program you used to work with the files you want to see.

3. Hover the mouse pointer over the arrow to the right of the program name. The recent files appear on the right side of the Start menu.

4. To open a file, click it. The program launches, and the file is displayed on your desktop.

How High Do You Want to Jump?

By default, Windows 7 displays in your jump lists the 10 most recent files that you have created or modified with the program you're pointing to. You can change that number—and make it larger or smaller—by clicking Start, right-clicking the blank area over the Shut Down button, clicking Properties, clicking Customize, and increasing or decreasing the value in the Number of Recent Items to Display in Jump Lists setting at the bottom of the Customize Start Menu dialog box. Click OK twice to get back to your desktop and check it out.

Jumping Off the Taskbar

Windows 7 also includes jump lists when you have multiple documents open on your Taskbar so that you can move quickly jump from one open window to another. Suppose, for example, that you have several pages open in Internet Explorer; you can position the mouse pointer on the IE icon to display a jump list of available pages and then click the one you want to view.

Learning the Taskbar

The taskbar is the place on your Windows 7 desktop where you work with open programs, move among files you are using, and find out about program updates and the status of system processes. By default, the taskbar stretches across the bottom of your desktop, and the Start button is located at the far left end.

Learning Taskbar Tools

The taskbar includes three important areas you'll use regularly in Windows 7.

Click the Start button to display the Start menu, launch programs, and open files.

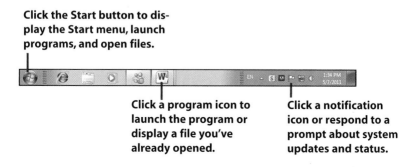

Click a program icon to launch the program or display a file you've already opened.

Click a notification icon or respond to a prompt about system updates and status.

Pinning Programs to the Taskbar

The taskbar automatically shows the program icons of any program you have open, and close to the Start button, the taskbar shows favorite Microsoft programs that are launched at startup, such as Internet Explorer, Windows Media Player, and maybe Windows Live Messenger. You can add favorite programs you use regularly to this "quick launch" area by right-clicking the program icon in the Start menu and clicking Pin to Taskbar.

Auto-Hiding and Displaying the Taskbar

As soon as you begin working with multiple windows, you'll realize that the amount of room you have on the desktop is really prime real estate. So instead of leaving the taskbar showing all the time, you may prefer to hide it when you don't need it. You can do this easily—and have it appear at just the right moment—by making a few simple changes.

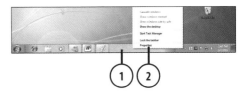

1. Right-click in a blank area of the taskbar.

2. Click Properties.

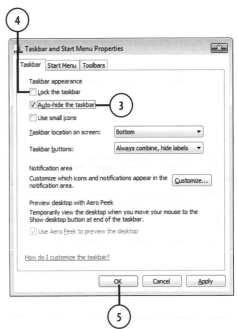

3. Click the Auto-Hide the Taskbar check box.

4. If you want to lock the taskbar in this Auto-Hide state, click the Lock the Taskbar check box.

5. Click OK.

Unlocking the Taskbar

If you decide that you'd rather keep things flexible and unlock the taskbar, you can do it easily. Right-click the taskbar and click Lock the Taskbar to remove the check mark. Now the taskbar is unlocked, and you're free to make changes as you see fit.

Moving the Taskbar

By default, the taskbar appears along the bottom of your desktop, but you can move it to a different area of the screen if you like.

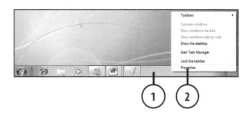

1. Right-click the taskbar.

2. Click Properties.

3. Click the Taskbar Location on Screen arrow.

4. Click the option that reflects where you'd like to position the taskbar.

5. Click Apply to preview your changes.

6. Click OK to save the change.

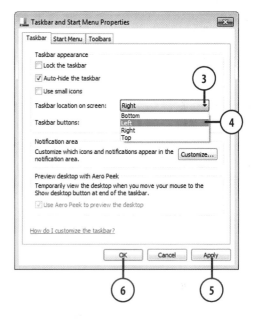

It's Not All Good

Mind Your Own Business, Taskbar!

The place you choose to position the taskbar will largely be a personal preference issue. The best idea is to place it where you can reach it easily with the mouse and access it when you need it.

If you position the taskbar along the right side of the screen, however, you'll soon notice—if you regularly use the vertical scrollbar in your favorite programs—that the taskbar pops up when you mean to click the scrollbar with the mouse pointer.

There are two ways to solve the dilemma: You can move the taskbar to another side of the screen, or you can turn off the Auto-Hide feature and lock the taskbar so that it's always visible. This way, you can always reach the taskbar easily, but it doesn't compete for space with your vertical scrollbar.

Changing the Look of the Taskbar

You may enjoy the large, colorful icons displayed by default in your Windows 7 taskbar. Most computers, right from the outset, show the Start button as well as a number of Windows standards—Windows Explorer, Windows Media Player, and Windows Live Messenger—pinned to the taskbar just to the right of Start. You can change the appearance of icons—as well as their order on the taskbar—and get just the look you want as you work with the programs and files you need.

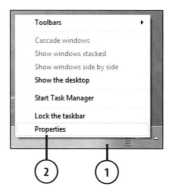

1. Right-click the taskbar.

2. Choose Properties.

3. Click Use Small Icons.

4. Click the Taskbar Buttons arrow.

5. Click the option that reflects what you'd like to see on the taskbar buttons;

   • **Always combine, hide labels** stacks open windows according to program.

   • **Combine when taskbar is full** groups icons when many programs are open.

   • **Never combine** keeps all window icons separate in the taskbar.

6. Click Apply to preview the changes.

7. Click OK to keep your changes.

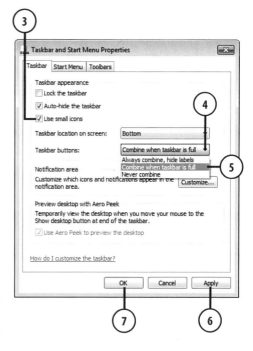

A Full Taskbar

When you choose Combine When Taskbar Is Full in the Taskbar Buttons setting and combine that with Display Small Icons, Windows 7 displays a small program icon, along with the first part of the filename in the buttons on the taskbar.

When the taskbar is full (both because you have a number of programs open and because descriptive taskbar buttons take up more room), Windows 7 stacks files according to the program you are using to create them. For example, the Excel files in the following image have been stacked, and you can display the open Excel files by hovering the mouse pointer over the Excel file item on the taskbar.

Hover the mouse pointer here

Pinning Applications to the Taskbar

With just a few clicks of the mouse, you can add the programs you use often to the Windows 7 taskbar so that you can open and work with them and switch among open programs easily. Right-click the program icon you want to add, and click Pin This Program to the Taskbar. The program icon stays in the taskbar whether any files that use that program are active or not. You can remove a program from the taskbar by right-clicking the icon again and choosing Unpin This Program from Taskbar.

Changing the Notification Area

The notification area on the right side of the taskbar contains the icons that indicate the status of various features on your computer. For example, one icon in the notification area shows your current Internet connectivity. Your new computer came with notification icons already set up in this area. You can change the icons by reordering them, hiding them, or moving them to a more visible place in the notification area.

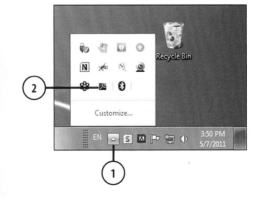

1. Click the up arrow in the notifications area to display the palette.

2. Drag the icon you want to display to the notification area.

3. Reorder the icons in the gallery by dragging one to a new location.

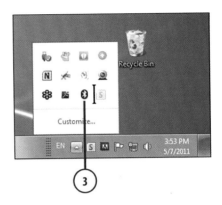

Managing System Icons

Some icons in the notification area have to do with the basic functions of your computer. For example, the Action Center, Clock, Network, Power, and Volume icons all have to do with items Windows 7 is managing for you.

If there are particular icons you don't feel you need, you can hide the system icon by dragging the icon to the Show Hidden Icons arrow to the left of the notification area. When you release the mouse button, the system icon galley appears and the icon you just added to the gallery appears there.

Navigation Basics: Using the Mouse and Keyboard

Getting around in Windows 7 is pretty simple business if you're comfortable using the mouse and know some keyboard basics. This section introduces you to the most common navigation techniques you are likely to use as you work with your programs.

Using the Mouse

For many of the basic operations you use Windows 7 to perform—start programs, find and open files, and choose program settings—you use the mouse. By now, this operation may be old hat, but here's a refresher.

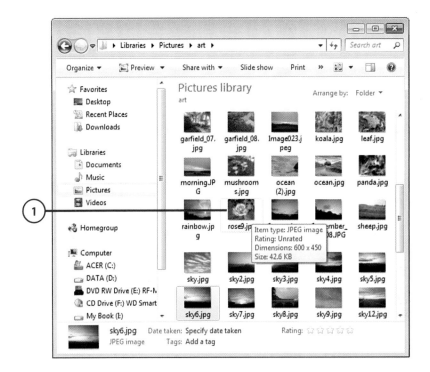

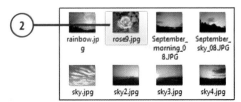

1. Move the mouse so the mouse pointer is positioned over the item you want to select. This is called *hovering*. The item may appear highlighted.

2. Click the left mouse button to select the item.

3. To display a context menu of commands related to a specific button or tool, click the right mouse button (this is known as *right-clicking*).

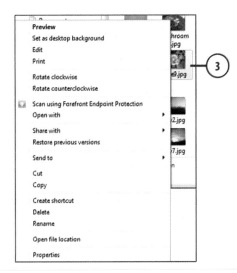

4. Drag an item from one place to another on the screen by clicking the item, holding down the left mouse button, and dragging the mouse pointer to the new location. Release the left button when the item is positioned where you want it to appear.

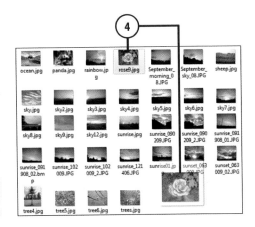

Selecting Multiple Items

You can also use the mouse and keyboard together if you want to select multiple items at once. If you want to choose several files in a folder, for example, you can click the first item and then press and hold the Shift key and click the last item you want to select. All items between the two clicked items are selected.

If you want to select multiple items that aren't next to each other, click the first item and press and hold the Ctrl key; then click all the other items you want to include.

Using the Keyboard

The keyboard also comes in handy, of course, when you need to type information or do calculations. But you can also use your keyboard for navigating in Windows 7. When you use your keyboard to move among programs and manage windows, you use special keys, shortcut key combinations, and function keys.

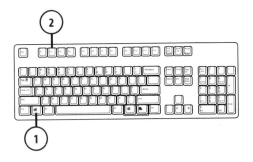

1. The Windows key, located on the lowest row of your keyboard on the left side between the Ctrl and Alt keys, opens the Start menu for you.

2. Function keys also carry out specific actions, such as displaying Help (F1) or showing items in the current list (F4).

3. You use the Tab key to move from option to option in a dialog box.

4. You can press key combinations (such as Alt and the underlined letter in a menu name) to perform operations.

5. You can use the arrow keys to move around in a document, expand or reduce a highlight, or select different items in a window.

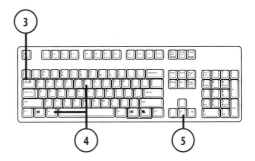

A Keyboard Is a Keyboard Is a Keyboard...Right?

Depending on the type of computer you are using, you may notice some differences in the ways certain keys appear on your keyboard The keyboard mentioned here is a "basic" keyboard layout. Your keyboard may or may not have a separate numeric keypad, function keys across the top, and a set of cursor-control keys that are separate from the alphanumeric keys. Additionally, you may notice that your Delete key or Backspace key is in a slightly different place than other keyboards you see. Take the time to learn where to find the common keys on your Windows 7 keyboard—once you know the lay of the land, finding the right key at the right time will be second nature.

SAY WHAT?!

>>> Go Further

Did you know you can control Windows 7 with voice commands? Turn on Windows Speech Recognition by clicking Start, clicking All Programs, choosing Accessories, clicking Ease of Access, and clicking Windows Speech Recognition.

Windows 7 walks you through a process that sets up voice recognition and prepares your microphone. You can also choose whether you want to use Manual Activation mode—which starts voice recognition when you press Ctrl+Windows key or click the microphone—or Voice Activation mode—which starts voice recognition when you say, "Start listening."

Windows 7 also offers you a printable command sheet you can keep as a reference so you will know what commands to use to get the software to respond correctly to your commands. If you decide to use speech recognition, be sure to take the tutorial to help Windows 7 learn the subtle patterns in your voice.

Working with Windows

So now you know how to use the Start menu, taskbar, and mouse and keyboard to navigate in Windows 7. That means you're ready to learn to start programs, find files, and work with windows on your desktop. This section introduces you to common tasks you'll do often in Windows 7.

Starting a Program

In the Start menu, you saw that Windows 7 organizes all the programs you have available on your computer. The ones you use most often are listed at the top of the Start menu, but you can also use All Programs to find other programs you may use less often.

1. To start a program from an icon on your desktop, point to the icon and then double-click it.

2. Alternatively, click Start.

3. Click a program icon at the top of the Start menu.

4. Or, click All Programs.

5. Click the folder containing the program you want to start.

6. Click the program icon to start the program.

Coming from the Document Side

Another easy way to start a program you want to use is simply to open one of the documents you've created with it. When you double-click a Word document icon to open that file, for example, the program also launches with it.

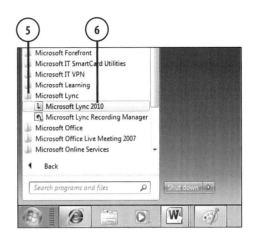

Finding the Folder You Want

Windows 7 includes a utility called Windows Explorer to help you easily find and work with the folders and files you want to use. You can also find files in common folders by selecting them in the Start menu.

1. Click Start.

2. Click Documents, Pictures, or Music in the upper-right corner of the Start menu and skip to step 4.

3. You can also click the Windows Explorer program icon.

4. Click the library containing the folders you want to view.

5. Alternatively, click the arrow to the left of the folder in the Navigation pane to display the subfolders.

6. Click the folder you want to view.

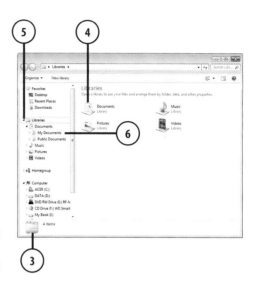

Displaying Your Favorites

You can also display a folder containing all the files you have created and saved that are affiliated with your user account. Just click your account name at the top right of the Start menu.

PREVIEWING FILES BEFORE YOU OPEN THEM

>> Go Further

When you're working in Windows Explorer, you can display a preview of the contents of the selected file by displaying the Preview pane on the right side of the window.

Click the folder containing the files you want to view; then click the file.

Click Show the Preview Pane in the right side of the Windows Explorer toolbar to open a pane that shows the contents of the file. You can continue choosing files until you locate the one you're looking for.

To learn more about working with Windows Explorer, changing folder views, and more, see Chapter 7, "Organizing Files and Folders."

Easy Opening

Perhaps the easiest way to open a folder is to locate it—whether it is on your desktop or nestled within another folder in Windows Explorer—and double-click it. The folder opens, and you can find the file you need.

Opening a Document

You can open files directly from folders in Windows Explorer, or you can open them within a program you're using.

1. If you have a document file on your desktop, you can simply double-click it to open it.

2. If the file is in a folder on your computer, click Windows Explorer in the taskbar.

3. Navigate to the folder containing the file you want to open.

4. Double-click the file.

Opening the Program First

You also can choose to open the program you used to create the program and then open the file from within the program itself. To do this, you start the program as described earlier in this chapter, click the File tab, and click Open. In the Open dialog box, navigate to the folder containing the file you want and click Open.

You may also be able to locate the file in the program's Recent tab. Click File to display Backstage view and then click Recent to display the recently used file. Open the file you want by clicking it.

Switching to a Different Window

One of the great benefits of the Microsoft Windows operating system is that you can easily have many different windows open on the screen at any one time. These windows might be program windows or folders of files. You might be running a video or listening to a tune in Windows Media Player while you work on an Excel worksheet. It can all happen at once. If you work with a number of programs open at one time, of course, you need to be able to get to the program you want when you need it.

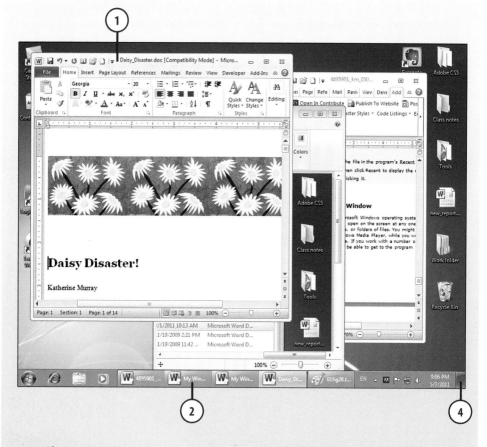

1. If several windows are open on the screen at once, click any part of the window you want to bring to the top.

2. Or you can click the button in the taskbar of the window you want to view.

3. Alternatively, you can press Alt+Tab to display a pop-up box that enables you to press Tab repeatedly to cycle through open programs.

4. You can click the gray bar at the right end of the taskbar to display your Windows 7 desktop.

Arranging Windows

Another important task when you are working with multiple windows open on the screen at one time is having the ability to arrange the windows the way you want them to appear. If you want to compare two documents, for example, it would be nice to show them side by side. Windows 7 can help you arrange windows the way you want.

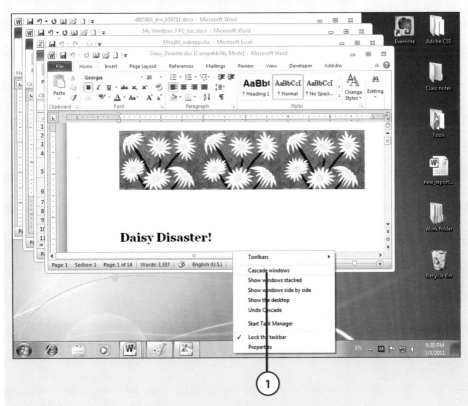

1. Right-click the taskbar and choose Cascade Windows.

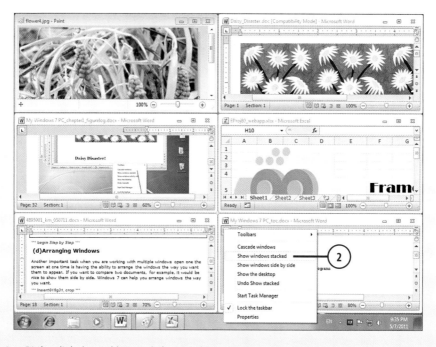

2. Right-click the taskbar and choose Show Windows Stacked.

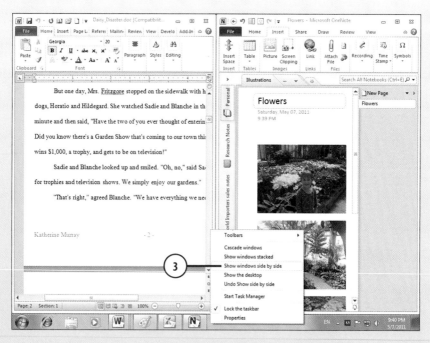

3. If you have two files you want to work with together on the desktop, right-click the taskbar and click Show Windows Side By Side.

If You're Having Trouble Arranging Windows...

If you begin the process with the desktop displayed, none of the arranging options are available to you. Right-click the taskbar and click Show Open Windows, and then all open windows appear on your desktop. Now you can choose one of the options in this section.

SHORTCUT KEYS AND SNAP FOR WINDOW WRANGLING

>>> Go Further

You can easily work with the windows on your desktop without ever taking your hands off the keyboard. A number of simple key combinations—called shortcut keys—makes it simple for you to open, close, and change which window is currently selected.

- Alt+spacebar displays the shortcut menu for the current window.
- Ctl+F4 closes the current window.
- Ctrl+Esc opens the Start menu.
- F5 refreshes the current window.
- Windows Logo key + M minimizes all open windows.
- Windows Logo key + E opens your computer library.
- Windows Logo key + D displays the desktop.
- Windows Logo key + Home minimizes all but the active window.

Windows 7 also includes a feature called Snap that makes it easy for you to align and resize windows at the same time. If you want to position the window so that it appears next to another window, for example, you can drag the title bar of the window to either side of the screen until you see an outline of the window appear. When you release the mouse button, the window expands, filling half your screen. You can arrange another window in a similar way by dragging the window to the opposite side of the desktop.

To maximize a window, drag the window to the top of the Windows 7 screen and, again, when you see the outline of the window change, release the mouse button; the window expands to fill the screen. To return the window to its smaller size, simply drag the window away from the top of the Windows 7 sceen.

Resizing and Closing Windows

You also have the option of changing the shape and size of windows that you display on the Windows 7 desktop. Perhaps you don't need a document to be shown full screen because you are reviewing only a small portion of it.

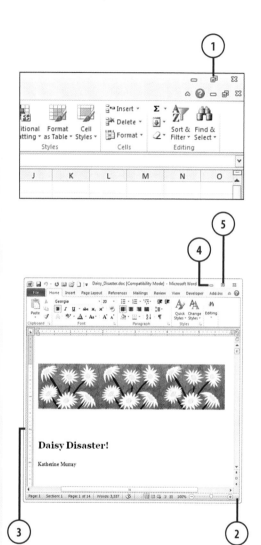

1. In the upper-right corner of an open window, click the center icon, which is called Restore Down.

2. Drag a corner of the window to make it larger or smaller.

3. Drag a side of the window to change the size horizontally or vertically.

4. Click Minimize to reduce the window to the taskbar.

5. Click the Maximize button to return the window to full-screen size.

Icons, Icons Eveywhere

If you're not sure what a tool or an icon on the screen is for, position the mouse pointer on the icon and leave it there. This "hovering" reveals a ToolTip that tells you the name of the tool. For some tools on the ribbon, the ToolTip tells not only the tool name but also a brief description about the way the tool is used.

Quick-Changing Windows

You can change the size of a window quickly by double-clicking the title bar. If the window was full-screen size (that is, maximized), it returns to its earlier smaller size. If the window is smaller than full screen, double-clicking the title bar maximizes it.

Old-Style Resizing

Sure, all these double-click tricks are fancy and fast. But if you prefer to choose commands from menus, you can display any window's control panel and choose the command you want—Restore, Move, Size, Minimize, and Close—from the list of options. You can find the control panel for the window in the upper-left corner; you can't miss it because it resembles a small program icon (in Word, you see a Word icon; in Excel, you see an Excel icon; and so forth).

Simple Moves

When a window is open on the screen, you can easily move it to a new location on your desktop by clicking the title bar and dragging it to the new location. Note that you can't move a maximized window, however, so you need to click Restore Down to make the window smaller before you move it.

Getting the Help You Need

Windows 7 includes a comprehensive and continually updated help system that can give you all kinds of information that will help you answer your questions and move forward in the tasks you need to complete.

Using Windows Help and Support

Your first stop when you're looking for help is in the Windows 7 Help and Support Center.

1. Click Start.

2. Click Help and Support.

3. Click in the Search box and type a word or phrase that reflects the type of information you want to find.

4. Click Search Help.

5. Click a link to find help information.

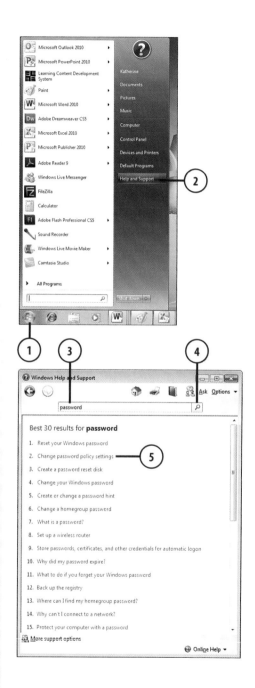

6. Click Browse Help.

7. Click a link to display topics and browse help articles.

Changing Text Size

You can easily increase the text size in Help by displaying Help and Support and then clicking Options in the upper-right corner of the Help window. Point to Text Size and then click the size you want from the list that appears.

Click to see other ways to get help.

Click to choose online or offline help.

Printing Help

If you find that you are looking up a certain task repeatedly, you might want to print the help information to keep close to your computer until you commit it to memory.

1. Search for the help information you need.

2. Click Print at the top of the help window.

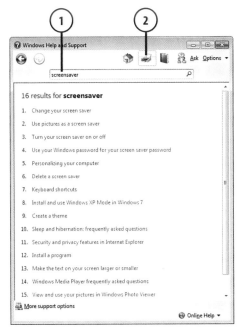

3. Choose your printer.

4. Set your print options.

5. Click Print.

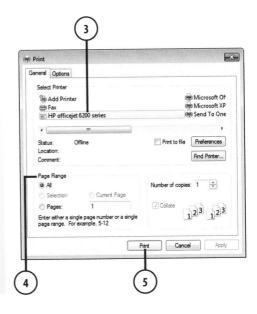

AND THAT'S JUST THE BEGINNING...

>>> Go Further

In addition to the help that's available to you in Windows 7 on your computer, you can visit Microsoft's Windows 7 site (www.windows.microsoft.com) to learn more about Windows 7 features, watch videos, and learn about basic tasks.

You can also click the Ask tool in the upper-right corner of the Windows Help and Support dialog box to find out more about Windows Remote Assistance, which enables a friend to log in to your computer to help you figure out what's wrong, and Microsoft Answers, which is an online community where you can ask and answer questions about Windows 7.

Windows 7 makes it easy for you to get your computer talking to all your devices—printer, scanner, phone, flash drive, and more—so that you can keep everything up to date.

With Windows 7, you can control settings for hardware and software.

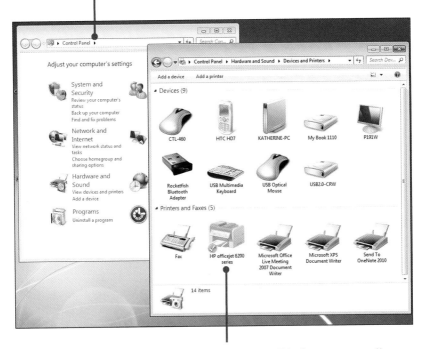

Windows 7 helps you get all your devices working properly.

This chapter shows you how to get your computer ready to work with programs, printers, and the Web:

→ Transferring files
→ Setting default programs
→ Setting up your printer
→ Getting ready to use hardware
→ Setting up Internet connections
→ Managing your PC power
→ Preparing for PC recovery

Preparing Your Windows 7 PC

Chances are, if you just purchased your new Windows 7 PC, you're probably looking forward to trying out the things you really want to do, such as browse the Web, play games, watch a video, or view your favorite photos. It's okay to do some of the fun stuff first, but don't neglect some of the necessary tasks. For example, you need to set up your computer to work with other devices, such as your printer, phone, or flash drive; make sure your Internet connection is working safely; manage the way your computer uses power; and create the tools you need to get things started again if a serious error should occur.

This chapter is all about the types of preparation that can keep things running smoothly as you head down the road with Windows 7.

Transferring Files

If your new Windows 7 computer is the latest in a line of computers you've used at home or at work, it's likely that you have files you'd like to transfer from one computer to another. How do you move the things you most need to be able to carry on your work? You have a few options:

- Use Windows Easy Transfer.

- Save the files to Windows Live SkyDrive or another online storage space.

- Add both computers to your home network and transfer files from one to the other.

Transferring Programs

The process for moving programs from one computer to another involves uninstalling the program on one computer and installing it on the new one, due to the licensing issues involved in legal copies of software you have purchased. Some programs enable you to log in to your account online and download the software from the company's website. Be sure to gather the following information from programs on your old PC before you uninstall the programs:

- Your user ID and password

- Your software registration number

- Any toll-free numbers or websites related to the software

- Any identifying information that shows your legitimate ownership of the software

Using Windows Easy Transfer

Windows Easy Transfer transfers files, settings, Internet favorites, email, and more from your old computer to your new one. Before you begin using the utility, log in to both computers as an administrator and make sure both have Windows Easy Transfer installed. (If not, you can download the tool from the Microsoft Downloads site.)

Begin by using Windows Easy Transfer on your old computer to prepare a transfer file that you can then install on your new Windows 7 PC. Then, when you have saved the transfer file (you can use these steps for both computers), add the transferred files to your computer by following these steps.

1. Click Start.

2. In the search box, type **Windows Easy Transfer** and click it in the results list.

3. In the Welcome to Windows Easy Transfer screen, click Next.

4. Choose the way in which you want to make the transfer.

5. Choose whether the current computer is the new computer or the old computer, and click Yes when the program asks whether you have copied the files to be transferred.

6. In the Open an Easy Transfer File dialog box, navigate to the external hard drive or flash drive containing the transfer files and click Open.

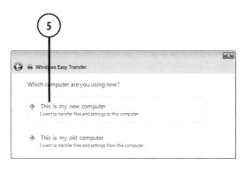

Checking Administrator Status

To make sure you're logged in as the administrator, click Start and click Control Panel. Choose User Accounts and Family Safety; then click User Accounts. Your user account appears on the right side of the screen. Click Change Your Account Type and select Administrator if needed; click Change Account Type to save your setting.

>>> Go Further

CHOOSING THE RIGHT TRANSFER METHOD

Windows Easy Transfer gives you three different ways to transfer your files, depending on the type of setup you have and how you want to copy the files:

- If you bought an Easy Transfer cable when you purchased your computer, you can use it to connect the two systems you'll be using to transfer the files. (Note that this is not a standard Universal Serial Bus [USB] cable. You can purchase an Easy Transfer cable online or by visiting your local electronics store.)

- If you've set up a home network and both computers are part of the network, you can transfer files as easily as you would copy them from one folder to another. You learn how to set up a home network in Chapter 3, "Getting and Staying Connected: Phones, Devices, and Tablets."

- You learn about networks and Home Groups in Chapter 12, "Networking—at Home and on the Road."

Setting Up Programs

One of the first changes you may want to make as you set up Windows 7 involves which programs start when you open a particular type of file. For example, suppose that you want to edit a photo you just captured. Which program do you want to use as an image editor? You can easily choose your favorite default programs and let Windows 7 know what you want to use for the various tasks you do.

Choosing Default Programs

Windows 7 includes a utility in the Control Panel that walks you through the process of setting up your default programs.

1. Click Start.

2. Click Default Programs.

3. In the Default Programs window, click Set Your Default Programs.

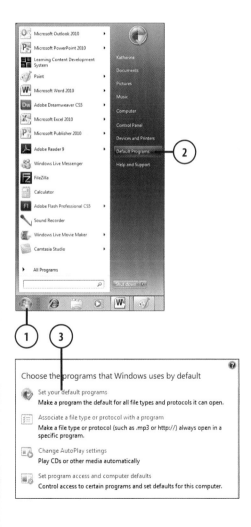

4. Click one of the programs in the list on the left.

A description of the program and options for setting the program as a default appear in the right side of the dialog box.

5. Click Set This Program as Default. Windows 7 stores your changes.

6. Click Choose Defaults for This Program.

7. In the Set Associations for a Program window, click the check boxes of extensions and protocols you want to be associated with this program.

This tells Windows 7 that you want files with the extensions you selected to be opened by the default program you chose.

8. Click Save.

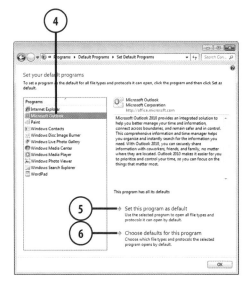

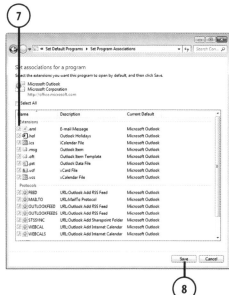

Setting Up All Your Defaults

Repeat steps 4 through 8 for each of the default programs in the Default Programs window. You can change your settings at any time—for example, you may want to change the program association of a specific file type later—by clicking Start and choosing Default Programs once again.

Removing Programs You Don't Need

Depending on the type of deal you got with your new Windows 7 PC, you may have a number of programs you doubt you'll ever use. For example, your computer may have come with an antivirus program, a suite of applications, games, and more that you don't think you need. Chapter 6, "Exploring, Downloading, and Running Programs," explains how to uninstall programs you don't need.

Adding Startup Programs

You can also have Windows 7 start certain programs automatically when you launch your computer. Some programs, such as your Bluetooth utility or the software that organizes your external hard disk, need to run for your other devices to operate smoothly. You may want to add other programs that you use continually, such as Microsoft Outlook, to the Startup folder so that those programs start automatically when Windows 7 does.

1. Click Windows Explorer in the taskbar.

2. Navigate to the folder containing the program you want to add.

3. Right-click the program icon and choose Create Shortcut; then right-click the shortcut and choose Cut. Alternatively, if you've selected a program shortcut, right-click it and choose Copy.

4. Click the folder for your hard drive.

5. Click in the search box and type **startup**.

6. Double-click the Startup folder to open it, and paste the shortcut into the folder.

Viewing Your Startup Files

After you add the shortcut to the Startup folder in Windows Explorer, the program launches automatically when you start Windows 7. You can also view the contents of the Startup folder in the Start menu by clicking All Programs, right-clicking Startup, and choosing Expand.

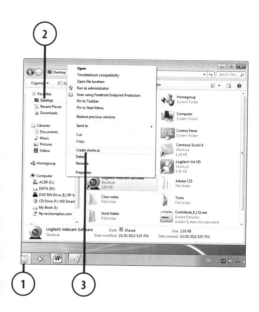

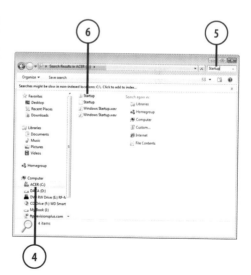

Launch Files Too

If you regularly work with a particular file—for example, perhaps you log all your work time in an Excel worksheet—you can create a shortcut for the file and add that to the Startup folder too. This automatically opens the file whenever Windows 7 starts.

Setting Up Your Printer

If you purchased a new printer to go along with your new Windows 7 computer, chances are all you need to do to prepare your printer for use is to plug it into one of the USB ports on your computer. If you have a wireless printer or an older model that doesn't support Plug and Play, you may have just a few more steps to follow.

Installing a New Printer

The first thing you should do when you want to add a new printer to your Windows 7 system is unbox it, plug the USB cable into a USB port on your PC, and plug the printer into a power outlet. Windows 7 checks to see whether it recognizes the printer and, if so, automatically installs the necessary driver for the printer.

You can also install a new printer without physically connecting the printer to your machine. You might want to do this, for example, when you're setting up your laptop to be able to print to the printer in another room. Use the following steps to install a printer manually.

1. Click Start.

2. Click Devices and Printers.

3. Click Add a Printer.

4. Choose whether you want to add a local printer or a wireless printer.

5. If you are adding a local printer, click to choose the port to which you want to attach your printer (in most cases, you can leave the default setting selected), click Next, and then choose your printer manufacturer from the list on the left. If you are adding a wireless printer, click the printer name from the list of wireless printers that appears and click Next.

6. Scroll through the list on the right and click the printer model.

7. Click Next twice. On the last screen, after you've connected your printer, you can click Print a Test Page to make sure your printer is operating properly.

Installing a Printer Driver
If Windows 7 can't find the driver for your particular printer, the program prompts you to provide the driver. Chances are a CD was included in the box with your new printer that will contain the driver you need. Insert the CD and follow the prompts onscreen to help Windows 7 finish setting up the printer.

Sharing Printers
After you set up a home network, you can easily set up a printer to share among the PCs on your network. To find out more about setting up a home network and sharing your printer, see Chapter 3.

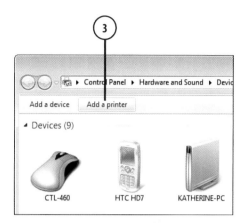

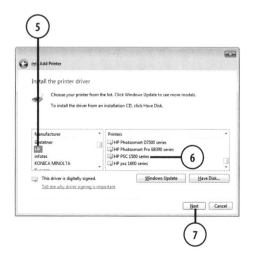

Setting the Printer as Your Default

After you've installed your printer, you can easily set it up to be the default printer that is selected whenever you want to print from a program running in Windows 7. Even after you choose a printer as your default, the other printers are still available, so you can change the printer selection at any time.

1. Click Start.

2. Click Devices and Printers.

3. Right-click the printer you want to set as the default.

4. Click Set As Default Printer.

Choose Printer Preferences

You can let Windows 7 know what your preferences are for printing by right-clicking the icon of your printer in the Devices and Printers window and choosing Printing Preferences. Different printers have different options, but in general, you can set advanced printing options, such as the default number of copies; whether the copies are collated; how graphics are handled; the paper type, size, and source you want to use; the type of print quality you want the printer to produce; the layout orientation and preview you prefer; and the way you want color to be used in print jobs. With some printer models, you can set all the options and save your printer preferences as a set specific for that printer. For example, some Hewlett-Packard printers enable you to create a Print Task Quick Set so that the settings are always available for the specified printer when it's time to print.

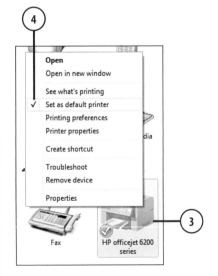

Go Further

>>>

ENTERING PRINTER PROPERTIES

For the standalone printer you use at home, you may not worry too much about the individual properties you set up when you want to print. After all, most of the settings—such as printing front and back or single sheets and paper size—are easy to select. But when you have other types of information you want your printer to remember—for example, who has permission to print from that device—you can add those properties to your printer setup so the printer always knows what it needs in order to print successfully.

Right-click the printer icon in the Device and Printer window and click Printer Properties. In the Properties dialog box, enter information about who has permission to use the printer, information on sharing the device, how (or whether) you want documents to be spools, and whether the printer prints by default in black and white or color.

Getting Ready to Use Hardware

Most devices you connect to your Windows 7 PC—scanners, cameras, drawing tablets, MP3 players, and phones—are super simple to install. You simply plug the device into an available UPS slot, and Windows 7's Plug and Play does the rest.

After your hardware devices are installed, you can tweak the properties to ensure they are working as they should. You can also use the Windows 7 Device Manager to look at the various hardware components in your system to make sure everything is working as it should.

Checking Device Properties

After Windows 7 installs the driver for the particular hardware component you've plugged in, the program tells you the device is ready for use. But you may want to take a look at the properties of the hardware item to make sure it will operate the way you want it to. To get started, open the Devices and Printers window from the Start menu and follow these steps:

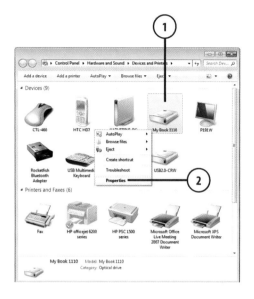

1. Right-click the hardware item.

2. Click Properties.

3. In the Properties dialog box for the device, click the Hardware tab.

4. Review the information displayed—the top list shows you what the device does, and the Device Status line tells you whether the hardware is working properly. Click Properties.

5. If you like, click the different tabs to review device properties.

6. Click OK.

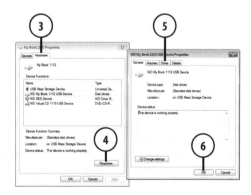

Go Further

GETTING HARDWARE INFORMATION IN DEVICE STAGE

Windows 7 has a new way of providing you with information about the hardware device you are connecting to your PC. Device Stage is a new feature that brings together relevant information about your device and enables you to see in one window the kinds of tasks being performed, along with control settings and preferences.

To display the Device Stage for, say, your printer, display the Devices and Hardware window and double-click your printer icon. The top of the window shows an image that looks very much like your printer. You also see the number of documents in queue (if any) and, in the bottom of the window, links that enable you to view and set preferences for printing.

Not all devices appear in Device Stage when you click them in Devices and Printers, however; some display the Properties dialog box instead.

Updating Drivers

The word *driver* is a bit of technospeak for the program that enables your hardware—your printer and other devices, like your camera, drawing pad, and phone—to talk successfully to Windows 7. Hardware manufacturers occasionally update the drivers they provide their devices; for example, every so often the maker of your MP3 player may release new driver software that enhances the product security or fixes a bug with music playback. The new drivers might help increase efficiency, fix problems, or make the hardware compatible with new equipment. Windows 7 makes it easy for you to update the drivers of your various devices and printers; you can do it from within the Devices and Printers window. Just open the Devices and Printers window from the Start menu and follow these steps.

1. Right-click the hardware item and click Properties.

2. In the Properties dialog box, click the Hardware tab.

3. If necessary, click the device function of interest.

4. Click the Properties button.

5. Click the Change Settings button.

6. Click the Driver tab.

7. Click Driver Details to check the date and maker of the driver.

8. Click Update Driver to get the latest version available. Windows 7 asks you to choose whether you want to search online for the latest driver or search your computer. If an installation CD came with the device you're updating, you can insert the CD in your drive so that Windows 7 will locate the driver. In most instances, however, you may want to let Windows 7 search online to find the most recent driver available. Click your choice, and after the update is done, click Close.

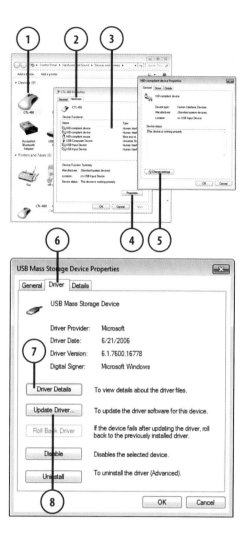

Organizing Your Drivers

Some of the devices you purchase, such as your printer, phone, camera, and video camera, come with CDs you can use to install the drivers on your Windows 7 PC. You may need these CDs only at first, when you initially set up the device to use with Windows 7. But it's a good idea to keep all your hardware CDs together in the event that you one day need to reinstall the drivers for the hardware devices.

Depending on the age of the item, you may be able to find more recent drivers for the various components available online. Search the manufacturer's website, using the model number of your device, to check for the most recent drivers. You can then download the drivers to your desktop and use the Update Driver utility to add the new driver to your settings in Windows 7.

Troubleshooting Hardware Devices

Luckily, most of the time, your printer, router, scanner, camera, and drawing tablet function the way they're supposed to. You plug them in to your Windows 7 PC, Windows finds the right drivers, and they're ready for you to use. Piece of cake.

But once in a while, devices have trouble. Your printer doesn't print anything. Your router is blinking, but you have no Internet connectivity. Your drawing tablet doesn't let you draw.

Windows 7 builds troubleshooting right into the work you do with your hardware devices, so help is always within reach. Begin by clicking Start and clicking Devices and Printers, and then follow these steps:

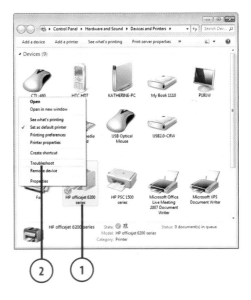

1. Right-click the icon of the device you're having trouble with.

2. Click Troubleshoot. The troubleshooter evaluates the device and displays the results, telling you what the problem was and (it is hoped) fixing the issue.

3. Click Explore Additional Options if you don't feel the issue was resolved and want to consider other possibilities.

4. Click View Detailed Information to display a report of issues the troubleshooter found and fixed.

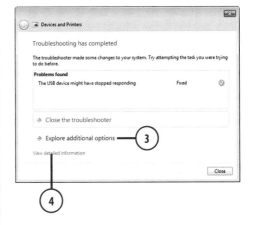

5. Review the report.

6. Click Next. The final page of the
   report shows the problems that
   were found and the fixes that
   were attempted. Click Close.

Keep Your Troubleshooters In-the-Know

The troubleshooters available to you
when you right-click a device in the
Devices and Printers window pull information from Microsoft's online help
content to keep fixes and suggestions
up to date. Be sure that you are online
before choosing Troubleshoot so, if necessary, the utility can access online help
information.

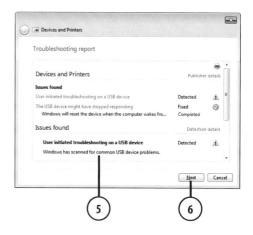

Review Troubleshooting Options

Windows 7 brings together resources to help you troubleshoot many of the most
common challenges in Windows 7. To display the Troubleshoot Computer
Problems window, click Start and choose Control Panel. Click System and Security,
and click Troubleshoot Common Computer Problems in the Action Center.

You'll find links in each of five areas—Programs, Hardware and Sound, Network
and Internet, Appearance and Personalization, and System and Security—that you
can use to solve the challenges with hardware or software you may be having.

Setting Up Internet Connections

Before you can begin to browse the Web, you need to have an account with an
Internet service provider (ISP). You might, for example, pay your phone or cable
company for a service package that includes DSL or cable Internet access.

When you know you will have access to the Internet, you need the equipment to help you get there. This means you need a modem and router
(sometimes these functions are combined in one device). Windows 7 will
help you make the necessary connections you need to get online so that you
can begin browsing, shopping, surfing, and sharing.

Router Types

You can use either a regular router or wireless router for your Internet connection. To learn more about router types, as well as how to set up a home and wireless network, see Chapter 12.

Connecting to the Internet

One of the first things you'll want to do with your new Windows 7 PC is get connected to the Internet and begin to browse the Web, check email, update social media, and more. Your startup utility when you turn on your computer and step through the process will likely help you establish an Internet connection right off the bat. You will need to have information from your Internet service provider—such as your email address and password—but the utility will help you establish a connection. If you find you're having trouble connecting to the Internet, follow these steps to do it manually:

1. Click the Network icon in the notification area.

2. Click Open Network and Sharing Center.

3. Click Set Up a New Connection or Network.

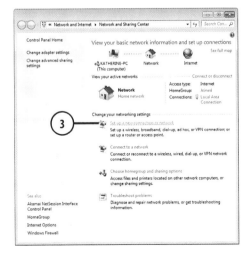

4. Click Connect to the Internet.

5. Click Next.

6. Click the type of connection you want to establish.

7. Enter the username your ISP gave you.

8. Type the password (also provided by your ISP).

9. Click Connect.

Seamless Internet
Not all types of Internet connection require you to enter a user name and password. Most cable Internet service providers, for example, don't require this type of login. So if you're not prompted for your user name and password but you still can access the Internet, you likely are using an ISP that doesn't require you to authenticate your login.

Remember That Password
If you want the connection to preserve your password (recommended), click the Remember This Password check box.

Naming Your Connection
Especially if you have created several different connections—perhaps one at home, one at work, and another at school—you can enter a unique name in the Connection Name field so that you can see easily which connection you are using at any given time. If you want to customize settings and change passwords for the different connection account later, the process is easier if the connections are clearly named.

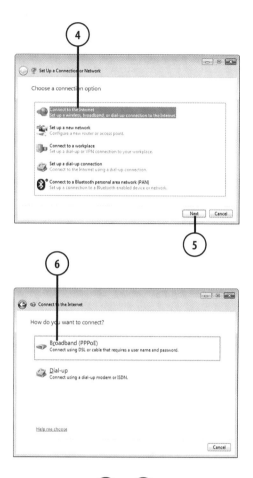

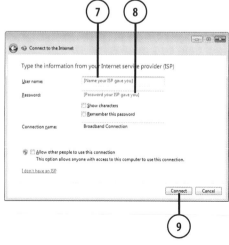

Managing Your PC Power

We don't often think about the amount of energy our computer and periph-
erals (printer, scanner, drawing tablet, and more) use on a daily basis. If you
leave your computer on 24/7 (which isn't really a good idea), your system is
burning fuel around the clock that could be going to other things. If your
monitor is gleaming into the dark of your home office but there's nobody
there looking at it, it is slowly wasting power and adding to your electric bill.

Luckily for you, Windows 7 includes power management plans you can use to
maximize the performance of your system while still cutting down on the
energy you use. You can choose from among different power management
plans or even create one of your own.

Choosing a Power Management Plan

By default, Windows 7 includes two
different power management plans.
The Balanced power plan balances
usage with performance, and Power
Saver reduces computer performance a bit to lower your energy use.
Selecting a plan is as simple as pointing and clicking.

1. Click Start.

2. Click in the search box and type
   Power Plan.

3. Click Choose a Power Plan.

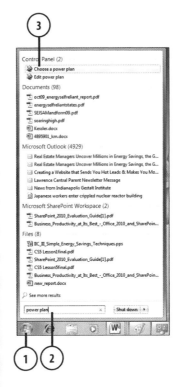

4. Click the power plan you want to use.

Show Additional Plans

Windows 7 comes with another ready-made plan for your selection. Click the Show Additional Plans arrow and click the High Performance plan if you want your computer to work as quickly and powerfully as possible without regard for the amount of energy you're using.

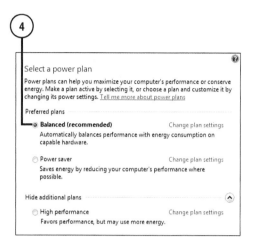

Changing Power Management Settings

Each of the power management plans you can choose with Windows 7 enables you to set priorities about the way you use Windows 7 and the type of power you use and save. For example, you can choose a plan that saves as much power as possible or select a plan that balances the power use with your computer's performance. You can view and change the settings to fit the plan you have in mind and tweak individual settings along the way.

1. In the Control Panel, click Hardware and Sound and review the Power Options area.

2. Click Change Power-Saving Settings.

3. Click the arrow to show additional plans.

4. Click Change Plan Settings for the plan you'd like to see.

5. Click the Turn Off Display arrow and choose the setting you want to apply.

6. Click the Put the Computer to Sleep arrow and click the setting you want.

7. Click Save Changes.

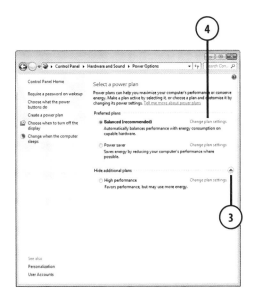

Wait, Reverse That

If you change the power settings and then have second thoughts and want to undo your changes, you can click the Restore Default Settings for This Plan link. Windows 7 returns the plan to its default settings.

Plan Differences

The settings available to you in both the Balanced and Power Saver plans are the same; the only difference is found in the settings already entered for each of the plans.

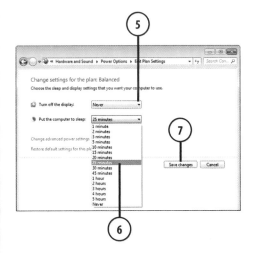

Preparing for Recovery

Nobody likes to begin using a new computer planning for catastrophe. But there's an old saying that "Fortune favors the prepared," so perhaps creating a system repair disc early in the process will help you safeguard your computer in case something bad should happen down the road.

A system repair disc gives you a way to start your computer in the unhappy event that something goes wrong with your hard drive or Windows 7 and your computer doesn't start properly. If you can use the system repair disc to start Windows 7 and begin to work with the software so that you can figure out what's going on, then the whole process is quick and painless.

Creating a System Repair Disc

The system repair disc tool in Windows 7 helps you prepare an emergency boot disc that jumpstarts your computer if anything ever goes seriously wrong and it doesn't start normally.

1. Click Start.

2. Click in the search box and type **system repair**.

3. Click the Create a System Repair Disc option.

4. Insert a blank recordable/ rewritable CD or DVD in the drive and choose the drive letter in the Drive selection.

5. Click Create Disc. Windows 7 begins copying the necessary files to the disc and lets you know when the operation is complete.

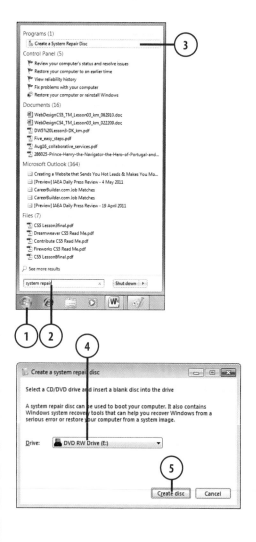

Creating a System Image

Windows 7 includes a tool that makes a complete image backup of your hard drive so that every file is carefully preserved, byte by byte. If you're using your computer primarily for gaming, social media, or entertainment, you might not want to worry about creating a system image of your complete system. But if you work with business-critical data, are working on the Great American novel, have loads of irreplaceable family pictures, or you have other important and complex files you need to be sure to preserve, creating a system image you know you can restore if necessary may help you sleep better at night.

1. Click Start.

2. Click the Control Panel.

3. Click Backup Your Computer in the System and Security area.

4. On the left, click Create a System Image.

5. Choose where you want to create the image by clicking the arrow and clicking your choice from the list.

6. Click Next, and follow the onscreen prompts to complete the image. Windows 7 shows you the status as the image is created and saved in the location you specified.

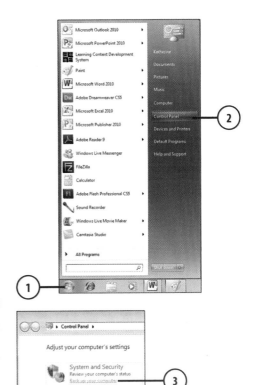

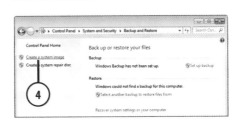

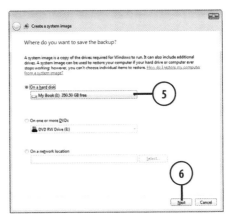

>>> Go Further

RESTORING A SYSTEM IMAGE

If you find yourself needing to use the system image you've created, you can restore the image of your hard disk. Be aware, however, that this is a complete job: All the files on your system currently will be overwritten with the restored files. You can't select specific files you want to restore. All the customizations you've done on your PC will be overwritten with the settings that were in place when you created the system image.

Microsoft recommends using Recovery in the Control Panel to restore the system image for your computer. Click Start, click Control Panel, click Find and Fix Problems, and click Recovering in the bottom of the left column. Then simply follow the prompts on the screen.

If you are having trouble starting Windows 7, you can insert and use the system repair disc to restore the image. When prompted, choose the Repair Your Computer option and follow the instructions on the screen.

Connection is the name of the game with Windows 7: Keep your phone, MP3 player, flash drive, and drawing tablet all communicating happily with your PC and trade files effortlessly among all devices.

With Windows 7, you can sync multiple devices.

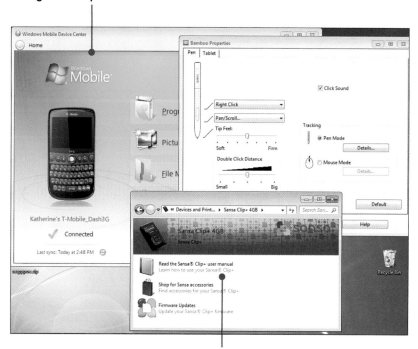

Use Device Stage and Control Panel to set your preferences for devices.

This chapter shows you how to connect your devices and sync your files by exploring these tasks:

- → Connecting devices to Windows 7
- → Synching your phone
- → Synching your MP3 player
- → Moving files from a flash drive
- → Setting up your drawing tablet

Getting and Staying Connected: Phones, Devices, and Tablets

Today we live in a connected age. We listen to music on our computers, our phones, and in our cars. It seems as if we're forever moving documents from our work PC to our home computer and over to our laptop, and maybe sending them to our mobile device before we're through. We type, doodle, paint, speak, and meet on just about every conceivable piece of technology, gathering information from our browsers, tablets, phones, and more.

All this connection is a great thing, but sometimes getting all the different pieces of technology communicating can be a bit of a headache. This chapter shows you how to connect your various devices to Windows 7 so that you can share files easily and get on with other, more creative tasks.

Connecting Devices to Windows 7

One of the challenges of being the program everybody wants to plug in to is that you need to be able to accommodate all kinds of different hardware and software. This means that even though Microsoft offers several ways devices can connect to Windows 7, the hardware manufacturer—the company that manufactured your mobile phone, for example—must provide the driver needed for the device to recognize the specific Windows 7 tool designed to help the device sync up.

This means that Device Stage, for example—the newest and smartest connectivity utility offered by Windows 7—is available for your device only if the device manufacturer has created the necessary driver for the device to be able to use Device Stage.

So depending on the device you're connecting to Windows 7 and the drivers available for that device, you may see the following:

- Device Stage, which was introduced in Chapter 2, "Preparing Your Windows 7 PC," helps you sync your device to Windows 7 and share photos, music, files, and more.

- Windows Mobile Device Center is a utility that was first made available for Windows Vista and now is part of Windows 7. If your device requires it, you need to download Windows Mobile Device Center from Microsoft Downloads. (You learn how to do that later in this chapter.)

Windows 7 Sync Center: For Networks Only

The Windows 7 Sync Center, although it might *sound* as though you could use it to sync your devices, is really intended to synchronize files when you're working on and off a network. The Sync Center keeps track of the files that have been synchronized and updates files as needed.

Yes, it's a little confusing, but the bottom line is this: Make sure your Windows Updates are turned on so that you always have the most current version of Windows 7. Chances are that the most important drivers you need to keep Windows 7 communicating happily with your devices will be updated automatically through the Windows Updates you receive. But it's a good idea to check your device manufacturer's website regularly or use the steps in the "Updating Drivers" section in Chapter 2 to make sure you have the most recent version of the driver available for your device.

Syncing Your Phone

No matter what kind of smartphone you're using, you can sync the phone with Windows 7 and transfer files—including pictures, music, videos, and Office Mobile documents—to your computer. This gives you great flexibility in the media and files you enjoy on your phone and enables you to share the files with your computer so you have access to them anywhere. The process is different, depending on the operating system of the phone you use.

Connecting Your Windows Phone 7

Excitement is growing about the Windows Phone 7 because of its beautiful touchscreen, full-featured mobile operating system, and easy integration with Microsoft programs. This phone—which is available from a handful of providers—enables you to make the most of touch capability and download and use more than 10,000 apps.

1. Begin by connecting your phone to a USB port on your computer.

2. When prompted, click Get Software.

3. You are taken to Microsoft's Zune site. Click Download Now.

4. In the File Download dialog box, click Run to download the software and click Run again.

5. Disconnect your phone as prompted and click Install.

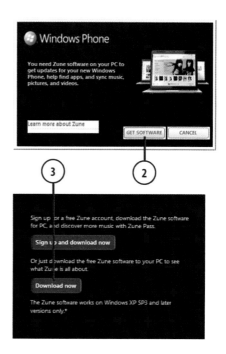

6. You are prompted to let the Zune software restart your computer and then reconnect your Windows 7 phone. The Zune software launches automatically.

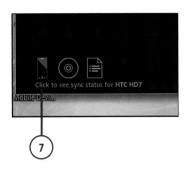

7. To begin the sync, click Start and then click Skip. Click the icon in the lower-left corner of the Zune window to check your phone sync status.

8. Click the phone and PC icon (alternately) to sync items from the phone to your computer and vice versa. Drag and drop the files you want to sync.

Subsequent Syncs

After you set up your initial synchronization, Zune updates your files automatically whenever you connect your phone to your PC. You can change your sync preferences by clicking Settings in the upper-right area of the Zune window.

Disconnecting Your Windows 7 Phone

Remember to remove your Windows 7 phone safely by clicking the Show Hidden Icons arrow in the notification area, clicking the Safely Remove Hardware icon in the gallery, and choosing to eject your phone.

Connecting Your Windows 6 Phone

If you're using a Windows phone model made prior to Windows Phone 7, your phone uses an earlier mobile operating system, such as Windows Mobile 6.5. This means that you need to download and install Windows Mobile Device Center (instead of Zune, for the Windows Phone 7) to be able to synchronize the files on your phone and your computer.

1. Using your web browser, go to Microsoft Downloads (www.microsoft.com/downloads) and enter **Windows Mobile Device Center** in the search box.

2. Click Microsoft Windows Mobile Device Center 6.1 for Windows Vista (32-bit or 64-bit, depending on which type of computer you have).

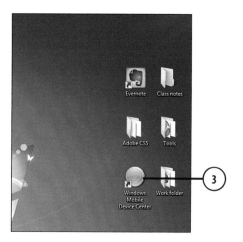

3. After you download and install the software (the utility will lead you through the steps), plug your phone in to an available USB port and double-click the Windows Mobile Device Center icon on your desktop.

4. Click Mobile Device Settings and choose how you want Windows Mobile Device Center to handle any conflict when syncing files between your phone and PC.

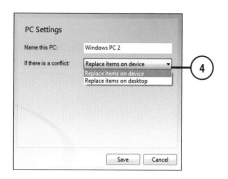

5. Set sync preferences for picture files by clicking Pictures, Music and Video.

6. Click Pictures/Video Import Settings.

7. Click the arrow and choose the location where you want imported files to be stored.

8. Change other import options as needed.

9. Click OK.

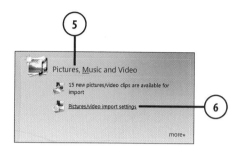

Yes, It's Okay That It Says "Vista"

Even though the Windows Mobile Device Center *says* Windows Vista, it works with Windows 7 as well.

Not Sure Whether You Have a 32-bit or 64-bit Computer?

There's an easy way to check the type of computer you have. Click Start, and on the right side of the Start menu, right-click Computer. Click Properties. The value to the right of the System Type item tells you whether you're using a 32-bit or 64-bit PC.

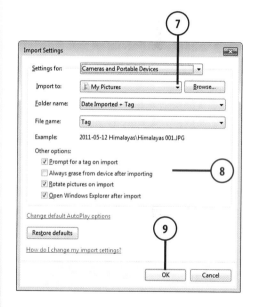

>> Go Further

WHATEVER HAPPENED TO ACTIVESYNC?

If you've use Windows phones previously with a Microsoft Windows operating system, you may be wondering what happened to ActiveSync, which was used to synchronize devices. Windows Mobile Device Center is an improved version of ActiveSync, which was originally designed for Windows Vista.

Windows Mobile Device Center works with Sync Center (remember that?) to create a mobile partnership and manage the synchronization of your files among the PC and supported devices. Sync Center also manages file relationships so that you have the most current versions of files whether you're working connected to a network server or using an offline PC or device.

You can check the sync status in Sync Center by clicking the Sync Center icon in the Show Hidden Icons gallery in the notification area. Sync Center tells you when the most recent sync was performed and lists any outstanding sync operations.

The Apple Doesn't Fall Far from the Tree

If you're using an iPhone or an iPod Touch, you still need to use Apple iTunes to sync your files. After you set up iTunes to run in Windows 7, however, all you need to do to synchronize your devices is to connect it with the cable that came with the device. You can find out more about Apple iTunes by going to www.apple.com/itunes/.

Syncing Your MP3 Player

Your MP3 player probably gives you lots of joy, enabling you to take your favorite albums, podcasts, and more basically anywhere you want to go—to the gym, on your bike, on the trail, at your desk. Windows 7 makes it easy to sync your MP3 player and transfer the audio files you want to listen to so you'll have your tunes on the road.

Many different types of MP3 players are available, of course, and some will have their own software requirements and sync with Windows 7 in different ways. Your iPod, for example, uses iTunes to sync your media. This section describes one way you can sync your MP3 player and set device preferences, but be sure to follow the on-screen prompts for your particular device if the process you experience is somewhat different from the ones described here.

Copying Files to Your MP3 Player

The easiest way to move files to your MP3 player is to choose the option Windows 7 presents to you as soon as you connect the device to your USB port.

1. Connect the device to your Windows 7 PC.

2. Windows 7 displays a message that the driver has been installed.

3. Choose Sync Digital Media Files to This Device from the AutoPlay dialog box that appears after the driver is installed.

4. In Windows Media Player, drag the files, playlists, or albums you want to sync to the column on the right.

5. Click Start Sync. Windows Media Player shows you the status of the synchronization and then lets you know that it's safe to remove your MP3 player from the USB port.

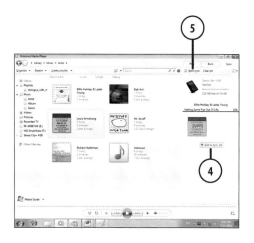

Where's Device Stage?

Not all devices appear in Windows 7 Device Stage. Because Device Stage is a new utility in Windows 7, not all third-party manufacturers have produced drivers that enable devices to use Device Stage for synchronizing and file management. You can check with the manufacturer of your device to see whether an update is available for the device model you have.

A Tiny Little USB

When you prepare to connect your MP3 player to your PC, you'll notice that the USB cable for connecting the device is different from the ones you use to connect other hardware to your computer. When you connect your printer to your PC, for example, the USB cable has what are called type A or B connectors at either end. Your MP3 player likely uses a mini or micro-USB cable, which has a small USB connector on one end and a traditionally sized USB connector on the other. Plug the small end into the port on your MP3 player and plug the regular-sized USB connector into an available USB port on your PC. Because the number of different USB cable connectors can get confusing, the important thing is to use the cable that came with your device. Windows 7 will do the rest!

Setting Connection Defaults

You can set up the way Windows 7 responds when you connect your MP3 player by changing the general settings for the device.

1. From the Device Stage window, click Change General Settings.

2. Click the arrow for the option that controls what happens when the device is connected to the computer.

3. In the list, click the action you want Windows 7 to take.

4. Leave the notifications check box selected.

5. Click OK.

Changing Connection Settings

You can change the connection behavior for your device at any time. In the Device Stage, click Change General Settings and repeat the steps in the list. If your device doesn't open Device Stage, click Start, click Device and Printers, right-click the device icon, and choose the option you want to set from the displayed list.

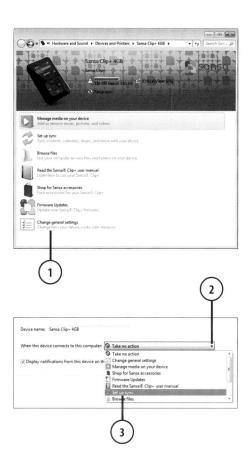

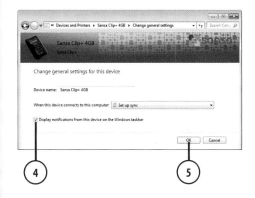

Specifying Sync Options

You can choose the way Windows 7 syncs the files on your device by choosing one-way or two-way synchronization. One-way synchronization syncs the files in one direction only—for example, from your media library on your PC to your MP3 player. Two-way synchronization syncs the device and the computer both ways, so both systems have the same files.

1. Click Set Up Sync from the device's Device Stage window.

2. Click Settings for the item you want to change.

3. Click to save as much music as you have room for.

4. Click to specify the folders, songs, or playlists you want to sync to your device.

5. Click to add specific folders to the sync.

6. Click to choose a playlist or songs.

7. Click OK to save the settings.

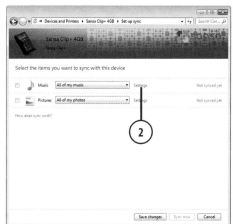

Keeping Track of Space on Your Device

Windows 7 shows you how much space is used on your device, how much is needed for the folders and files you want to sync, and how much space is left over.

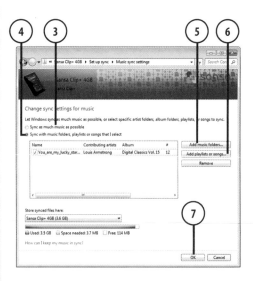

Moving Files from a Flash Drive

Small storage devices, called *flash drives* or *thumb drives*, enable you to easily move files from one device to another when you don't have the option of sharing a network or when the files you want to share are too big to attach to an email message.

Viewing and Moving Flash Drive Files

When you first connect the flash drive to your USB port, Windows 7 automatically senses the addition and displays the AutoPlay dialog box so that you can tell the program what to do next.

1. Click Open Folder to View Files.

2. In Windows Explorer, select the file(s) you want to transfer.

3. Click a folder arrow to locate the subfolder you want to use to store the file(s).

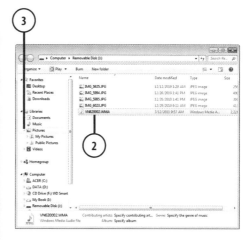

4. To move the file, press and hold the Shift key and drag it to the folder.

5. Release the mouse button and Shift key.

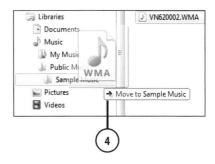

Selecting Multiple Files

Of course, you don't have to move files one by one. If you want to select all the files on the flash drive, press Ctrl+A. If you want to choose a couple of the files that happen to be next to each other, click the first file you want, press and hold Shift, and click the last file in the set you want to move. If you want to choose different files on the flash drive that are not beside each other, press and hold Ctrl and click each file you want to move.

Copying Files from the Flash Drive

If you want to leave the files on the flash drive and copy a version of the files to your Windows 7 PC, click the files you want to copy and then drag them to the destination folder. By default, Windows 7 copies the files you drag, leaving the originals intact in the original folder.

Compressing Many Files

If you have many different files you want to move or copy to a new location, you can compress all the files into one before you move them. To get the specific steps on compressing files, see Chapter 7, "Organizing Files and Folders."

Removing the Flash Drive

When you're ready to remove the flash drive, it's a good idea to let Windows 7 close the drive properly before you remove it. Chances are everything will be fine if you just pull the drive out of the port, but why take a risk when removing it the safest way takes only two extra clicks?

1. Click the Show Hidden Icons arrow in the notification area.

2. Click the Safely Remove Hardware icon.

3. Click the flash drive in the list.

4. When you see the Safe to Remove Hardware message, remove the flash drive.

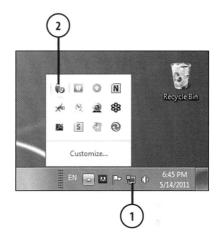

On Second Thought...

If you decide you want to check something on the flash drive after you've used the Safely Remove Hardware tool, Windows 7 isn't able to view the contents of the drive unless you remove the drive from the port and reinsert it.

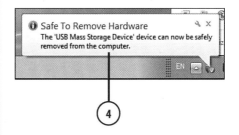

>>> Go Further

BOOSTING PERFORMANCE WITH READYBOOST

If you love the idea of optimizing the performance of your computer and accessing your files as quickly as possible, you may want to use your flash drive as additional memory. Windows 7 includes a feature called ReadyBoost that enables you to use the flash drive as a disk cache, or a segment of memory that stores data in such a way that it can be accessed more quickly.

You can use a number of different storage devices with ReadyBoost: a USB flash drive, SD card, flash memory, or CompactFlash. When you connect the device, the Windows AutoPlay dialog box appears. You can click the ReadyBoost tab to set the amount of space you want to use as the disk cache.

Setting Up Your Drawing Tablet

Depending on the type of work you do, a drawing tablet may be part of your normal toolkit. No matter what manufacturer made the drawing tablet you have, the device came with a CD that includes installation software, drivers, and possibly a manual for your device. Install the manufacturer's software before you plug the device into Windows 7. The software probably walks you through the steps of calibrating the tablet so that it responds to your hand-writing and gestures. You can also specify settings (or tweak things that aren't working well) by using the Control Panel.

Getting Started with Your Drawing Tablet

Windows 7 includes a number of settings you can customize so that your drawing tablet will work the way you want it to in Windows 7. The types of settings may vary depending on the capabilities of your tablet model, but the steps here give you a sense of how to find and set drawing tablet options.

1. Click Start.

2. Click Control Panel.

3. Click Hardware and Sound.

4. Scroll down to the area that reflects your tablet and click Set Up Your Pen and Tablet.

5. Click the arrows and click your choice to select the way you want the pen buttons to function.

6. Adjust the Soft-Firm slider to change the feel of the pen tip.

7. Choose whether you want to hear an audible click when you use the tablet.

8. Click Advanced.

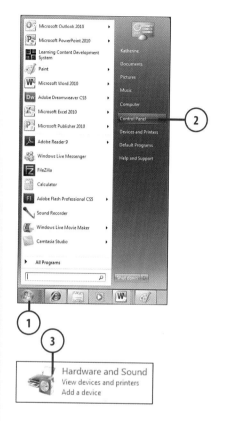

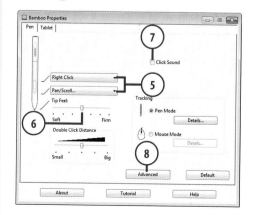

9. Choose how you want Windows 7 to recognize right-clicks on the pen.

10. Click OK.

11. Click Tablet for more options.

12. Click to choose right-handed or left-handed use.

13. Click the close box to save your settings.

Different Strokes for Different Folks

The settings shown here are part of the configuration for a Bamboo drawing tablet, so if you are using a tablet made by a different manufacturer, you may see different options from the ones shown here.

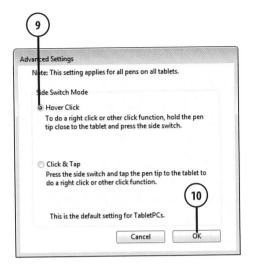

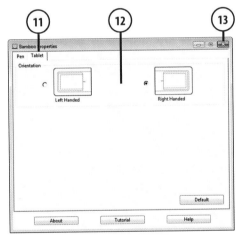

Choosing Preferences for Your Tablet

Windows 7 includes a number of settings you can customize so that your drawing tablet works the way you want it to in Windows 7.

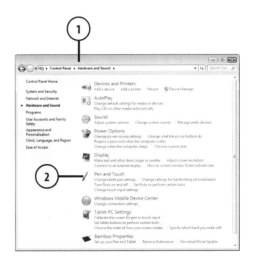

1. Display the Hardware and Sound screen of the Control Panel.

2. In the Pen and Touch area, click Change Tablet Pen Settings.

3. In the Pen Options list, click Double-Tap.

4. Click Settings.

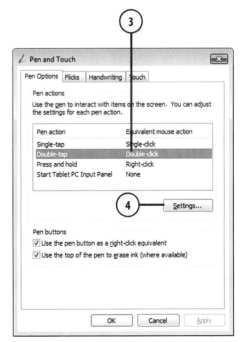

5. Adjust the slider to control the speed for double-tapping.

6. Change the Spatial Tolerance setting to allow space in the double-tap.

7. Click OK to save your settings.

8. Click the Flicks tab.

9. Click whether you want to use flicks to navigate onscreen or use them for both navigation and editing.

10. Choose how sensitive you want the tablet to be to flicks and touch.

11. Click the Handwriting tab and choose whether you want Windows 7 to learn automatically from your handwriting on the tablet.

12. Click Touch and choose your preferences for using touch on the device.

13. Click OK to save your preferences.

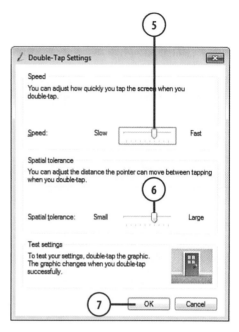

Customizing Flicks

If you click Navigational Flicks and Editing Flicks, the Customize button becomes available. You can click Customize to adjust the flick controls for all directions of the pen and even create your own custom flick actions.

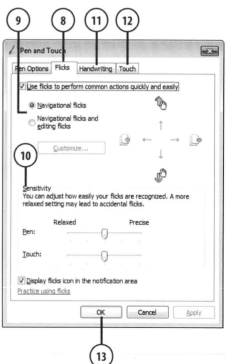

Keeping your Windows 7 PC secure is an important part of your entire computing experience. The Sharing and Security tools in Windows 7 help you protect your information and keep your computer virus-free.

The Action Center shows you security or maintenance issues that need your attention.

Turn on Windows Firewall to protect your computer from unwanted changes.

This chapter shows you how to make sure your Windows 7 PC is as secure as possible by showcasing these tasks:

→ Working with the Action Center
→ Setting up user accounts
→ Setting a password
→ Using Windows Defender
→ Turning on your Windows Firewall
→ Changing User Account Control settings

Securing Your Windows 7 PC

Today, computer protection is nothing to sneeze at; there are many potential dangers lurking out there that are all too eager to infect your hard drive, hijack your email, or steal your sensitive financial information. Luckily, Windows 7 includes a number of tools and features that can help you ensure your system and data are as safe as possible. This chapter shows you how to take the necessary steps to effectively use these features.

Working with the Action Center

The Windows 7 Action Center is a feature available in the Control Panel that displays in one place information about all the updates your computer needs for both security and regular maintenance activities. For example, if your antivirus program expires, the Action Center lets you know so that you can renew your subscription or find another antivirus program.

You can use the Action Center to review the status of your system security and to set alerts so that you'll know when something important comes up. What's more, you can customize the information in the Action Center so that it displays just what you want to see when an alert is in order.

Reviewing System Status

You can easily see which security tools are in place on your computer, change settings, and update your software in the Action Center. You can find all the tools you need in the System and Security page of the Control Panel.

1. Click Start.

2. Click Control Panel.

3. Click Review Your Computer's Status in the System and Security area. The tag color to the left of the issue indicates the urgency of the issue—yellow warns you that the item should be resolved eventually; red indicates that your attention is needed immediately.

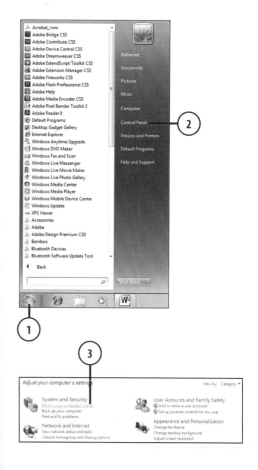

4. Check the various settings currently active on your system. On the computer shown here, the Action Center shows that the Network Firewall is turned on, Windows Update is set to download and install program updates automatically, and a virus protection program is being used. The settings also show that spyware protection, Internet security settings, and User Account Controls are all actively protecting your computer. Your computer may show different settings from the ones shown here. Windows 7 will prompt you by displaying a yellow or red alert for items that need your attention.

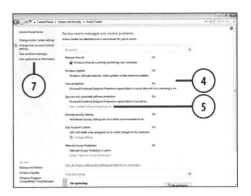

5. Click a link to get more information about the topic. The link might enable you to change settings or view more information about the installed program.

6. Click the button that is provided on issues you need to resolve. The name of the button and the task performed will vary depending on what Windows 7 is prompting you to do.

7. Change security settings and preferences. You can modify the way User Account Control settings are handled, look through past Action Center messages, or check the performance of your system.

WHY WORRY ABOUT USER ACCOUNT CONTROL?

It's not unusual today when you're surfing the Web to encounter websites and online programs that want to make changes to your computer. Some of these downloads are legitimate—perhaps you need the latest version of Microsoft Silverlight or Adobe Flash in order to play a movie trailer. But some programs are not so well-intentioned; and these are the ones you need User Account Control to block.

User Account Control makes it easy for you to find out when a program wants to make a change to your computer. You can set up User Account Control so you'll be notified when a program tries to change your system settings. (It's set to do this by default.) Windows 7 offers four different settings— ranging from Always Notify to Never Notify—and you can easily change the settings by clicking Change User Account Control Settings in the left panel of the Control Panel. Although User Account Control prompts can be annoying, before you disable them, remember that they're there for your protection.

Working with an Action Center Alert

The Action Center divides the various alerts into two main categories: Security and Maintenance. These alerts offer you ways to find out more information about the specific issue and provide a button offering an action you can take to complete the task involved.

Alerts let you know about issues that need your attention, and they are color-coded to help you know what's most important to focus on first. Depending on the needs of your particular computer, you may see both yellow and red alerts. Yellow alerts are cautioning you that the issue needs some action from you, and red alerts let you know that an important matter needs to be addressed.

1. Click the button to get more information about the next steps in resolving the issue. The buttons you'll see vary depending on the topic of the alert. For example, View Message Details provides more information about the alert, and Check for Solutions helps you troubleshoot a problem the alert has identified.

2. Review the information provided. This again will vary depending on the topic of the alert.

3. Click a link to go online if necessary to solve the problem. A new browser window will open over your Control Panel window with links you can use to troubleshoot the issue.

4. Rate the message solution to give Microsoft feedback about whether the suggestions were helpful.

5. Click OK.

Yelling Help

The Ask for Help link is at the bottom of the message details window. Clicking this link displays additional information in Windows Help and Support that enables you to use Windows Remote Assistance to ask a friend for help, post a question about the problem in the Microsoft Answers discussion forum, or contact the tech support department of your computer manufacturer or Microsoft Customer Support. Additionally, links are provided so that you can search the Windows or Microsoft TechNet websites for additional information.

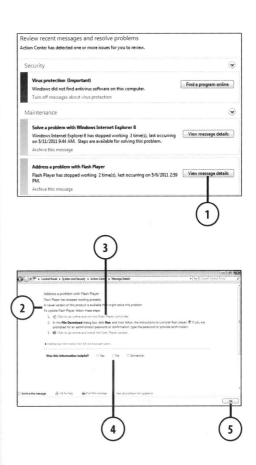

ARCHIVING MESSAGES

After you open and review a message displayed in the Action Center, Windows 7 archives the message automatically for you and removes it from the alert list. You can view a message you've already opened, however—perhaps you didn't take action on it earlier and now you want to do something with it—by clicking View Archived Messages in the Action Center window. The Archived Messages list shows you the title of the original message, the date on which the issue occurred, and the status of the issue. Open an archived message by double-clicking it. When you're finished viewing archived messages, click OK.

Changing Action Center Alerts

Within each message displayed in the Windows 7 Action Center, you see a link offering you next steps in how to deal with the alert. You may choose to turn off messages about that particular issue, archive the message, or ignore the message. You can change which issues you receive alerts for so that you are notified about only the ones you want to see.

1. In the Action Center, click Change Action Center Settings.

2. Click to uncheck any security item you *don't* want Windows 7 to check for.

3. Click to uncheck any maintenance messages you don't want Windows 7 to display.

4. Click OK.

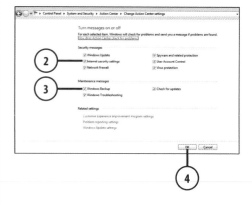

Choice—It's Your Prerogative

Of course, you can change the items Windows 7 checks for and the messages you receive at any time. If you turn off an item and then get concerned that maybe you need it after all, simply go to the Action Center, click Change Action Center Settings again, and click to check any unmarked boxes of items you want to add. Click OK to save your settings.

Out of Sight, Out of Mind

Although being alerted for every little thing can be annoying, unless you have a specific reason for turning off an alert—for example, Windows 7 doesn't recognize the antivirus program you're using on your PC and keeps telling you there's no antivirus program installed—the best practice is to leave all the alerts turned on. Why would you want to do this? Because there may be issues that Windows 7 will raise that you aren't aware of in the moment, and if you turn off the alerts altogether, you could potentially miss something that might put your system at risk.

Updating Problem Reporting

When Windows 7 experiences a problem of some sort—perhaps your version of Word locked up when you were saving the file, or Internet Explorer hung without loading a page for a long time, which caused an error—the program by default looks for a solution and displays it in a pop-up message on your desktop. You can tailor the way Windows 7 handles that, however, if you want to reduce the amount of background searching your computer is doing without your knowledge.

1. In the Action Center, click Change Action Center Settings.

2. Click Problem Reporting Settings.

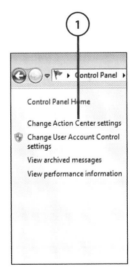

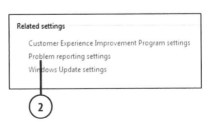

3. Click the setting you want to apply.

4. Click OK.

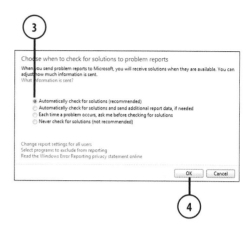

Changes for Everyone!

You can change the problem reporting settings for other users who use
your computer as well (if you're the
Administrator) by displaying the
Problem Reporting Settings page
and clicking Change Report Settings
for All Users. You can then choose the
setting you want Windows 7 to use,
or you can leave Allow Each User to
Choose Settings as the default and
enable individuals to specify their
own preferences.

CHOOSING A PROBLEM REPORTING SETTING

Setting	Choose When
Automatically Check for Solutions	You want Windows 7 to search help content and search online for possible solutions to the problem.
Automatically Check for Solutions and Send Additional Report Data, If Needed	You want Windows 7 to search your computer and online for solutions and send error reporting information to Microsoft for data-gathering purposes.
Each Time a Problem Occurs, Ask Me Before Checking for Solutions	You want Windows 7 to give you the choice of searching online for solutions.
Never Check for Solutions	You don't want Windows 7 to look for solutions on your computer or online.

PROGRAMS UNDER THE RADAR

If you're working with a program that is having repeated problems but you don't want it to be included in the problem reporting, you can turn off reporting for a particular program. Display the Action Center and click Change Action Center Settings. Then click Problem Reporting Settings below the list of message options.

Click Select Programs to Exclude from Reporting, and in the next page, click Add to display the Problem Reporting dialog box. Navigate to the folder containing the program file you want to exclude, click it, and click Open and then click OK. Windows 7 adds the program to the list, and in the event you have a problem with that program in the future, Windows 7 will not take action to find a solution or report the problem to Microsoft.

Setting Up User Accounts

If you share your Windows 7 PC with others in your household, it's a good idea to create separate user accounts for each person involved. This helps you keep your files and programs straight, set the permissions you want, use your own passwords, and limit the access others have to your personal information. You can set user accounts with different privileges (for example, you might want to set up different accounts for your children and use parental controls to make sure they are online only during the hours it's okay with you). You can also easily change and customize any user accounts you create at any time.

Creating User Accounts

Each individual user of your computer can have his or her own user
account so that specific program
preferences, histories, favorites, and
more can be kept separately. This
makes using the computer more
convenient for you, because you can
find just what *you're* looking for as
opposed to sorting through dozens
of files created by others.

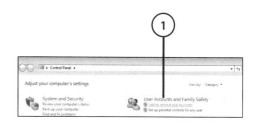

1. From the Control Panel, click Add
   or Remove User Accounts.

2. Click Create a New Account.

3. Type a name for the new account.

4. Click Create Account.

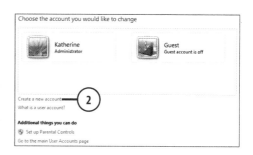

Why Standard Is Fine

Sure, we all have that overachiev-
er's tendency. But when it comes
to user accounts in Windows 7, it's
best to reserve the Administrator
setting to one or two people who
will oversee the usage of the various user accounts in Windows 7.
The Administrator can set up and
manage accounts, reassign passwords, set parental controls, and
more. It's also a good idea to add
a password to your Administrator
account so that basic settings
aren't up for grabs (or inadvertent
edits) by others who may use
your computer.

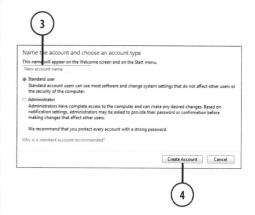

Tailoring User Account Settings

You can customize the settings for your own account or those of others—if you're the Administrator—by using the tools in the User Accounts and Family Safety area of the Control Panel. You can change the account name and picture, set other account controls, or even delete the account if you like.

1. From the Control Panel, click Add or Remove User Accounts.

2. Click the account icon of the account you want to change.

3. Click to change the name on the account.

4. Click Change the Picture. You can use one of the sample photos Windows 7 provides for you or add one of your own custom pictures.

5. Change the account type (from Standard to Administrator or from Administrator to Standard).

6. Click to return to the Manage Accounts page, where you can choose to display the settings for another account.

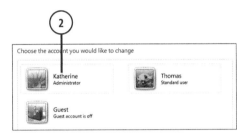

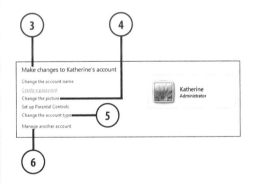

Passwords and More

This is the spot in Windows 7 where you can add and change passwords for various user accounts. You can also add parental controls to make sure your kids stay safe while they use your computer. This is the topic of the next section, so we go into more detail on that process there.

Setting Parental Controls

Parental controls in Windows 7 are tools that enable you to set the amount of time you want your kids to be allowed to use the computer, choose the specific programs you want your kids to have access to, and identify content you want Windows 7 to block when your kids are using the computer.

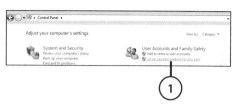

1. From the Control Panel, click Set Up Parental Controls for Any User in the User Accounts and Family Safety area.

2. Click the user account of the person for whom you want to change account settings.

3. In the Parental Controls area, click On, Enforce Current Settings.

4. Click Time Limits.

5. Click and drag to display in blue all the times you want the user's access to the computer to be blocked.

6. Click OK.

7. Click Games.

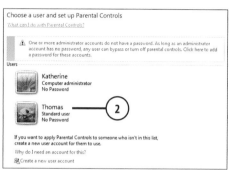

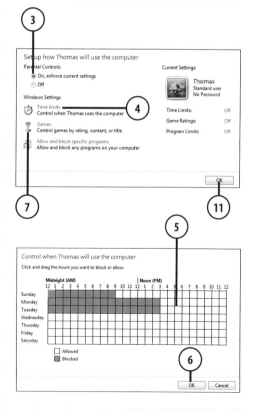

8. Click to use game ratings to manage your child's access to games or block specific types of content you don't want your child to see.

9. Click to choose specific programs you want to block your child from using.

10. Click OK to close the Games Controls page.

11. Back on the Setup page, click OK.

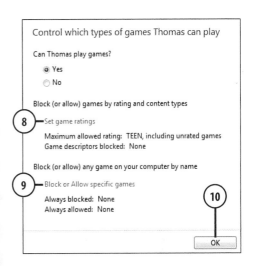

Control which types of games Thomas can play

Can Thomas play games?

◉ Yes
○ No

Block (or allow) games by rating and content types

— Set game ratings

Maximum allowed rating: TEEN, including unrated games
Game descriptors blocked: None

Block (or allow) any game on your computer by name

— Block or Allow specific games

Always blocked: None
Always allowed: None

OK

Not Sure How to Schedule Computer Time?

If you're struggling with when to allow your kids to use the computer—or having trouble deciding who gets access when—consider starting with the big picture. Use the timing schedule in parental controls to simply block out the time your kids should be at school and then consider how much time you want them to have on the weekend. It's okay to allow more than one user account access to the computer at any given time, so you don't have to get too detailed as you create the schedule. In other words, blocking out the definite "off limits" times is much easier than deciding which nights Thomas can use the computer and which nights are Sara's turn.

Hey, Don't Forget the Password!

Windows 7 is very consistent about reminding you that you need to set a password for Administrator accounts. You'll see the alert text, complete with yellow exclamation point symbol (!), anywhere the software notices your account is unprotected. You learn how to set passwords in the next section, never fear.

UNDERSTANDING GAME RATINGS

Rating	Age	Description
Early Childhood	3+	Content is suitable for all ages over 3.
Everyone	6+	Game content is fine for all ages over 6. The game may include small amounts of violence, comic mischief, or some mild language.
Everyone 10+	10+	Game content includes some mild language or violence and could include some suggestive themes.
Teen	13+	Game content could include violence and strong language.
Mature	17+	Game content may include strong violence, strong language, and sexual themes.
Adults Only	Adults	Game content may include graphic depictions of sex or violence.

ADD WINDOWS LIVE FAMILY SAFETY

>>> Go Further

Microsoft beefs up the family security factor by offering Windows Live Family Safety (http://explore.live.com), a free online tool that is part of Windows Live Essentials 2011. This tool works alongside the parental controls you set up in Windows 7 and enables you to see whom your kids are talking to online and produce reports of their online activity.

Additionally, a feature called SafeSearch filters search results in Bing, Google, and Yahoo! search engines to make sure that unwanted content stays out of the mix. And you can also use Windows Live Family Safety to safeguard your child's email and instant messaging and even monitor the whole thing remotely by logging in online and displaying a report of recent activity.

Setting a Password

A strong password is your first line of defense against a person, company, or program that wants to access your accounts, steal your information, or harm your computer or files in any way. You can easily set and change your password on your Windows 7 system, and each individual user can set up his or her own unique password as well. Using a password safeguards your programs and files and makes sure that your private information stays that way.

Creating a Password

Adding a password to your account is a simple matter. In fact, if you're the account administrator and haven't added a password yet, Windows 7 prompts you repeatedly to do so—and includes the link to the tool in the message box it displays. What could be more convenient?

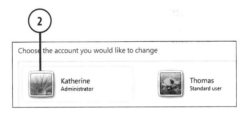

1. In the Control Panel, click Add or Remove User Accounts.

2. Click the account you want to set the password for.

3. Click Create a Password.

4. Enter a new password.

5. Retype the password.

6. Enter an optional password hint if you want a reminder in case you forget the password you created.

7. Click Create Password.

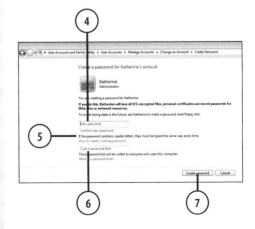

What Makes a Strong Password?

A strong password is at least eight characters long and doesn't include any recognizable words or number sequences. What's more, you should vary the capitalization of letters, mixing the upper- and lowercase letters. Windows 7 remembers your password as case sensitive, which means that 45GoT37 is a different password than 45gOt37.

>>> Go Further

WORRIED ABOUT FORGETTING YOUR PASSWORD?

Windows 7 provides a way to give you access to your programs and files in the unhappy event that you forget your password at some point. You can create a password reset disk (or USB flash drive) containing a file that enables you to reset the password without losing access to your information.

You'll need a disk or USB flash drive to be able to create the reset file. Display the Control Panel, click User Accounts and Family Safety, click User Accounts, and click Create a Password Reset Disk in the links on the left. The Welcome to the Forgotten Password Wizard screen appears, and you can click Next to move through the onscreen instructions and create the disk or USB flash file you need to get into your computer later if you lose track of the password you set.

Changing a Password

Changing your password from time to time is good practice whether you're working at your computer or safeguarding files online. In Windows 7, you can easily modify your password by following just a few simple steps.

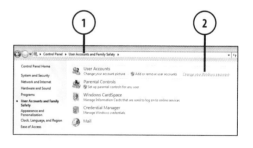

1. In the Control Panel, display User Accounts and Family Safety.

2. Click Change Your Windows Password.

3. Click Change Your Password.

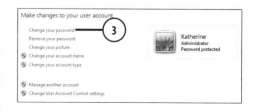

4. Type your current password.

5. Type the new password twice. Click the link How To Create a Strong Password to get suggestions on creating a secure password.

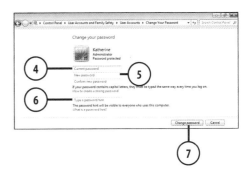

6. Add an optional hint, if you like, to jog your memory in case you forget your password at some point.

7. Click Change Password.

Setting Your Account Free

If you decide after some period of time that the password on your Windows 7 account is an annoyance—and you don't have parental controls or other user accounts set up on the system which make it a smart thing to have your Administrator account set up separately—you can do away with your password relatively easily. In the Control Panel, click Add or Remove User Accounts and click your Administrator account. Click Remove the Password, enter your current password, and click Remove Password. Simple.

Administering Passwords

If you have set up user accounts for your kids, your spouse, your roommates, or your pets (no, wait, scratch that), you need to be able to assign, recover, and change passwords if need be. As the Administrator, you can do this easily by clicking Add or Remove User Accounts in the Control Panel and then selecting the account of the user whose password you'd like to change. Click Create a Password (or Change the Password, if you've already added one) and type the password (twice) and provide a hint to remind you about the password later—just in case.

Using Windows Defender

Windows 7 comes with an antispyware utility already built in: Windows Defender. Spyware is software that can download to your computer without your knowing it, and the makers of the spyware can find out about your usage habits or gain access to important files and data. Windows Defender runs automatically in the background as you use your computer, blocking any attempts by spyware to download to your computer and notifying you when programs try to change your Windows settings.

You can also use Windows Defender to regularly scan your system and remove any suspicious files that have been added to your system without your knowledge.

>> Go Further

ADDING MALWARE PROTECTION TOO

In addition to the need for a program that nets out all the spyware that wants to infiltrate your computer, you need an antivirus program that makes sure your computer doesn't catch any bugs from wayward programmers intent on doing harm to you or your data.

Microsoft Security Essentials is a free downloadable program you can add to your computer to protect it against viruses, spyware, and malware (or software with malicious intent to cause harm). To find out more about Microsoft Security Essentials, go to the Microsoft website and search for the product. The free download installs directly from the Web, so you can simply click Download Now and follow the onscreen prompts to set up the service. Microsoft Security Essentials updates regularly so that your software always includes information about the latest viruses and malware.

Scanning with Windows Defender

Although Windows Defender works in the background, you can also do a scan of your system periodically to make sure no worrisome files have snuck in under your radar.

1. Click the Start button.

2. Click in the Search box, type **Windows Defender**, and press Enter.

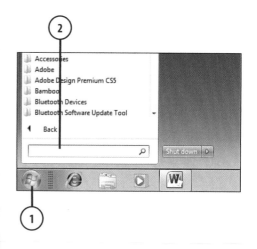

3. In the Windows Defender window, click the Scan arrow.

4. Choose the option you want for the type of scan you want Windows Defender to perform.

5. After the scan completes, Defender reports on any findings. Click the Close box to exit Defender.

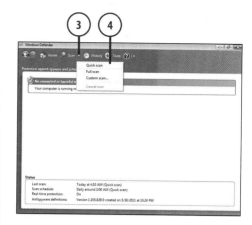

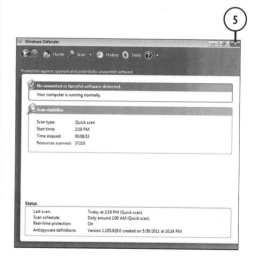

SCANNING STYLES IN WINDOWS DEFENDER

Type of Scan	Description
Quick Scan	Windows Defender checks all files that have been downloaded to your computer since the date of the last scan.
Full Scan	Windows Defender checks all files on all drives and folders in your computer.
Custom Scan	You can choose the drives and folders you want Windows Defender to check.

Changing Windows Defender Options

You can also change when and how Defender scans your system looking for suspicious files so that you can ensure the scan is done after hours, for example, or at a time when you know you won't be using your computer.

1. In the Defender window, click Tools.

2. Click Options.

3. Click the option you want to review or change.

4. Modify the settings in the right side of the window. Choose the Frequency setting you want to specify for how often Windows Defender scans your computer. You can choose the approximate time for the scan so that it occurs when you won't be using your computer. And in the Type setting, choose whether you want a Quick Scan, a Full Scan, or a Custom Scan.

5. Click Save to save your settings.

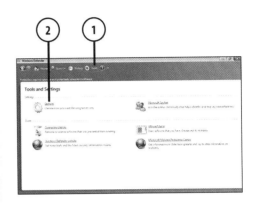

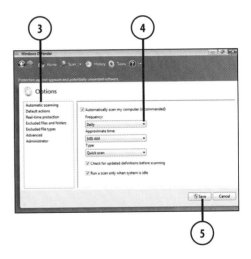

Changing What Happens Next

Windows Defender uses what's known as a *definitions file* to determine what should be done with risky files found on your computer. You can change what happens to files that trigger different alert levels (Severe alert, High alert, Medium alert, and Low alert) by clicking Default Actions in the Windows Defender Options window and choosing a new action (Recommended Action Based on Definitions, Remove, or Quarantine).

It's Not All Good

It's Not All Good

One of the challenges of working with antivirus, spyware, and malware protection programs is that they don't play nicely together. As you can imagine, they are suspicious of everyone; that's their job.

This means that if you have installed another type of antivirus or spyware program, such as Lavasoft's Ad-Aware, Windows Defender may be disabled. Or even when you download and install Microsoft Security Essentials (which includes all the basics of Windows Defender but adds a malware checker too), Windows Defender is turned off so that the other program is turned on.

If you'd rather have Windows Defender operating, you may need to uninstall the other antivirus or spyware software before you can activate Windows Defender. Yes, it's a hassle, but it's one of the prices we pay for secure systems that don't crash every few minutes.

Turning on Your Windows Firewall

You may be feeling as though your computer is pretty secure by this point, but there's another piece to this security puzzle that you really need to have. Windows 7 includes a firewall utility that enables you to further protect the programs and data on your computer from unwanted attacks. A firewall checks all the information coming to your computer from the Internet or from a network you may be connected to, to see whether the sender is a trusted contact and the information can be considered safe for your computer. If any suspicious information is found, your Windows 7 Firewall alerts you so that you can block the sender.

Activating the Firewall

Chances are that Windows Firewall is already turned on by default on your computer. But you can check the settings easily and turn on the utility if necessary.

1. Display the Control Panel and click System and Security.

2. Click Check Firewall Status in the Windows Firewall area.

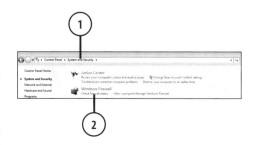

3. Review the settings in the Home or Work (Private) Networks area.

4. Click the Public Networks arrow to see settings saved for networks in public places such as coffee shops or libraries.

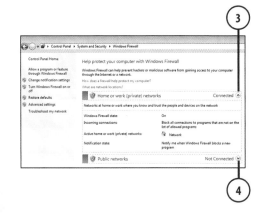

Changing Firewall Settings

When Windows Firewall is active, you are prompted each time a program tries to make changes to Windows 7 on your computer if the sender is not on your trusted contacts list. You can change the settings for Windows Firewall so that you receive different alerts if you like.

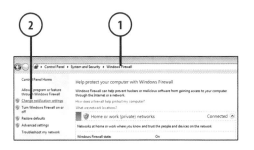

1. Display the Windows Firewall window from the System and Security section of the Control Panel.

2. Click Change Notification Settings.

3. Change the settings in the Private network area. You can choose whether you want to block incoming connections or be notified when Windows Firewall blocks a program. You can also choose to turn off Windows Firewall for your private network, but that's not recommended.

4. Click to change your Public network settings, if applicable. You can make the same choice—block everything or get notified about the programs Windows Firewall blocks—for your public network.

5. Click OK.

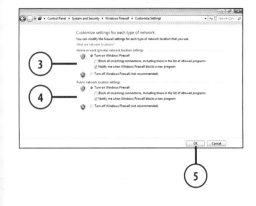

Changing User Account Control Settings

Windows 7 uses the User Account Control settings you choose to determine how sensitive you want the software to be about notifications when an outside company or website tries to make changes to your Windows settings. You can tailor your User Account Control settings so that the other spyware and antivirus programs you use know how responsible to be to potential threats.

Changing User Account Control Settings

You'll find you have only a few different settings you can apply for User Account Control. By default, Windows 7 notifies you when outside programs try to make changes to your computer by dimming the desktop and displaying an alert in the center of your screen. You can also have Windows 7 notify you when your own actions make changes to the operating system (this is the highest setting for the notifications) or remove the dimming. Finally, you can turn off User Account Control settings, which of course isn't recommended.

1. Click System and Security in the Control Panel.

2. Click Action Center, and if necessary, click the Security arrow to display all your security settings.

3. Under User Account Control, click Change Settings.

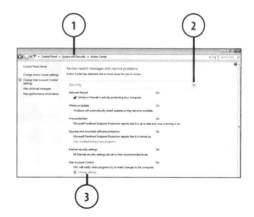

4. Drag the slider up if you want to increase your notifications. The one level of security above the default setting notifies you every time you or a program changes your computer settings.

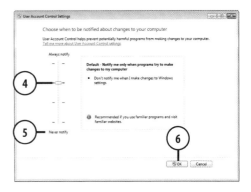

5. Drag the slider down to decrease the notifications. You'll find two levels of security lower than the default setting; one level notifies you only when a program tries to make changes to the desktop (but your desktop doesn't not "dim" to get your attention), and the lowest level never notifies you when changes are made. This is not safe to do.

6. Click OK.

Annoying Prompts

Some users find User Account Control annoying because of the number of times they are interrupted with prompts as they are using their computer and browsing the Web. The trade-off, however, is that you get a more secure system with the necessary safeguards in place to ensure that it's more difficult for unwanted programs and sites to download harmful code to your computer. In the end, safety is a good investment and managing security—through passwords, the firewall, User Account Control, and more—is all part of a safe and secure computing experience.

As your experience with your computer grows, you will collect all kinds of files—music, documents, pictures, videos, and more. Luckily, Windows 7 includes super-fast, smart search tools that help you find what you're looking for quickly.

Windows instantly displays files that include the phrase you specified.

Enter a search phrase.

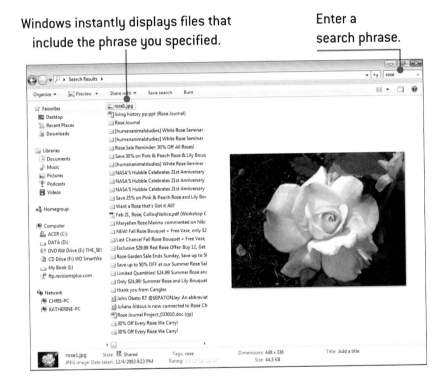

This chapter shows you how to find the files you need—as quickly as possible—on your Windows 7 PC:

→ Performing a simple search

→ Extending a search

→ Customizing and saving a search

Find What You're Looking for—Fast!

Whether you use your Windows 7 PC for work or entertainment—or a combination of both—you will soon find that learning how to find the files you need is a natural part of your computing landscape. When you want to listen to a particular song, you need to know how to locate the song you want Windows Media Player or your Zune to play. When you want to send a photo to your aunt in Amherst, you need to be able to locate the picture file you need and attach it to an email message addressed to her.

Similarly, for your work tasks, you need to be able to locate the files you want whether they are stored in a folder on your hard drive, tucked away on a flash drive, or stored online somewhere. Windows 7 includes a comprehensive search feature that enables you to find the files you need quickly by knowing a few simple search techniques. And that's the subject of this entire chapter.

More About Files Coming Soon

In Chapter 7, "Organizing Files and Folders," you learn all about working with Windows 7 file libraries, creating folders and subfolders, and moving and copying files so they'll be where you want them to be on your Windows 7 PC. This chapter focuses solely on searching for specific files to help you locate what you're looking for as quickly as possible.

Performing a Simple Search

When you're looking for a specific file on your computer, you may be at a bit of a loss about where to begin. Should you open a program that you used to create it? Or go back to the place where you first downloaded it to your computer? What's the simplest way to find what you're looking for? Luckily, Windows 7 offers several different ways to find the files you need—and each tool is within a click or two of where you are right now.

Using the Start Menu

The easiest place to begin finding the files you want is in the Start menu.

1. Click Start.

2. Click in the search box.

3. Type a word or phrase that is part of the file you want to find.

4. Click the search result you want to view.

5. Right-click to complete a task without opening the file.

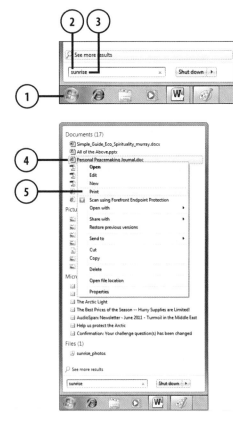

Searching Shortcuts

You can add filters to your search in the Start menu by typing the name of the filter you want to use in the search text. For example, instead of typing **roses** and getting results with documents, email messages, and more, you can type **kind:picture** as part of the search phrase, and Windows displays picture files that meet your criteria at the top of the list.

Using the Search Box

When you are working in Windows Explorer (the tool in Windows 7 that helps you organize files and folders), you can easily use the search box to find files and folders that match what you're looking for.

1. Click Start.

2. Click Pictures (or Documents).

Click to edit the file

③ ④

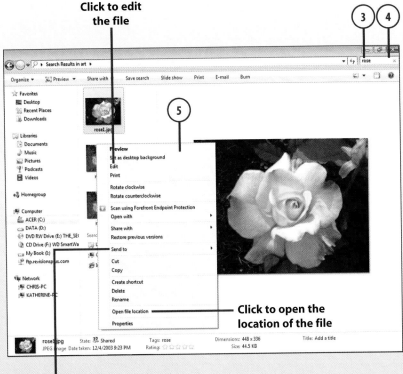

⑤

Click to open the location of the file

Click to send the file to a person or device

3. Click in the search box.

4. Type a word or phrase you think will be in the picture filename.

5. Right-click the desired result to see a list of options suggesting ways you can work with the file.

TAGGING FOR BETTER SEARCHES

You can add tags to images and files to help Windows 7 locate them faster in searches you perform. Right-click the file you want to tag and click Open File Location. At the bottom of the folder display in Windows Explorer, you see a number of file properties you can assign to the file.

Click in the Tags field and begin to type a tag for the file. As you type, Windows 7 displays a list of tags already in the system that begin with the letters you type. Click the check box of one on the list if it fits the tag you want to add; if you don't see a tag that fits, type a new tag in the box.

The more consistent you can be in the use of file tags, the better search results you'll get.

Using the Search Folder

Windows 7 also includes a Search folder that you can use to locate your files. The Search folder is part of Windows Explorer; you can also view and use any saved searches in the Search folder.

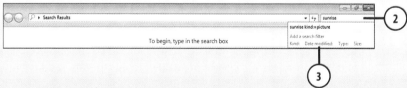

1. Press the Windows key and F.

2. Type the word or phrase you want to find.

3. Click a search filter if you want to narrow your search.

4. Review the search results.

5. Close the search.

What's This About Filters?

If you want to filter out unwanted search results, you can click one of the filters that appear beneath the search box when you begin typing a new search. To learn more about using Windows filters and creating your own, see "Understanding Search Filters," in the next section.

Extending a Search

If you don't find what you're looking for the first time out of the gates, you can extend your search to others areas of your computer—and even search places online where you have stored files. In addition to expanding your search into new areas, you can narrow your search by applying a search filter. You can also change the way your computer indexes files so that the results you want arrive quickly and accurately.

Filtering Your Results

You can apply one of the Windows
filters to your search so that the
results you receive are more relevant
to what you're looking for.

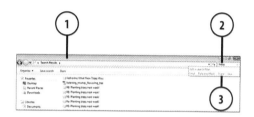

1. Display the Search window.

2. Click in the search box.

3. Click the search filter you want to
   use to narrow your search results.
   For this example, click Date
   Modified.

4. Click the date of the files you
   want to view, or click and drag to
   select a range of dates.

5. You can also click one of the Date
   Modified filters to provide a more
   general time frame.

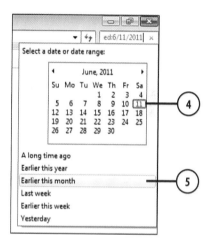

Understanding Search Filters

You can choose the filter you want to apply by clicking the filter type in the search
box. The following table explains the differences among the search filters.

Filter	Description
Kind	Displays files of a certain kind, including Calendar entries, folders, games, instant messages, and more.
Date Modified	Shows files that were created or modified on the date you select; you can also choose phrases like "last week" or "a long time ago" to indicate time frame.
Type	Displays a list of file types so that you can choose the type of file you want to see (for example, .jpg or .bmp).
Size	Displays files within a certain range of sizes, from Empty (0) to Gigantic (>128MB).

Use Multiple Filters

You can apply multiple search filters to reduce unwanted results and zero in on the ones you want to see. For example, you might use the Kind filter to choose instant messages and use Date Modified to display all IM communications within the past week.

Filters, Filters Go Away

If you've added a search filter that you regret, you can easily delete it by clicking in the search box and pressing Backspace, or selecting the filter name and pressing Delete. If you want to cancel the search, click the Cancel Search button in the right side of the search box.

Expanding Your Search

If the search results didn't bring back the file result you were hoping for, you can expand your search to include other areas and devices.

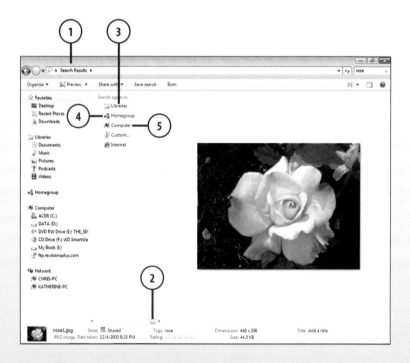

1. Display the Search window.

2. Scroll the results to the last entry.

3. Click Libraries to search all the libraries on your computer (Documents, Pictures, Music, Podcasts, and Videos).

4. Click HomeGroup to search all the drives on the computers that are part of your HomeGroup.

5. Click Computer to search all the drives and folders on your computer.

Narrowing and Expanding at the Same Time

You can choose which folders you want Windows to index and search by default, which gives you the chances of skipping unnecessary folders and speeding up your search results. You find out how to change the locations Windows indexes in the section "Changing Indexing Options," later in this chapter.

Searching Online

Did you know you could do an online search from within Windows 7? If you're not finding what you need on your local computer, you can launch a web search from your search results. Here's how.

1. Display the Search window.

2. Scroll to the end of your search results.

3. Click Internet.

4. Click the search result you'd like to see.

5. Click Advanced at the top-right of the center column to streamline your search.

Changing Indexing Options

Windows 7 indexes the files on your computer so that it can retrieve the files you want quickly and display accurate results. You can customize the folders and devices Windows uses to generate the index to help speed the process and ensure that the most relevant files appear in the results list.

1. Click Start.

2. Click Control Panel.

3. In the Indexing Options dialog box, review the current locations Windows 7 indexes.

4. To change the index locations, click Modify.

5. In the Indexed Locations dialog box, click to add check marks to locations you want to add.

6. Click to deselect locations you don't want to include in the index.

7. Click OK.

Indexing Encrypted Files

If you frequently protect your files by encrypting them, you can change an indexing option so that Windows 7 will included encrypted files in the search index. Display Indexing Options and click Advanced. Under File Settings, click Index Encrypted Files and click OK.

Fight the Temptation to Index Everything

Although it may seem like a great idea to index all the drives and folders and devices attached to your Windows 7 PC, Microsoft says that it's best to resist that desire. Indexing everything could actually have the opposite effect you're hoping for, by slowing down your searches dramatically. Better to have Windows 7 index only the folders and drives you use most; that's where the files you need are likely to be found anyway.

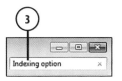

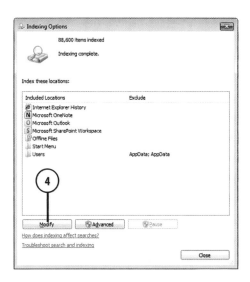

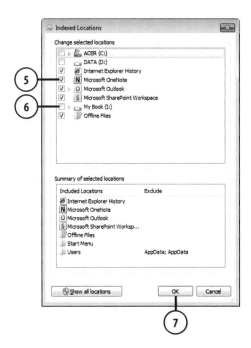

Customizing and Saving a Search

Windows 7 makes it easy for you to create your own custom searches that find the files you want within a drive and folder you specify. What's more, you can save searches that you perform often so that you can easily call up a saved search to use again later.

Creating a Custom Search

As you learned previously, Windows indexes the files in selected folders on your computer. You can customize the search so that only specific folders are included in the search.

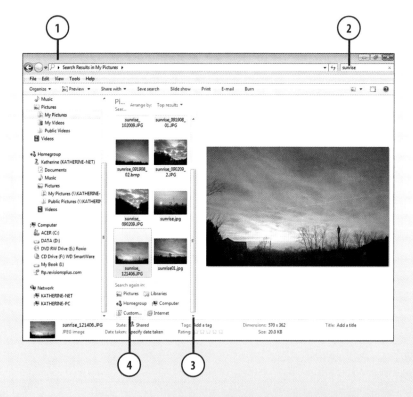

1. Press the Windows key and F to display the Search window.

2. Type your search phrase.

3. Scroll to the end of the search results.

4. Click Customize.

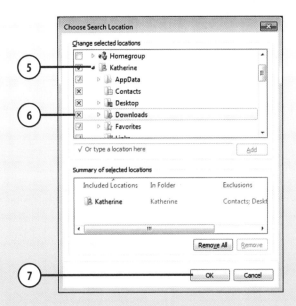

5. Click the triangle to the left of a folder that includes subfolders.

6. Click to remove subfolders from the search.

7. Click OK.

Changing Search Options for Folders

You can change the way Windows searches a particular folder by setting the folder properties. You can choose whether to include compressed files, find partial matches, and include subfolders in your search.

1. Display the Control Panel.

2. Click in the search box and type **Folder Options**.

3. Click the Folder Options link in the Search window.

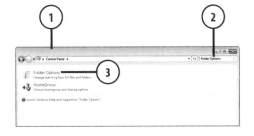

4. Click the Search tab.

5. Choose whether you want Windows 7 to search only the filenames of non-indexed locations.

6. Choose whether you want to include subfolders in your search, display results that partially match your search text, use natural language search, or bypass the index when you're searching system files.

7. Choose whether you want to include system directories and compressed files.

8. Click OK to save your changes.

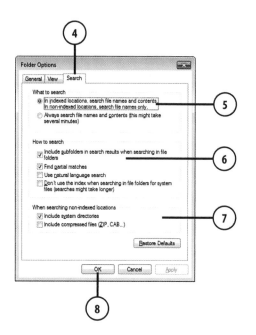

Undoing Changes

If you want to return the search options to their default values, click Restore Defaults before clicking OK.

Displaying Hidden Files

By default, Windows 7 hides some of the files you work with regularly. These system files are hidden from view so that you don't accidentally delete them or move them from folders in which they need to appear. When you're searching your computer for files and folders, however, there's a chance that some hidden files won't appear in your results unless you display them prior to searching.

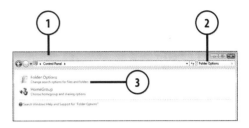

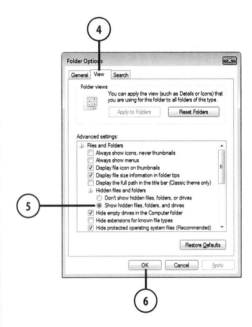

1. Display the Control Panel.

2. Click in the search box and type **Folder Options**.

3. Click the Folder Options link in the Search window.

4. Click the View tab.

5. Click the Show Hidden Files, Folders, and Drives radio button.

6. Click OK.

Saving Your Search

After you create a search you particularly like—perhaps one that you intend to use in the future—you can save it so that you can use it again. Windows 7 displays your saved searches in the Search window where you can access them easily.

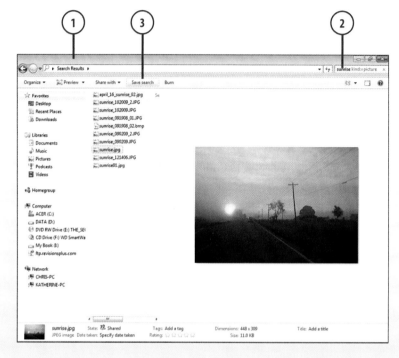

1. Press the Windows key and F to open the Search window.

2. Enter the search phrase and choose any filters you want to apply.

3. Click Save Search.

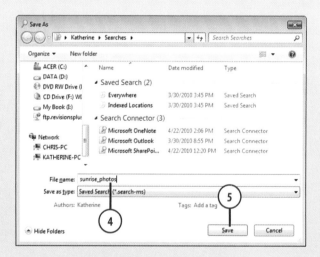

4. Enter a name for the search.

5. Click Save.

The search is added to the Favorites area in the navigation pane of Windows Explorer so that you can use it easily by simply clicking it. The results will appear automatically in the details area.

Windows 7 makes it simple for you to find, launch, and work with multiple programs at once.

You can run multiple programs at once and switch among them in Windows 7.

Windows 7 gadgets.

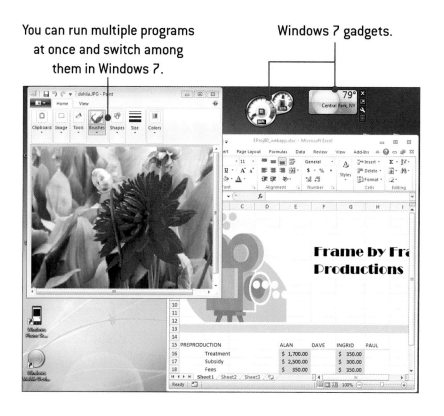

This chapter shows you how to work with programs and gadgets in Windows 7 by spotlighting these tasks:

→ Finding and starting a program
→ Working with program windows
→ Closing a program
→ Downloading a program
→ Installing and uninstalling programs
→ Working with gadgets

6

Exploring, Downloading, and Running Programs

Whether you are using your computer primarily to stay in touch with friends and family, to finish the work you didn't get done at the office, or to watch your favorite media and shop your favorite sites, programs are at the heart of all you do on your Windows 7 PC. Microsoft Word is an application program you use to create documents, mailing labels, and more. Internet Explorer is a web browser program that enables you to move from site to site on the Web. The Calculator, in Windows 7, is a small program you can use to do calculations quickly.

In addition to programs like these, which help you accomplish specific tasks, your Windows 7 PC also relies on many system programs to help it keep running safely and efficiently. In this chapter, we focus on the application programs you use for work and play with Windows 7.

Finding and Starting a Program

Depending on the type of system setup you purchased when you bought your Windows 7 PC—or whether you're upgrading to Windows 7 on a computer you already owned—you may have all kinds of programs installed on your computer, or you may have next to none.

Whether you have a huge collection of programs or only one or two on your computer so far, you can find them listed in the Start menu under All Programs.

Starting a Program from the Start Menu

The easiest way to start a program on your computer is to begin with the Start menu. You can find programs as well as recently accessed files, libraries, and system settings available when you click Start.

1. Click Start.

2. Click the icon of the program you want to start.

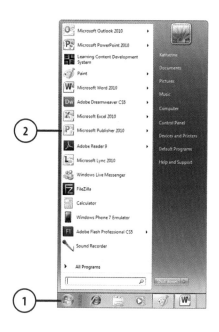

Be My BFF Program

It's a good idea to position the programs you use most often so they appear automatically at the top of the Start menu program list. That way, you can find and select them easily when you're ready to work with the program. You can keep a program at the top of the Start menu list by pinning it to the list. Right-click the program you want to pin in the All Programs list and click Pin to Start Menu.

Starting a Program from the Jump List

When you point to a program name that shows an arrow off to the right, a list of recently used files appears on the right side of the Start menu. If you want to launch the program *and* open one of the files in the list, click the filename; otherwise, click the program name and icon on the left side of the Start menu to launch the program with a new blank document open on the screen.

1. Click Start.

2. Point to a program showing an arrow to the right of the program name.

3. Click a filename to launch the program and open the file.

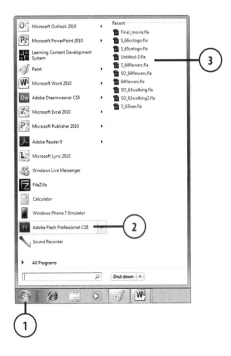

Do More Before You Jump

Jump lists give you an easy way to start a program and open a file at the same time, but you can perform other file actions as well. Right-click the file in the jump list to display a context menu that enables you to open, print, copy, or display the file properties. You can also pin the file to the list or remove it from the list altogether.

Searching for a Program

One of the great things about the search box at the bottom of the Start menu is that you can use it to search for just about anything—programs, emails, files, music, pictures, help content, and more. Follow these steps to find the program you're looking for:

1. Click Start.

2. Click in the search box and type the first few characters of the program name.

3. Click the program in the results list.

WHAT IF YOU CAN'T REMEMBER THE NAME OF THE PROGRAM?

Use Windows Explorer to scan program files or search for either the file extension created by the program (if you know it) or a word or phrase the program helps you accomplish (for example, *video editing*).

Simply type the characters you remember in the search box and scroll through the results list. If your search doesn't produce the program you're looking for, open Windows Explorer by clicking it in the taskbar (or by clicking it in the All Programs list in the Start menu) and click the Program Files folder to scan the various folders for the program you seek.

Finally, if neither of these techniques helps you locate the program, you can search for it in the Control Panel's Programs window. Click Uninstall a Program. A list of programs that are installed on your computer appears. You can click the column heading to sort the program by the program name or installation date, for example. After you discover the name of the program, close the Control Panel, return to the Start menu, type the program name in the search box, and click the program icon when it appears in the result list.

Creating a Program Shortcut

For those programs that you use often and want to access quickly, you can create a program shortcut that you keep directly on your desktop. When you double-click the program icon, the program launches automatically, and you don't need to click Start to search for the program in the All Programs list.

1. Right-click the Windows 7 desktop.

2. Point to New.

3. Click Shortcut. The Create Shortcut wizard launches.

4. Click Browse.

5. Choose the program you want to create the shortcut for.

6. Click OK.

7. Click Next.

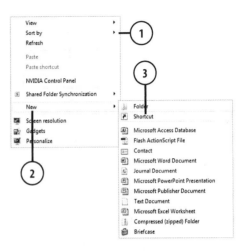

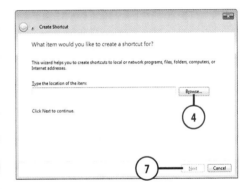

8. Type a name you want to assign to the shortcut.

9. Click Finish.

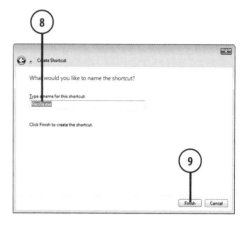

Finding the Program You Want

In the Browse for Files or Folders dialog box, click the triangle to the left of a folder name to display subfolders within it. If you are unsure where to look for the program you want, click the icon that represents your hard drive (usually, C:) and expand the Program Files subfolders to view the various programs installed on your computer. Click the .exe file for the program and click OK.

Working with Shortcuts

You can easily launch the program by double-clicking the program shortcut. You can rename the shortcut, pin it to the Start menu or taskbar, or view shortcut properties by right-clicking the shortcut icon and clicking the option you want. Note that if you delete the shortcut icon from your desktop, the program itself is not deleted; the program remains intact on your computer.

Working with Program Windows

The windows in which your programs appear have some common elements that make working with them easier. Whether the program is designed to help you plan a landscape, calculate loan payments, surf the Internet, check email, or run a virus checker, the program windows all have certain elements in common. The great thing about this is that you can move from program to program and feel confident that you know your way around the window and can find the tools you need.

Switching Among Open Programs

Remember that you can cycle through open programs by pressing Alt+Tab. A small message box appears in the center of the desktop area showing you all your current open programs. Each time you press Tab while holding Alt, Windows 7 moves to the next open program available on your computer.

Exploring a Program Window

In Chapter 1, "Getting Started with Windows 7," you learned some basic techniques on how to arrange and resize windows. The program windows you work with as you use all kinds of programs in Windows 7 all have a similar feel and function, but there are some differences that can help you use your program even more effectively. For simplicity's sake, this figure shows the Microsoft Word 2010 and Windows Paint program windows. Non-Microsoft programs generally follow the same format but may have their own unique features, such as palettes or drop-down menus.

Quick Access toolbar   Title bar   Ribbon   Window controls

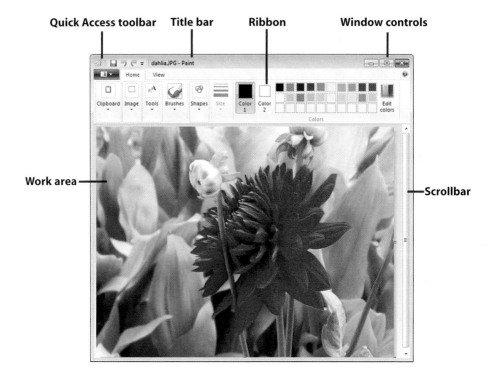

Work area ——

——Scrollbar

- **Title bar.** The title bar of the window shows you the name of the file you're working on and the name of the application program in which it was created.

- **Quick Access toolbar.** The Quick Access toolbar displays common file tools—as well as Undo and Redo—in the upper-left corner of the window where you can reach them easily.

- **Window controls.** In the upper-right corner of the program window, you can find three tools to change the state of the window. Minimize reduces the window to the taskbar; Restore Down reduces the window to its previous smaller size (or, if the window is already at a smaller size, it changes to Maximize, which makes the window full size); and Close, which closes the file and, if no other files are open for that program, closes the program as well.

- **Ribbon or menu bar.** The Office Ribbon is a feature that is common among all Microsoft programs, offering the tools and options you need for working with various programs. If the program is not a Microsoft program, you will likely see a menu bar listing menu names close to the top of the window. You can click a menu name to display a list of tools you can use in your program.

- **Scrollbars.** Depending on the size of your file and the type of program you are using, you may see horizontal and vertical scrollbars

- **Status bar.** Some programs display helpful information about commands and procedures in the status bar at the bottom of the window.

- **View controls.** Some programs offer tools for changing the display of the file—magnifying the display or changing to a different view—in the lower-right corner of the window.

- **Work area.** The work area of the window is the place where you write documents, create worksheets, edit photos, and more. The file you open and work with appears in the work area.

Finding the Desktop Again

If you have multiple programs open on the screen, it may be hard to find your Windows 7 desktop again. Go directly to the desktop by clicking the Show Desktop button, which resembles a small gray rectangle on the far right end of the Windows 7 taskbar. All programs are hidden for the moment, and the desktop appears.

How Many Programs at Once?

One of the beauties of Windows is the ease with which you can have programs open on your desktop. Depending on the size of your monitor and the number of programs you need to use, you can open a dozen program windows if you like; of course, it is difficult to see anything helpful in so many small windows! You can arrange the windows on the screen by right-clicking the taskbar and choosing Show Windows Stacked or Show Windows Side by Side.

Copying Content Between Programs

Depending on the types of programs and program information you are working with, you may be able to copy content from one program to another. Suppose, for example, that you want to add a picture from Windows Paint to your Word document as easily as possible. You can follow these steps to move the information you need:

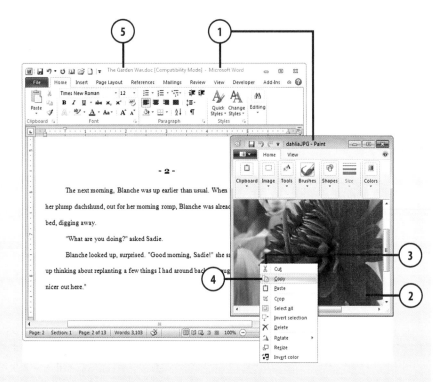

1. Begin with both programs open on the desktop.

2. Select the information you want to copy.

3. Right-click the selection.

4. Click Copy.

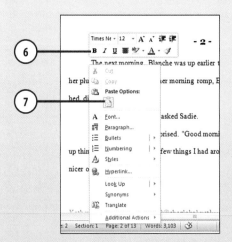

5. Select the other program window.

6. Click to position the cursor where you want to paste the information.

7. Right-click to show the context menu. Click Paste. The information is pasted at the cursor position, and you can use it in the program as usual.

Drag and Drop

With some programs—for example, when you're working with Office applications—you can drag content from one window to another. Suppose that you've created a table in one document and you'd like to include it in a report you're creating. Simply select the entire table and drag it to the new window. A copy is placed in the second window, and the original content stays intact.

Closing a Program

Years ago, computers were much more finicky about the way you close a program than they are today. Windows 7 offers a safety net for you, so if you begin to close a program without saving any changes you made to the file, the program stops and asks whether you want to save your changes before closing. You can exit a program several different ways: by clicking the close box on the program window, by using the program's Exit command, or by choosing to close the program in the Task Manager.

Exiting the Program

When you're ready to close the program you've been working with, shutting it down is a simple matter. First, save any file you were working with and then follow these steps:

1. Click the File tab or, if the program is a non-Microsoft program, click the File menu. This is typically the menu farthest left on the menu bar.

Quicker Closing
You can also exit a program by clicking the X button at the top-right corner of any open window.

2. Click Exit. Some programs may ask you to confirm that you do in fact want to close the program. If you see a prompt, click Yes to finish exiting the program.

It's Not All Good

Occasionally even stable, reliable programs hit a glitch and hang up in the middle of an operation. You'll notice that your screen updates slowly, or when you save a file, it seems as though it's taking an unusually long time. Although Windows 7 is a reliable, friendly operating system and chances are you won't have to deal with too many lockups, this does happen from time to time. So how do you shut down your program the right way when everything seems to have frozen on your desktop?

The best technique for exiting gracefully when things appear to be locked up involves pressing the Ctrl, Alt, and Del keys all at once. This key combination displays a Windows 7 screen. Click Start Task Manager. When the Task Manager appears on top of your frozen windows, click the Applications tab, click an open task in the list (which is actually the programs you have open), and click the End Task button. This technique closes the running program successfully.

Downloading and Installing Programs

Sooner or later, you are sure to discover a program you want to download and use on your computer. This is a common occurrence these days. Perhaps you learn about a trial version of a paint program you've been wanting to try so you download it to give it a test run before you buy it. Downloading the file to your computer, and then installing it successfully, is a fairly straightforward process, but it is important that you know you are downloading a reliable program from a secure site and not making your computer vulnerable to a virus or malware.

Think Before You Click!

All kinds of ads abound on the Web, and one sneaky way some not-so-reputable vendors get unsuspecting users to their site is to display an ad banner across the top of the screen that tells you (urgently) that something is wrong with your PC. The ad is designed to alarm you and get you to click quickly without thinking. Fight the temptation! It's much better to use your computer's virus-scanning software to check for problems with your PC.

Getting Ready to Download a Program

Chances are you purchased your computer along with some basic software included. In addition to Windows 7, you may also have received Microsoft Office, Internet Explorer, and one of the popular antivirus programs. When you discover a computer program you'd like to download free or purchase online, how do you know the site from which you're purchasing the software is a reputable one? Here are some things to watch for as you're looking for a secure site.

Download only from sites you trust.

Be sure Protected Mode is on.

- In Internet Explorer, look for the lock icon in the status bar or look for the words *Protected Mode: On*. This means the site is secure and your transaction will be protected.

- Download software only from sites you recognize. Sites such as Microsoft Downloads, CNET, Apple iTunes, or other well-known sites can generally be trusted to offer a secure download environment.

User ratings and reviews

- Look for user ratings and reviews. On a site where downloads are completed successfully in a trusted environment, users are able to rate and review their downloads so that other users can benefit from their experiences.

Do Your Homework

It's a good practice, when you have discovered a program you want to download, to search online to see how many different online stores offer it for sale and download. Finding a number of sources enables you to choose the one you recognize most (and you may find a better deal, too).

Purchasing, Downloading, and Installing a Program

After you decide on a program and you're set to download it, the process is fairly simple. If the program is free, you can download the program and install it directly. If the program has a cost, you need a credit card or another means—perhaps a PayPal account—of paying for your purchase.

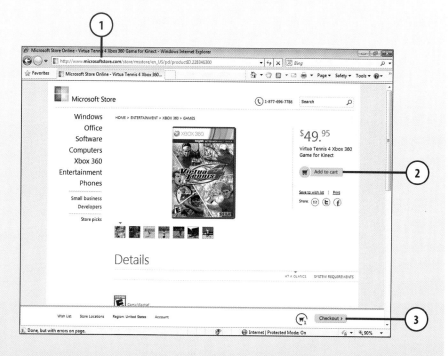

1. Go to the site with the product you want to download.

2. Click Add to Cart. Different sites may name this purchase button differently, but each shopping site includes a button or link you can click to begin the purchase process.

3. Click Checkout. Again, the wording on the button may vary, but a link or button enables you to finish shopping and make your purchase.

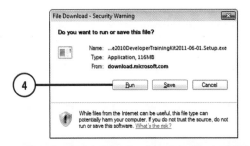

4. You may receive a link you can click to begin the download of your purchase, or the File Download dialog box may appear. Click Run. The program downloads and the installation utility launches.

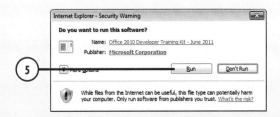

5. After downloading, you may be asked whether you want to run the program. Choosing to do so launches the installation utility. Click Run.

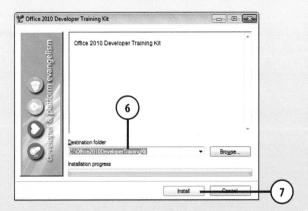

6. Follow the prompts on the screen to accept the user agreement and choose where you want to store the program. The default folder Windows 7 presents is usually the best one to use.

7. Click Install to install the software.

Let's Get the Install Started

If you have downloaded a new program and the installation utility *didn't* start automatically, you can launch it yourself by navigating to the folder where you stored the file and double-clicking the name of the downloaded file.

Go Further

CHANGING AUTOMATIC UPDATES

Some programs on your computer—like Windows 7—update automatically whenever program updates are available. You may see pop-up prompts from Windows Update, Adobe Application Updates, as well as other programs you've installed.

To view your automatic update settings for Windows, click Start and click Control Panel. Choose System and Security and click Windows Update. Click Change Settings to view and change your update status, and click the Close button when you're through.

Repairing and Uninstalling Programs

Windows 7 includes a utility you can use for installing and uninstalling programs safely. What's more, you can also check program status, look for updates, and even repair programs that are having problems or behaving strangely. You can find what you need in the Programs category of the Control Panel.

Repairing Installations

If your program begins acting strangely at some point—locking up when you apply a certain template, taking forever to check for your email, giving you errors when you try to choose a specific tool— Windows 7 may be able to repair the installation for you. Not all programs offer this option, but for the ones that do, you can use the tools in the Programs category of the Control Panel to correct any errors that are making your program behave inconsistently.

1. Display the Control Panel and click Programs.

2. Click Programs and Features.

3. In the program listing, click the name of the program you want to repair. The Repair option appears in the menu bar above the program listing.

4. Click Repair. Windows 7 launches the installation utility.

5. When the repair operation finishes, click the Close button to exit Control Panel.

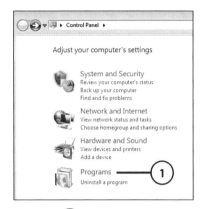

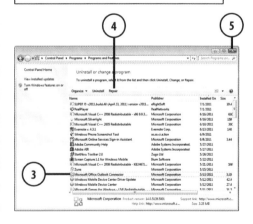

Uninstalling Programs

You can also remove programs you no longer need to free up space on your hard drive and allow room for other programs. When you know you don't need one of your programs anymore, uninstall it by clicking Start and choosing Control Panel and then follow these steps:

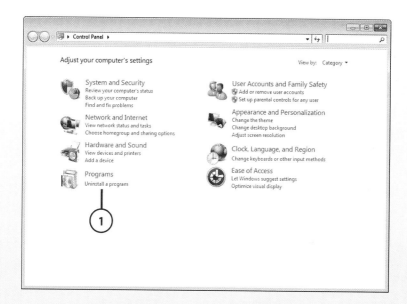

1. In the Control Panel, click Uninstall a Program.

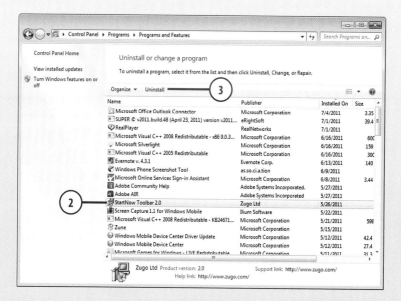

2. Click the name of the program you want to uninstall.

3. Click Uninstall. The uninstall wizard for that particular program begins.

4. Click Next. The uninstall utility shows you where the files will be uninstalled from.

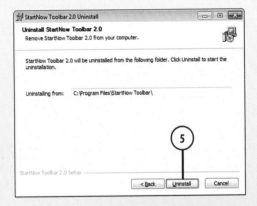

5. Click Uninstall. The uninstall utility shows you the status of the uninstall, and then a message box lets you know that the uninstallation process is complete.

6. Click OK to close the uninstall message box.

It's Not All Good

Most programs that you install with Windows 7—especially those programs that are designed to work with Windows 7—will work properly after you install them. Occasionally, you may run into a program that causes your computer to crash. This will be a rare occurrence, thankfully, but you do need a way of turning back the clock so that you can return your computer to the way it worked before you installed the program that made everything go wonky.

System Restore is a utility that is like a trip back in time. The best practice is to create a new restore point before you install the new program. Then, if you need to, you can return Windows 7 to that restore point—a restore point is a day and time at which Windows saved all the settings on your computer—so that you can use the settings that were in effect before you installed the program. And although the settings on your computer return to the way they were previously, you don't lose any files or data you've created since that time.

To create a restore point, click Start, click in the Search box, and type *create a restore point*. In the System Protection tab of the System Properties dialog box, click Create, enter a name for the restore point, and click OK. To use System Restore, display the Control Panel and click System and Security. In the Action Center area, click Restore Your Computer to an Earlier Time. Click the Open System Restore Button and click Next. Choose a restore point from the displayed list (choose a time just before you installed the program that caused the trouble) and click Next. Windows 7 displays a message box and restores your settings to a time prior to the software installation.

Working with Gadgets

Gadgets are small, functional, fun utilities that were first made available with Windows Vista, and now they are available in Windows 7 as well. Gadgets give you specific bits of information—for example, displaying your local weather, showing you how much power your computer is using, or listing the headlines from your favorite RSS feeds—displayed in a small visual icon that appears on your desktop where you can see it easily.

Windows 7 gadgets aren't displayed by default, but you can easily change that. You can also set up your preferences for gadgets and even download additional free gadgets from Microsoft.

Display Running Gadgets

Windows 7 comes with nine gadgets you can add to your desktop. Whether you're looking for fun, function, or both, the gadgets give you access to information you need without taking up a lot of room. The default gadgets Windows 7 includes are

The Calendar gadget can display the day only or the day and the month (shown here). You can click through the various months by using the arrows on either side of the month name.

The Clock shows the time currently showing on your computer. You can choose different clock styles, name the clock, and choose to show a different time zone if you like. You can also display the clock's second hand.

The CPU Meter shows you, in the larger dial, how much of its processing power your microprocessor is currently using. In the smaller dial, the CPU Meter shows you how much of your available computer memory (RAM) is being used.

The Currency gadget displays the current exchange rate, using the U.S. dollar and the euro by default. You can add additional currencies by clicking the plus symbol in the bottom-right corner of the gadget and adding a country to the comparison.

The Feed gadget displays a running series of RSS feed headlines from a variety of sources. You can choose the sources you want to display and also control the size of the feeds and the number of feeds that appear.

The Picture Puzzle gadget enables you to choose from a set of 11 different puzzles. You can drag and drop the pieces to their correct position to solve the puzzle.

The Slide Show gadget displays pictures in an ongoing rotation that you control. You can choose the folder from which the pictures are chosen, select the amount of time each picture appears, and determine whether to add a transition between pictures.

The Weather gadget enables you to display the weather in any area you choose. You can select the city and the way in which the temperature is displayed (Fahrenheit or Celsius) and show a minimal or expanded view.

The Windows Media Center gadget enables you to access Internet TV and control the channel, shows, trailers, and clips you watch in the gadget.

Add Gadgets to Your Desktop

The process of adding Windows 7 gadgets to your desktop is a simple one. You can add the existing gadgets that you like, and you can also download more gadgets from Microsoft. To display one of the existing gadgets on your desktop, follow these steps:

1. Click Start.

2. Click in the search box and type **gadget**.

3. Click Desktop Gadget Gallery.

4. Double-click the gadget you want to add. The gadget is added to your desktop in the upper-right corner.

Gadgets, Fast

A quick way to display the Gadgets gallery is to right-click your desktop and click Gadgets.

Maybe Not

If, after you add the gadget to the desktop, you decide it's not your cup of tea after all, you can remove it easily by clicking the close box at the top of the tools row that appears to the right of the gadget when you point to it with the mouse.

Changing Gadget Settings

Depending on which gadget you've added to your desktop, you may be able to change the settings that control the way the gadget looks. Some gadgets have limited settings; for example, with the CPU Meter gadget, you can only choose whether you want to display the gadget in large or small size. Other gadgets offer a greater range of settings. To change the settings for the Slide Show gadget, for example, follow these steps:

1. Hover your mouse pointer over the gadget you've added to your desktop.

2. Click Settings.

3. Click to choose the folder with the pictures you want to display.

4. Choose whether you want subfolders to be included.

5. Click to choose the time each picture is displayed.

6. Click to select the type of transition you want between pictures.

7. Click OK.

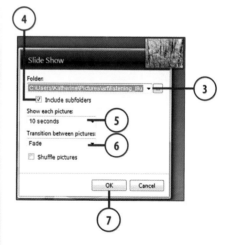

Choosing Other Folders

If the folder you want to use isn't displayed in the Folder list, you can click the Browse button and navigate to the folder or subfolder you want to use. Click it, click Open, and the gadget adds it as the source of the photos displayed in the Slide Show gadget.

Go Further

GET MORE GADGETS

You can search for more gadgets for Windows 7 by displaying the Desktop Gadget Gallery and clicking Get More Gadgets Online in the lower-right corner of the gallery. The Microsoft Windows site opens, offering a number of desktop gadgets you can download to your computer. Click the Get It Now link and then click Download. When prompted, read the message about downloading and click Install. In the File Download dialog box, click Open, and Windows 7 installs the gadget. The next time you display the Desktop Gadget Gallery, the new gadget will be visible there.

With Windows 7, you can easily create, find, and organize your files, folders, and libraries so that what you need is always at your fingertips.

Find the options you need to work with files and folders.

Windows 7 libraries help you find files by file type.

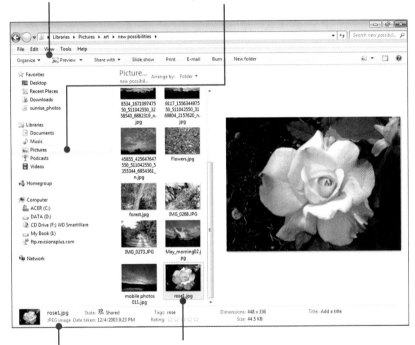

Display and add information about the current file.

Work with the selected file.

This chapter shows you how to work with Windows 7 libraries, folders, and files by exploring these tasks:

→ Working with Windows 7 file libraries
→ Managing folders
→ Finding, organizing, and sharing your files

Organizing Files and Folders

Files and folders have a funny way of multiplying. You may start out with only a few important files—a couple of reports, some letters, an article you're working on, some photos—but soon you'll discover you are collecting dozens, if not hundreds, of documents, pictures, music files, video clips, and more. Organizing this mass of files is important, and it's a good idea to start sooner rather than later. Luckily, Windows 7 gives you the tools you need to make this task super simple.

This chapter introduces you to Windows 7 libraries and shows you how to organize your files and folders in such a way that you can easily find and work with what you need. You learn about Windows Explorer and discover how to create your own libraries and folders, organize and manage your files, and share what you create with others.

Working with Windows 7 Libraries

A library in the real world is a place you can go to find the information you seek—whether you want to find a book, article, audio tape, video, or other information. The information is gathered from many different sources into that one location where you can access it.

Windows 7 libraries are similar grouping files in such a way that you can find them easily. Libraries are in effect indexed locations of various files, and when you click a library to view its contents, what you're really seeing are links to the files stored in their respective folders. Windows 7 libraries organize the files by type into one of five default categories: Documents, Music, Pictures, Podcasts, and Videos.

Clickable Locations

The various library and folder names in the Location bar are clickable, which means that you can move directly back to the library or to another folder by clicking the item you want in the Location bar. You can also click one of the arrows between the folder names to display a list of folders you can select. Simply click the one you want and move right to it. Nice.

Getting Started with Windows 7 File Libraries

You are likely to use some libraries more than others. All the files you create are stored by default in your My Documents library, for example, so you will probably be looking for files in that folder fairly often. Your photos may be in your My Photos folder, and—you guessed it—your music files go in the My Music folder. Each of these libraries is directly available on the Start menu.

1. Click Start.

2. Click the library you want to see.

3. Scroll to the file you want to display

4. Click the file with which you want to interact.

5. Use the tools in the toolbar to work with the file.

It's Not All Good

You may notice that the various Windows 7 libraries appear both as "Pictures" and "My Pictures" in different places. Both terms point to the same library, but when you are viewing items in relation to your user account (for example, you click your username on the top right of the Start menu and then click the library you want to see), the libraries have the word "My" in front of them. When you click Libraries in Windows Explorer, the library names say simply Documents, Music, Pictures, Podcasts, or Videos.

Taking a Look at Windows Explorer

Windows Explorer is the Windows 7 tool you use to manage your libraries, folders, and files. You can launch Windows Explorer a couple of different ways: You can click the library you want to view in the Start menu (as you just saw in the preceding section) or click the Windows Explorer icon in the taskbar. The Windows Explorer window contains a number of different elements you use to find and work with files and folders.

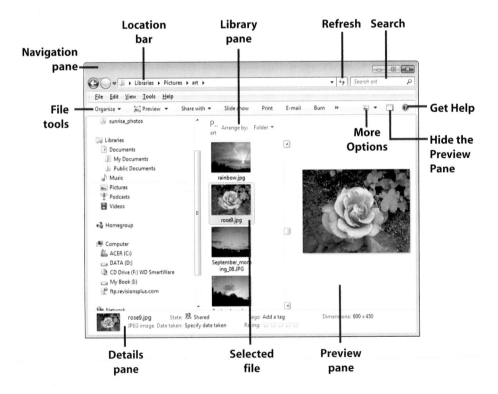

- **Address bar.** The Location bar shows the library, folder, and any subfolders that contain the currently selected file.

- **Refresh button.** The Refresh button updates the display to show the files in the current folder.

- **Search box.** You can use the search box to find folders, files, and libraries in Windows Explorer.

- **Details pane.** The Details pane displays information about the selected file, such as the name and size of the file and the date the file was created.

- **Preview pane.** The Preview pane displays a preview of the contents of the file.

- **Navigation pane.** The Navigation pane displays your favorites, libraries, and folders and files on your computer.

- **Selected file.** The selected file appears with a blue highlight, and a thumbnail of the file appears in the Details pane.

- **Library pane.** The Library pane displays the name of the library, the name of the selected folder, and a tool for choosing the way in which the files are arranged.

- **More Options.** Click More Options to change the way in which Windows Explorer displays the files in the current folder.

- **Hide the Preview Pane.** The Hide the Preview Pane tool is a toggle, meaning that when the Preview pane is hidden, the tool's name is Show the Preview Pane. Click the tool alternately to hide and display the Preview pane.

- **Get Help.** Click Get Help to display a pop-up window of help information related to the task you were performing in Windows Explorer.

- **File tools.** Use the file tools to work with the currently selected file.

Changing Tools

When a file is selected in Windows Explorer, the File tools appear above the Windows Explorer work area. When a folder is selected, a set of Folder tools appears. You learn more about working with folder tools in "Managing Folders," later in this chapter.

Using the Navigation Pane

The panel on the left side of Windows Explorer is known as the *Navigation pane*. This pane lists all the libraries, folders, and subfolders on your computer and any devices that are currently connected to it. You can do all sorts of things in the Navigation pane, including moving and copying folders and files and adding, deleting, and renaming folders.

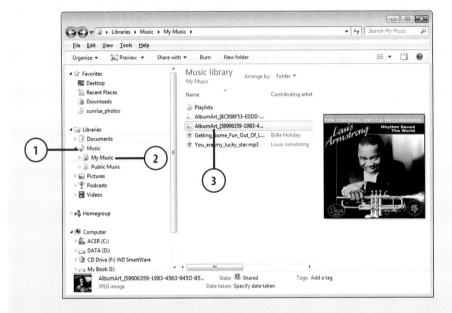

1. In Windows Explorer, click the arrow to the left of the library you want to view. Any subfolders in that library appear.

2. Click the folder with the files you want to view.

3. Click the file you want.

Folder Fun

You learn more about adding, copying, moving, renaming, and deleting folders in the section "Managing Folders," later in this chapter.

Changing the Windows Explorer Layout

You can hide and redisplay the different panes in Windows Explorer: Details pane, Preview page, Navigation pane, and Library pane. Click Organize and point to Layout, and click the pane you want to hide to clear the check mark. To redisplay the pane, click the pane to display the check mark.

Adding Folders to Libraries

Because Windows 7 libraries are actually indexes of folders and files that you want to be able to find in each of these different categories (Documents, Pictures, Podcasts, Video, and Music), it's important that you be able to add folders to the library that Windows 7 may not be picking up. For the most part, Windows 7 does this automatically for you. But if you discover a folder Windows 7 missed that you'd like to include in a library, you can use these steps to add it to the library of your choice.

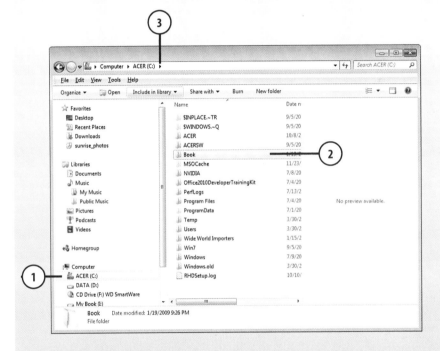

1. In Windows Explorer, click the item in the Navigation pane that contains the folder you want to add.

2. Click the folder in the center panel. The file tools change to include an option called Include in Library. (If you don't see this option, it means that the folder is already included in a Windows 7 library.)

3. Click the Include in Library arrow.

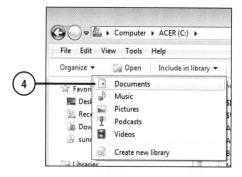

4. Click the library to which you want to add the folder. Windows Explorer displays a message letting you know the folder is being included in the library you selected. The new folder appears in the subfolders below the library name in the Navigation pane and will remain in that library.

Nothing Really Moved

Even though it may look as though the folder you added to the library is now in a new location, in reality nothing moved. Windows Explorer maintains a link to the folder so that the files are included and easy to access any time you choose to work with that library.

Creating a Library

Because a library is essentially a stored, indexed search that keeps together all your favorite files of a certain type, you can create your own libraries if your interests differ from the libraries Windows 7 has already provided for you. When you are adding a folder to a library, you may decide instead to make it its own library. You could create a library that collects links to all the folders you are using for a specific project, for example.

1. In Windows Explorer, click the item containing the folder you want to use to create the library.

2. Click the folder.

3. Click the Include in Library arrow.

4. Click Create New Library. Windows Explorer automatically adds the folder you selects in the Library area of the Navigation pane, and you can click the folder name to display the contents of the folder.

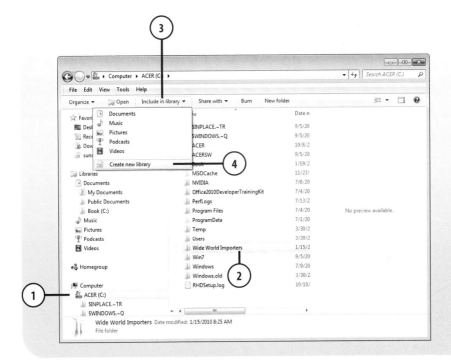

It's Not All Good

Windows Explorer no doubt needs some kind of organizing mechanism to keep us from creating libraries all over the place with folders that are already in libraries. But one slightly frustrating aspect about libraries is that you can't easily create a new library from a folder that's already included in one of the default libraries. You *can*, however, remove the folder from the library (using the technique in the next section) and then select the folder again and create a new library.

Removing Folders from a Library

When you no longer need to include a certain folder in a library—perhaps you completed the project you were working on and don't use the folder anymore—you can remove it easily.

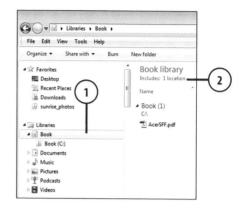

1. Click the folder in the Navigation pane.

2. Click the Includes link in the Library pane at the top of the center column.

3. In the Library Locations dialog box, click the name of the folder you want to remove from the library.

4. Right-click your selection and click Remove.

5. Click OK. Windows Explorer removes the folder from the library for you.

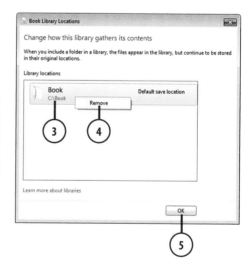

Fast Removal
You can also remove a folder quickly from a library by right-clicking the folder in the library and choosing Remove Location from Library.

Your Files Are Safe
Remember that removing a folder from a library doesn't do anything at all to the files contained in the library. Because a library is really an indexed collection of links to the various folders and files related to that topic, only the link is removed when you remove a library.

Arranging Library Display

Chances are your libraries contain lots of files, and that means you need to think about the best way to display them so that you can easily find what you need. In the Library pane at the top of the center column in Windows Explorer, you can use the Arrange tool to choose the filter by which the files in your folder are displayed. You might choose to arrange the files by Author, Date Modified, Tag, Type, or Name.

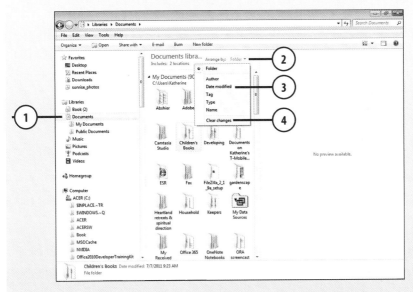

1. Click the library you want to arrange in the Navigation pane.

2. Click the Arrange By link in the Library pane at the top of the center column.

3. Click the setting that arranges the files the way you want them to appear. Author lists the files and folders alphabetically by author; Date Modified lists files with the most recently modified files shown first; Tag arranges files alphabetically according to any tags you've assigned to the file; Type shows the files organized by file type; and Name lists the files alphabetically (from A to Z).

4. When you want to return the folder to normal display, click Clear Changes.

More Display Controls

Later in this chapter, in the section "Changing Folder Views," you learn how to use the More Options tools to further organize and change the display of files in Windows Explorer. You can use the tools in More Options to change the display of library files as well.

Hiding and Redisplaying a Library

Depending on the type of information you store on your computer—and who else uses your computer in addition to you—you may want to hide a library so others can't see it. Perhaps you created a library for sensitive household information, such as your insurance account information, mortgage refinance data, and so on. You can easily hide a library in Windows Explorer. Here's how.

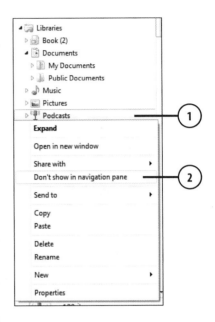

1. In Windows Explorer, right-click the library you want to hide.

2. Click Don't Show in Navigation Pane. Windows Explorer removes the display of the library from the Navigation pane.

3. When you want to return a hidden library to display in the Navigation pane, click the Libraries category.

4. Right-click the library in the list in the center column.

5. Click Show in Navigation Pane.

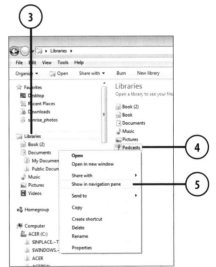

Hiding Whole Libraries

Windows Explorer doesn't allow you to hide specific folders within a library; you must select the top folder in the library (Documents, Music, Pictures, Podcasts, Videos, or one you created yourself) before you can hide it from display. You can, however, remove the folder location from the library, if you like, which removes it from display as part of the library in the Navigation pane.

Managing Folders

The folders you create on your computer will likely store files grouped in specific ways. You can just save all the files you create to your desktop, but sooner or later your desktop will be one crowded and disorganized place! Creating and using folders to store your files helps you know how to locate files easily later, and it also gives you a specific location in which to store files you want to keep. After you create folders, you can do all sorts of things with them: Move them around, rename them, add them to your Favorites, and more.

Finding the Folder You Want

Windows 7 wants you to find what you're looking for. And that means you have more than one way to find the folder you're looking for. You can click Start and type the folder name in the search box, as you learned in an earlier chapter, or you can click in the Windows Explorer search box and do the same thing. Windows Explorer quickly looks for the folder you need and displays the results in the center column of the window.

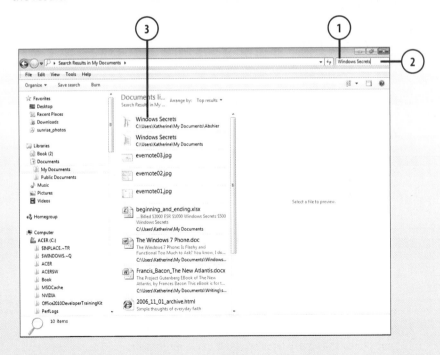

1. Click in the search box of Windows Explorer.

2. Type the folder name you're looking for. You may see a message indicating that Windows is searching for the folder you seek.

3. Double-click the result you want to move directly to that folder.

Opening the Folder Location

If you want to display the folder that contains the subfolder you're looking for (as opposed to opening the subfolder you searched for), right-click the search result for the folder and click Open Folder Location.

SAVING YOUR SEARCHES

If you find that you often perform the same searches—perhaps you search for the latest sales reports or look for new MP3 files that have been added to your computer—you can save the search in your Favorites area so that you can use it again later.

Enter the search information as usual, and then, when the search results appear in the Windows Explorer window, click Save Search in the Folder tools row. The Save As dialog box appears. Type a filename for the saved search and click Save.

Now you can use the search at any time by clicking the saved search in the Favorites area of the Navigation pane.

SETTING SEARCH OPTIONS

You can change the way Windows Explorer handles searches by setting search options in the Folder Options dialog box. Display the dialog box by choosing Organize and clicking Folder and Search Options. Click the Search tab. Leave the setting in the What To Search area set to the default; this causes Windows Explorer to search more efficiently using the index Windows 7 has created of the files on your computer and to use the names only in nonindexed files.

You may want to change the settings in the How to Search area. These options control whether Windows Explorer includes subfolders, displays partial matches, uses natural language in search results, and uses the index for searches that include system files.

Finally, the When Searching Non-Indexed Locations area enables you to choose whether you want to include system directories that are not in the index as well as any compressed files that have not been indexed. These options are good to include if you want the most thorough search results possible. Click OK to save any changes you made.

Creating New Folders

Creating new folders—and subfolders within them—is a simple task in Windows Explorer. You can add as many folders as you like. The trick is to think through the way they are organized so there is a logical order to the folders you create. In your Household folder, for example, you might have the following subfolders: Financial Info, Health, School, and Friends and Family. You can then store files related to each of those topics in their respective folders.

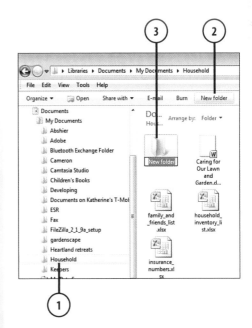

1. In Windows Explorer, click the folder in which you want to create the new folder.

2. Click New Folder.

3. Type a name for the new folder and press Enter.

Adding Files to the Folders

You can now add files to your new folder. You learn how to do that later in this chapter, in the section "Moving Files."

Moving Folders

After you create new folders and store the files you need in them, you may decide you want to move them to other folders or consolidate sub-folders you've already got. You can rearrange your folders as easily as you can click and drag the mouse.

1. Click the folder you want to move.

2. Drag it to the new folder in the Navigation pane, below which you want it to be placed, and release the mouse button. The folder moves and appears in the Navigation pane.

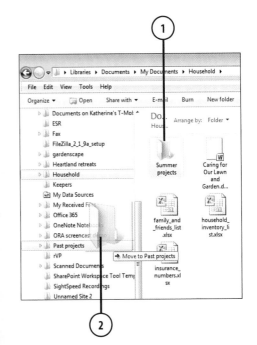

And Moving Again

If you don't like where you placed the folder or you decide it belongs better somewhere else, you can simply click and drag the folder to the new location. You can also press Ctrl+Z to undo your last operation, or simply press Del to delete the folder. Windows 7 asks you to confirm that you want to delete the folder and all files it contains.

Changing Folder Views

Windows 7 gives you a number of different ways you can view the files in folders in Windows Explorer. The technique you learn here can be applied in any folder you're viewing. Changing the view involves choosing tools in the More Options list or using the choices in the View menu.

1. Click the library you want to display.

2. Click the More Options button.

3. Click the view you want to use for the display of the files in the current folder. Extra Large, Large, Medium, and Small Icons all display the file images or icons in different sizes. List, Details, Tiles, and Content all use small or medium file icons. Details provides the most information about the file, giving size, filename, and the opportunity to rate the file. List simply lists the files by name. Tiles displays medium-sized file icons and also gives the file name, size, and type of file. Content shows small file icons but enlarges the filename so that you can read it easily.

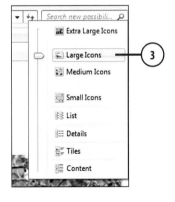

>> Go Further

WHICH VIEW IS RIGHT FOR YOU?

The view you choose to display the files in Windows Explorer is primarily a personal preference issue. If you like images and want the file icons to be large, you choose Large or Extra Large Icons. The trade-off is that the larger the file icon, the fewer the number of files Windows Explorer can display in one window. That means if you like a large icon display, you may be scrolling quite a bit.

If you want to fit the greatest number of files in the window at one time, choose List. To see medium icons with a fair amount of data, choose Tiles. You get the idea: experiment until you find the view that best fits the way you like to work.

Renaming Folders

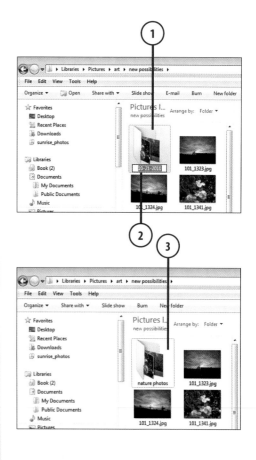

You can easily rename a folder in Windows Explorer. You might want to rename a folder when you want to give it a more descriptive name, for example. Note that this process also works for renaming files.

1. Click the folder you want to rename.

2. Click the folder name beneath the folder icon to select the name.

3. Type the name you want to assign to the folder and press Enter.

Conventional Renaming

If you'd rather use menu options to get the job done, you can right-click the folder and click Rename. This selects the folder name so that you can type the name you want to apply. Press Enter to save the change.

Making a Folder a Favorite

At the top of the Navigation pane, you see the Favorites area. This area shows any folders you've added to your favorites as well as any saved searches you've created. Add a folder to your Favorites list when you know you will want to access it often—and as easily as possible.

1. In Windows Explorer, click to select the folder you want to add to the Favorites area.

2. Drag the folder to Favorites. A black bar shows you where the folder will appear in the Favorites list.

3. Release the mouse button to add the folder to your favorites.

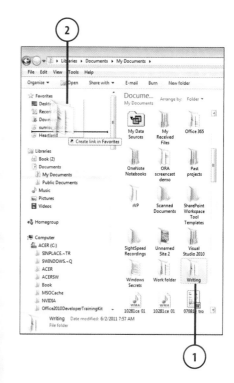

Linked, Not Moved

Similar to the way libraries work, the folders in your Favorites list are not actual folders containing files. Instead, they are links that enable you to move directly to your favorite folders and searches quickly.

Removing Folders

Deleting your folders is so easy it's almost scary. Luckily, Windows Explorer asks you to confirm that you really do want to delete the folder before it's removed. Otherwise, we might delete a lot of things we really need! (Of course, you can retrieve a deleted folder from the Recycle Bin if you choose.) Here are the steps for deleting folders (and the files they contain) in Windows Explorer.

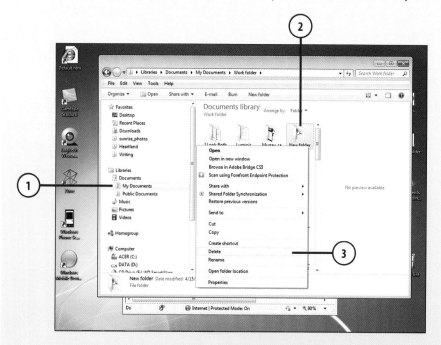

1. Click the folder containing the subfolder you want to remove.

2. Right-click the folder you want to delete.

3. Click Delete. The Delete Folder message box appears, asking you to confirm that you want to delete the folder.

4. Click Yes to delete the folder or click No to cancel the operation.

Recovering a Deleted Folder

If you delete a folder and then suddenly remember something you needed in it, don't panic. You can recover a folder right after you deleted it by pressing Ctrl+Z. This reverses your last operation, and the folder is returned to its previous location.

Finding, Organizing, and Sharing Your Files

Now that you know how to work with libraries and folders in Windows Explorer, what about the files? The files you create are the building blocks of all your work on your computer. Chances are you work with document files, picture files, music files, video files, and more. Knowing how to locate, copy, move, sort, and get information about your files is an important part of staying organized and up-to-speed with all the data you're collecting. You'll find that the process is very similar to the techniques you used for managing your folders in Windows Explorer.

Finding Files

Finding files in Windows Explorer is really the same process you used to find folders. Click in the search box and apply filters if you'd like to narrow your search according to Author, File Type, Date Modified, or File Size.

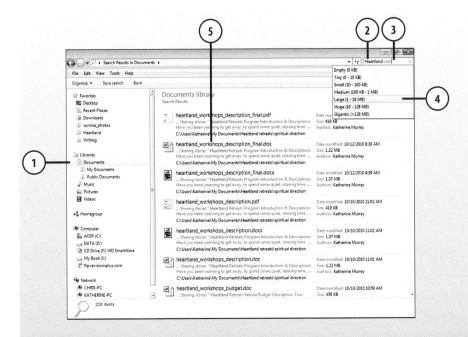

1. In Windows Explorer, click the library or drive in which you want to search.

2. Click in the search box and type a word or phrase to describe what you're searching for.

3. Click a search filter—Authors, Type, Date Modified, or Size—to apply to the search.

4. Click the filter options to narrow the search.

5. Click the search result you want to see.

Finding Specific File Types

When you want to find files in a specific format—for example, .jpg, .wmv, .docx, or .mp3—use the Type filter in the Windows Explorer search box. When you click Type, Windows Explorer displays a list box of file formats you can choose to narrow your search.

Previewing Files

The Preview page in Windows Explorer shows you a preview of the selected file. If the file you've selected is a Word document, for example, the first page of the Word document is previewed for you in the Preview page. If the Preview page is not visible, you can display it by clicking the Show the Preview Pane tool on the right side of the Windows Explorer window.

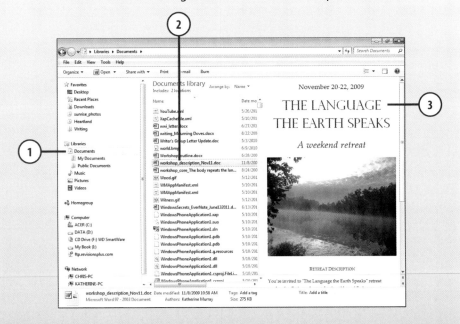

1. Click the folder containing the file you want to see.

2. Use Search if necessary to locate the file.

3. Click the file and review the file in the Preview pane.

Scanning the Previewed File

You can read through the entire previewed document by dragging the scroll box in the vertical scrollbar down the screen. If you'd like to make changes to the file, you can open it in its original application by double-clicking the file.

Displaying and Updating File Information

The Details area of Windows Explorer gives you information about the selected file. You can see the filename, size, and the date it was last modified. You can also see any tags that have been assigned to the file, review the authors' names, and in some cases, see any rating that has been applied to the file.

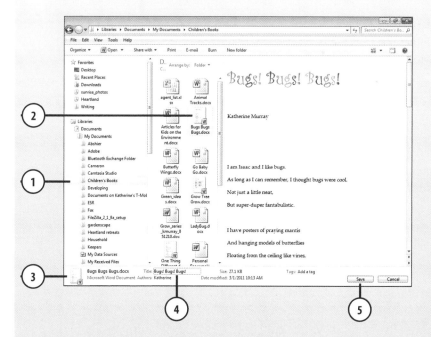

1. Click the folder containing the folder you want to see.

2. Click the file.

3. Review the information in the Details pane. You may see information including Title, Authors, Date Modified, Size, and Tags.

4. Click Title, Authors, or Tags and add information as needed.

5. Click Save to save your changes.

DISPLAYING FILE PROPERTIES

>> Go Further

In addition to the file details visible in the Details pane at the bottom of the Windows Explorer window, you can view the file properties of individual files by right-clicking the file and clicking Properties.

The Properties dialog box for the selected file contains four tabs: General, Security, Details, and Previous Versions. For the most part, you don't need to change file properties, but you can choose to hide a file or mark it as read-only, change the permissions of people who are allowed to access the file, remove file properties and personal information, and view any previous versions of the file you have created. After you finish viewing the file properties, click Apply if you've made any changes and click OK to close the dialog box.

Tagging Files

You can easily tag the files you work with in Windows Explorer to make them easier to locate in a search later. For example, if you have a set of figures related to your parents' 50th anniversary party, you could tag them with Anniversary Party and then display them all in a search later by searching for files with the tag you assigned.

1. Display the file you want to tag in Windows Explorer.

2. In the Details area, click in the Tags field. Type tags that you can use to identify or categorize the file, separating multiple tags with commas. A list box appears, suggesting tags that match the characters you are typing.

3. Click the check box of any tag you want to add.

4. Click Save to save your tags.

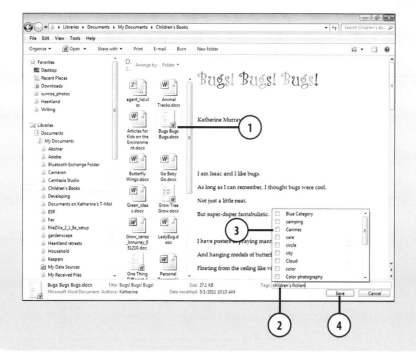

Rating Files

In the Details pane of your picture files, you can also assign a rating value to your image files. Rating the files on your computer helps you prioritize the ones you love over the ones you don't. This can help you choose the right files when you're searching, for example, for the best photos you have of a particular event. If you've rated the files, you can search for the files with the highest rating, which will give you a results list that is the cream of the crop. Select the file you want to rate in Windows Explorer and then click the number of stars (one to five) you want to assign to the image. Click Save to save your rating.

Copying and Pasting Files

Copying and pasting files are two of the most common file operations we perform in Windows Explorer. You can easily copy and paste the files you select in several different ways: You can drag and drop files; you can use menu options; or you can use shortcut keys.

1. In Windows Explorer, select the files you want to copy.

2. Right-click your selection.

3. Click Copy.

4. Navigate to the folder where you want to paste the files.

5. Click the Edit menu.

6. Click Paste.

Quick Key-Based Copy and Paste

If you want to use shortcut keys only to copy and paste files, you can select the files you want to copy, press Ctrl+C, and then navigate to the folder where you want to paste the files and press Ctrl+V.

Drag-and-Drop Copy and Paste

You can copy files to a new folder by dragging and dropping them as well. Select the files, press Ctrl, and drag them to the new location; then release the mouse button. The files are copied to the new folder.

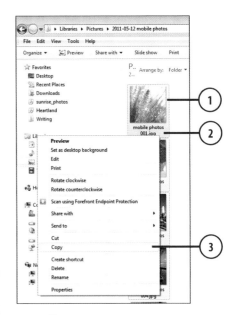

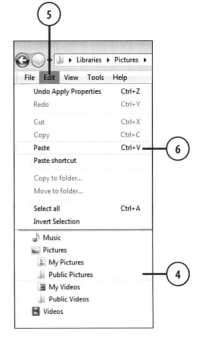

Moving Files

When you're ready to move files
from one folder to another, you
begin by selecting the files you want
to move and then drag them to the
new folder or choose Move to Folder
from the Edit menu in Windows
Explorer.

1. Begin in Windows Explorer by
   selecting the files you want to
   move.

2. Press and hold Shift and drag
   your selection to the new folder.

3. Alternately, click the Edit menu.

4. Click Move to Folder.

5. Click the folder to which you
   want to move the files.

6. Click Move.

Moving Shortcut Keys

You can also move files by selecting the files, pressing Ctrl+X, and
then navigating to the receiving
folder and clicking Ctrl+V.

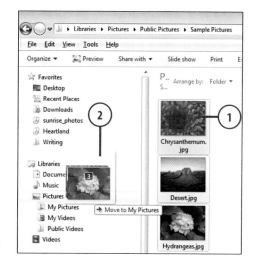

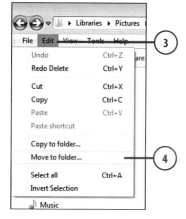

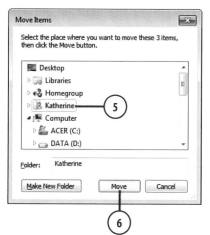

Sorting Your Files

When you have a number of files in a folder—perhaps with similar names—it's helpful to be able to sort your files so that you can easily locate the ones you're looking for. Windows Explorer makes it easy for you to sort your files a number of different ways. Begin by hiding the Preview page so that you have more room in Windows Explorer (click Hide the Preview Pane in the right side of the window).

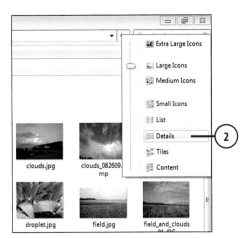

1. Click More Options.

2. Click Details.

3. Click the arrow to the right of the column heading by which you want to sort the files. If you click the Date arrow, you can choose a specific date or range of dates, or select A Long Time Ago, Earlier This Year, or This Week.

   The files are arranged according to the sort criteria you selected. You can return the file display to normal display by clicking the column heading and clearing the criteria you selected.

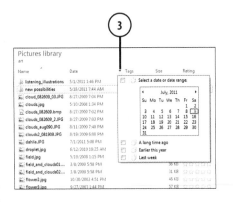

Sorting Quickly

You can quickly sort your files according to the various columns in Details view by clicking on the column heading. If you click Names, for example, the order reverses so that the files are displayed alphabetically ordered from Z to A. Similarly, if you click Size, the files with the largest file sizes are displayed at the top of the list, in descending order to the smallest files.

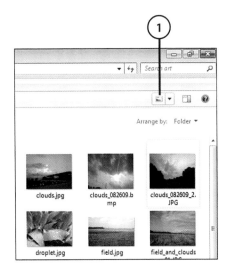

7. Click Browse if necessary to choose a folder for the extracted files. (It's okay to leave the default setting if that folder is where you want the uncompressed files to be placed.)

8. Click Extract. Windows Explorer extracts the files and places them in the folder you specified, ready to use.

Sharing Files

When you're ready to share your files with your HomeGroup or specific people, click the file or group of files you want to share and click Share With in the File tools at the top of the Windows Explorer window. You'll learn more about creating and working with a HomeGroup in Chapter 12.

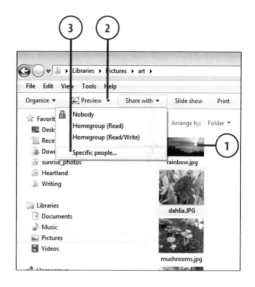

1. Select the file or files you want to share.

2. Click the Share With arrow.

3. Click Specific People.

4. Click the arrow to choose someone to share the file with.

5. Click Add.

6. Click Share.

Putting Files in Public Places

You can also place files in Public folders on your computer so that others who have the necessary permissions are able to view the files in that location. To move a file to a Public folder, simply drag and drop the file to that location.

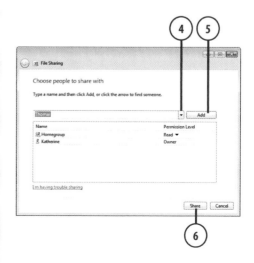

With Internet Explorer 9, you can enter a web address, search, and pin a site to the taskbar.

You can have more than one site open at a time and switch among them by clicking the tabs.

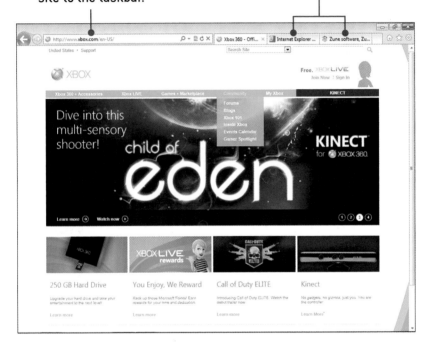

Windows 7 includes Internet Explorer, the web browser you can use to visit websites, connect with your friends, play games, shop, and more.

In this chapter, you learn how to browse the web securely and find what you seek using Internet Explorer. Specifically, you learn how to use your web browser for the following tasks:

→ Getting online with Internet Explorer

→ Browsing the web

→ Adding and managing favorites

→ Setting Internet options

→ Understanding web slices

→ Working with RSS feeds

→ Setting security options

→ Securing your browsing experience

→ Getting email with Windows Live Mail

Doing the Web Thing (Plus Email and Calendars, Too)

Where would we be without our web browsers?

Today we can't go very long without needing to get on the web to find something—a quote, new shoes, directions to a new restaurant—or to catch up with what all our friends are doing on our favorite social media sites. Windows 7 includes Internet Explorer to provide you access to the web, along with a set of powerful web tools that help keep your browsing experience safe and secure and give you what you need to organize all your favorite sites so that you can return to them easily.

Getting Online with Internet Explorer

Internet Explorer is one of the tools included with your version of Windows 7. After you set up your Internet connection, which we covered in Chapter 2, "Preparing Your Windows 7 PC," you are able to get online by simply opening Internet Explorer and typing a web address you want to visit in the address bar at the top of the browser window.

Starting Internet Explorer

Your first steps begin in the Start menu. Depending on how your computer was set up initially, you may also find in Internet Explorer icon on your desktop. For this process, we use the Start menu to launch the program.

You can also click the Internet
Explorer icon on the taskbar.

1. Click Start.

2. Point to Internet Explorer. Notice that a jump list of recently visited sites appears on the right side of the Start menu.

3. If you want to go directly to a site on the jump list, click the site you want to visit.

Looking in All Programs

If you don't find Internet Explorer pinned to your Start menu, click All Programs at the bottom of the list and scroll down until you see it in the alphabetical listing. Click its icon to start the program. You might also have an Internet Explorer shortcut icon on your desktop. If you see the icon on your desktop, simply double-click it to launch the program.

WINDOWS 7 AND INTERNET EXPLORER TOGETHER

>>> Go Further

One of the great things about Internet Explorer 9 (IE9), which is used in the examples throughout this chapter, is that it works seamlessly with a number of features in Windows 7. For example, the Snap technique, which enables you to snap an open window to the side of your screen so that you can compare two open files easily, is also available when you're working with web pages in Internet Explorer 9.

The Internet Explorer icon on the taskbar also has its own jump list. When you click the icon, the sites that you visit most often appear in the list. You can click one to move right to it.

You can also pin your favorite websites to the taskbar so that you can return to them quickly later. When you point to a website that's been pinned to the taskbar, a thumbnail preview of the page appears, and you can click it to open that page. Some sites also display what Microsoft calls *icon overlays*, which give you additional information about the site; for example, the number of new posts or messages you've received on that site.

A Look Around the Internet Explorer Window

Most browsers have features in common as well as their own unique tools and approaches. Internet Explorer 9 is the newest version of Microsoft's popular web browser. Chances are, if you bought your Windows 7 computer new, your version of Windows 7 included Internet Explorer 8. The new version of Internet Explorer is streamlined to give you maximum room onscreen, the page tabs have been changed and are now color-coded, and the address bar at the top of the window is now called One Box because it is a combination web address, search, and navigation tool.

You'll most likely use the following items as you browse the web with Internet Explorer 9.

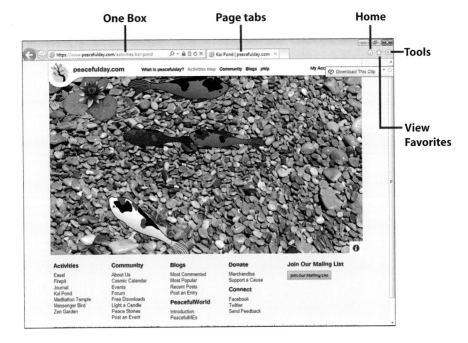

- **One Box.** Now you can search for information or browse the web by clicking and typing in the same box. Formerly called the *address bar,* One Box enables you to surf, search, refresh the site, and display security information all in the same box.

- **Page tabs.** When you're working with more than one web page at a time, Internet Explorer 9 displays each web page in a separate tab. Now the tabs are color-coded to help you navigate among them easily.

- **Home.** Clicking Home at any point returns you to the website you've set as your browser home page.

- **View Favorites.** Click View Favorites to access websites you've saved as your favorites or to add a new favorite to the list.

- **Tools.** Click Tools to access the various menus in Internet Explorer 9 and to print, check site security, check your downloads, and more.

Making the Menus Visible

If you like to see the menus stretched across the top of the browser window, you can put the menus back where you're familiar with them. Simply right-click the top of the browser window and click Menu Bar. The menus appear just below One Box, where you can reach them easily.

A Quick Look at the Menu Bar

If you just want the menu to appear briefly, until you click your choice, press Alt. The menu bar appears at the top of the browser window, and after you click the option you want, the menu disappears again.

Displaying Browser Toolbars

Different people have different browsing styles, and part of making your web experience your own involves being able to arrange the browser window the way you like it. In Internet Explorer 9, you can display three additional tool-bars to help you find what you need as you look around online.

The Favorites bar displays the sites you've added so that you can access them easily; the Command bar includes common tools you use while browsing; and the Status bar appears at the bottom of the browser window, giving you information about the current operation you're performing.

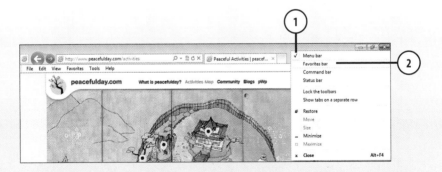

1. Open Internet Explorer and right-click the area at the top of the window.

2. Click the name of the toolbar you want to add: Favorites bar, Command bar, or Status bar. The check mark acts as a toggle; when the item shows a check mark, the bar is displayed. When the item does not show the check mark, the bar is hidden.

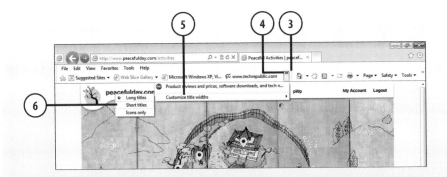

3. You can adjust the length of the toolbar by clicking and dragging the divider at the left end of the bar.

4. Click the double-arrow to display additional choices for the toolbar.

5. To edit the name of titles on the Favorites bar so that more choices fit in the displayed space, click Customize Title Widths.

6. The default is Long Titles; click Short Titles or Icons Only to shorten the titles in the Favorites bar.

Locking the Toolbar

When you get the toolbars just the way you want them to appear, you can lock them so that changes aren't made to the layout inadvertently. Right-click the top of the browser window and click Lock the Toolbars. You aren't able to move or hide the toolbars until you select Lock the Toolbars a second time to remove the check mark.

Using the Notification Bar

In previous versions of Internet Explorer, when the browser had a message for you—for example, perhaps the site was trying to download a file and your browser was letting you know—the message appeared as an alert at the top of the browsing area. Typically, you had to click a button or take some action before you could carry on with your browsing experience. In Internet Explorer 9, the message appears at the bottom of the screen in the new notification bar, and it doesn't interrupt your browsing and force you to take action.

Different notifications ask different questions, depending on the task that needs to be performed. You may be asked to take one of these actions:

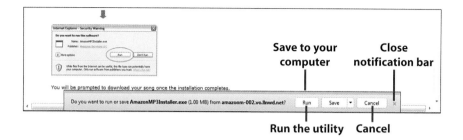

Save to your computer

Close notification bar

Run the utility

Cancel

You will be prompted to download your song once the installation completes.

- Run the utility that is being downloaded.

- Save the utility to your computer.

- Cancel the operation.

- Close the notification bar without taking any action.

The Automatically Disappearing Navigation Bar

Microsoft purposefully designed the navigation bar to be less intrusive than the message bar used in previous browser versions. So instead of insisting that you take action, the navigation bar gradually fades away when you continue browsing and take no action.

Gold Means Look

The most important messages the navigation bar displays have to do with your computer's safety. So if a website is trying to download a utility to your computer, the navigation bar flashes and appears in gold, letting you know this is a message worth viewing. You can click your response to let Internet Explorer 9 know whether you want to run, save, or cancel the operation.

Selecting Your Home Page

Which web page do you want to see first thing when you fire up your Internet Explorer 9 browser? Perhaps you want to see your favorite news site or your company's web page. Whatever it might be, you can add the site—and others too—in the Home Page area of the General tab in the Internet Options dialog box.

1. Start Internet Explorer 9 and display the web page you'd like to use as your home page.

2. Click the Tools icon.

3. Click Internet Options.

4. In the Home Page area of the General tab, highlight the existing web addresses and press Del.

5. Click Use Current.

6. Click OK. Now whenever you launch IE9, the browser opens right up to the web page you specified.

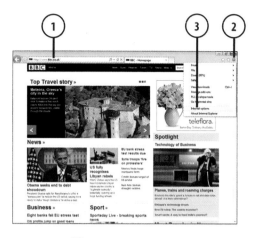

Multiple Home Pages

If you have several sites you like to check first thing in the morning, you can add them all to the Home Page area of the General tab in the Internet Options dialog box. Simply put each web address on its own line and then click OK. When you launch IE9 the next time, all the web pages you entered will open automatically.

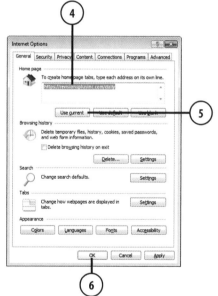

Browsing and Searching the Web

Ah, the fun of browsing the web! What *can't* you do on the web today? You can chat with your friends, call your mother, buy school supplies, order your groceries, work on a document, plan your vacation, watch videos, and much, much more. Internet Explorer 9 promises a faster-than-ever browsing experience and far-reaching search results, and it makes the whole process seamless and simple.

Turn On Searching

Before the One Box feature will display search results automatically for you when you type a word or phrase, you need to turn on the search capability by clicking Turn On Suggestions (Send Keystrokes to Bing) in the One Box drop-down list. Click in One Box and begin typing a word; the list appears. Click Turn On Suggestions (Send Keystrokes to Bing) to enable the search feature. You can also add all sorts of other search utilities to Internet Explorer 9's quick search. You learn how to do that in "Adding a Search Provider," later in this chapter. If you choose to turn off the Bing Suggestions later, you can do so by clicking Turn Off Suggestions (Stop Sending Keystrokes to Bing) at the bottom of the One Box list.

Displaying Web Pages with One Box

Internet Explorer 9 has renamed the address bar, where you used to click and type the web address you wanted to see, One Box. The new name is meant to remind you that you can now basically use "One Box" for everything, whether you want to search, get security reports, or go directly to a web page.

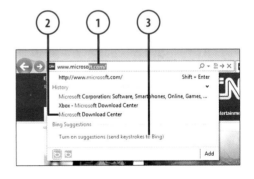

1. Click in One Box. Type the web address of the page you want to view. Internet Explorer 9 attempts to autocomplete the phrase for you, so if you want to use the site provided, press Enter. If not, just keep typing the full address.

2. You can also click a link in the History area. These suggestions match the characters you typed that you used recently browsing.

3. Click if you want to turn on site suggestions in Bing, Microsoft's search engine. Bing will display suggestions that match the phrase you typed.

Using Compatibility View

If the website you are viewing looks strange—maybe the text is out of alignment or the photos overlap the text—it's possible that the site was designed for an earlier version of Internet Explorer. Click the Compatibility View tool on the right side of the One Box to correct the problem.

>> Go Further

KEYBOARD SHORTCUTS FOR BROWSING

If you'd rather skip the clicking and navigate through the web using your keyboard, you can use the following shortcut keys:

- Press Alt+Home to display your home page.
- Press Alt+C to display your favorites, feeds, and history.
- Press Ctrl+B to organize your favorites.
- Press Ctrl+D to add another web page to your favorites.
- Press Ctrl+L to highlight the web address in One Box.
- Press Ctrl+J to display the Download Manager.

Navigating the Web

The tools Internet Explorer 9 provides for you to use as you move from one web page to another are pretty intuitive. Chances are you already know from other web experiences which tools to click to move forward or backward from page to page. Here's a quick look at the main tools IE9 provides to help you move among pages on the web.

Forward   Click a link   Scroll down the page

Back

Click to visit another web page

Click to sort page content

Click a linked image

Scroll across the page

- **Back.** Clicking the Back button takes you back to the page you were pre-viously viewing. IE9 also includes the name of that page in the tool name; for example, Back to Wildflowers.

- **Forward.** Clicking Forward takes you to the web page you previously viewed *after* viewing the current one. This capability is helpful if you're moving back and forth between pages. If you haven't moved ahead to another page yet, this button is not active.

- **Click a link.** Click a link on the page to get more information about the topic at hand. What that link does—for example, takes you to a new page, opens a pop-up window over your current one, or plays a media clip—depends on what the website designer programmed the link to do.

- **Scroll down the page.** Use the vertical scrollbar as you would in any other program to display content that is currently out of view along the bottom of the page.

- **Scroll across the page.** Use the horizontal scrollbar to scroll across pages that are too wide to be displayed at one time on your monitor.

- **Click to sort page content.** This particular page enables visitors to click a link to sort the images displayed by the various categories shown here.

- **Click to visit another web page.** Click a link to move to sites that are linked to the current one.

IE9 Has Got Your "Back"

One of the nice things about the simple, elegant Back and Forward buttons in IE9 is that during your current browsing session, you can go back and back and back if necessary. Suppose that you start off shopping for shoes, find a pair you like, and then get distracted by something else and go browsing along happily for 10 minutes or so. And then you suddenly realize you've wandered away from those shoes! No worries—just click Back to retrace your steps through the web links and return to that early page.

You can also view the sites you've visited recently by clicking the Show Address Bar AutoComplete arrow in the One Box tools (it resembles the down arrow). A list of sites you've visited in this session appears, and you can click the one with the shoes you liked and go directly there.

Go Further

WHO SAYS YOU CAN'T GO BACK?

Internet Explorer 9 also gives you a way to return easily to sites you browsed earlier—or go back to your last browsing session. Click the New Tab box to the right of the last tab open in your browsing window, and, if you want to revisit earlier sites, click Reopen Closed Tabs. A list of sites you visited earlier appears. Just click the site you want to display.

If you want to return to your last browsing sessions, click the Reopen Last Session link, and Internet Explorer 9 automatically opens the web page you were visiting the last time you used the browser.

Searching for Information

With Internet Explorer 9, you can click in the One Box and type a word or phrase that describes what you'd like to find—for example, entering **tennis** brings suggestions like *tennis channel, tennis elbow,* and *tennis.com.* Bing is the default search engine Microsoft uses to display a list of search suggestions related to your search; you can click the suggestion you like to narrow your search and display a page of results with links to web pages you may want to visit.

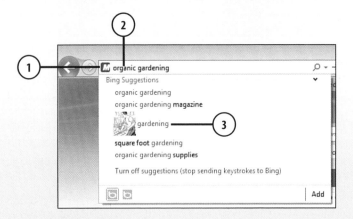

1. Click in One Box.

2. Type a word or phrase describing what you want to find.

3. Click the suggestion that best narrows your search.

**Click to display
different types
of results**   **Paid
result
placement**   **Paid
advertising**

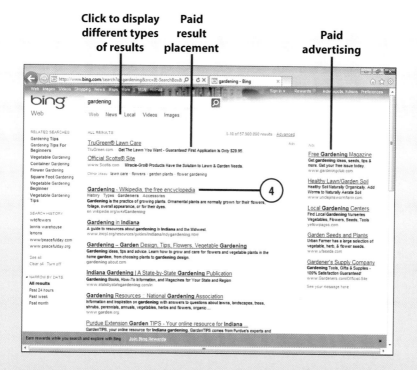

4. Your search provider—which is Bing until you tell IE9 otherwise—displays a list of search results, ranked from those that match your search phrase most closely to those that are not as close a match. Click a link you'd like to view.

It's Not All Good

It's important to know the difference between the various links you see in your search results. Some of those links are paid ads, which means that companies are paying the search utility for the space on the page where their link and description appears. It's a bit like print advertising, when people buy space to advertise their new washing machine or magazine or what-have-you. On the web, paid advertising is marked in some way—either with the word *Ads* as you see in the Bing search engine or by displaying ads with a second-color background.

Companies also pay for result placement so that their links appear at the top of your results list. When you're in the habit of thinking that "top means best result," you could easily click one of these paid-placement links, which is really an advertisement. Look closely at the web page results before you click anything. Generally, the first link in the results list that is a nonpaid link is a least two or three links down the page.

That's not to say, of course, that these companies aren't legitimate or that the products they are offering don't really fit the topic you were searching for. They could have just what you need. But the point is to know what's behind the result placement of these links so that you know what you're getting into before you click.

>> Go Further

QUIET SURFING WITH INPRIVATE BROWSING

In some cases, you may not want to track your browsing activity for others to see. Perhaps you're shopping for a holiday gift for someone and you don't want him to inadvertently discover it. You can turn on InPrivate Browsing to tell Internet Explorer 9 to skip recording your web activity. This means that the sites you visit won't be available in your browsing history, cookies, form data, temporary Internet files, or in the usernames and passwords Internet Explorer 9 usually keeps.

To turn on InPrivate Browsing, click the Tools icon in the upper-right area of the Internet Explorer 9 window. Click Safety and click InPrivate Browsing. Internet Explorer 9 opens a new browser session independent of the current one you have been using, and none of your browsing information is stored in the new session. When you're ready to end the InPrivate Browsing session, simply close the browser session.

Adding a Search Provider

You can add other search providers—in fact, you can choose from all kinds of search providers—to the One Box experience so that the search suggestions you receive are focused in a particular area. For example, if you are currently on a job hunt, you might want to add the CareerBuilder Job Search search utility. You can add in Google search or Google Translate. Or if you love to know how to do new things, choose the eHow Search. Or, of course, if eBay is a weakness (or a joy), you can add the eBay.com Visual Search.

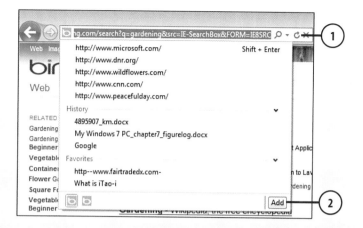

1. In the Internet Explorer 9 window, click Show Address Bar AutoComplete.

2. At the bottom of the One Box list, click Add.

3. In the Internet Explorer 9 Gallery, scroll to find a search provider you'd like to add. You can hover the mouse on the edge of the page to scroll in either direction.

4. Click the search provider you want to add.

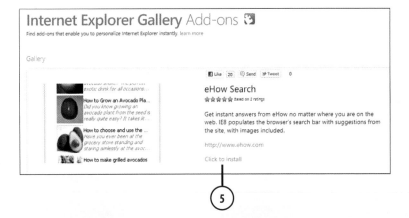

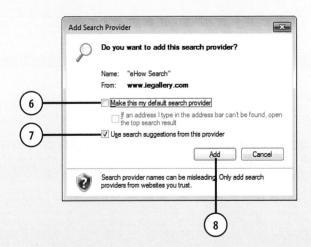

5. Select the Click to Install link. The Add Search Provider dialog box appears.

6. Click Make This My Default Search Provider if you want this search utility to be the one used automatically when you enter a word or phrase in One Box.

7. Click Use Search Suggestions from This Provider to add the utility to One Box search.

8. Click Add. The search provider is added to the bar at the bottom of the One Box list.

Take Some Time to Find Your Favorites

The list of search providers in the Internet Explorer 9 gallery is truly amazing. You are likely to find something that connects with your interests—recipes, sports, travel, news, and more. You can add more than one search provider to Internet Explorer 9 and then choose the provider you want to use as the default.

MANAGING SEARCH PROVIDERS

Go Further

Over time, you may want to change the search provider you've selected as the default or remove search providers you no longer need. How do you do that? Begin by clicking the Tools icon on the far side of the Internet Explorer 9 window. Click Internet Options.

In the Internet Options dialog box, click Settings in the Search area of the General tab. The Manage Add-Ons dialog box appears. You can click the various search providers you've added and click Set As Default or Remove to change the status or remove the provider from the list. Click Close when you're finished.

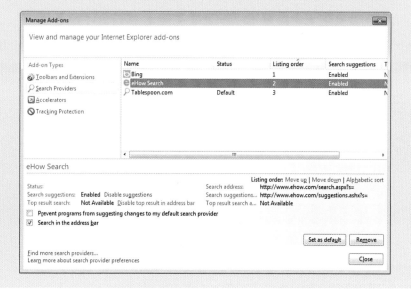

Working with Tabs

Being able to have more than one website open on the screen at one time is an important feature if you are used to searching on multiple sites, comparing what you find, or gathering information from more than one place. Or perhaps you're into multitasking—keeping your email or social media site open while you're doing some work at the same time. Either way, tabs in Internet Explorer 9 enable you to move easily among the open sites in your browsing session.

Opening a New Tab

You can easily open a new tab in your browser window so that you can open a web page in addition to the one you're currently viewing.

1. In Internet Explorer 9, click the New Tab button.

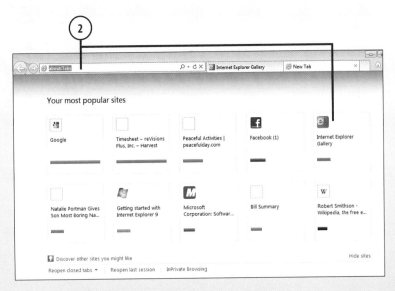

2. In the New Tab page, you can see site panels of the most recently viewed websites you've visited. You can click one of the panels or click in One Box and type the web address of the site you want to visit. Alternatively, you can enter a word or phrase and search for the content you want to find.

Double-Display Duty

You can view two or more pages at the same time by clicking a tab and dragging it toward the center of the Internet Explorer 9 window. The page comes
"undocked" from the browser window, and you can position it onscreen wherever you want it by clicking and dragging the top of the window.

Changing the Tab Display

The tab display in Internet Explorer 9 looks a little different than it appeared
in earlier versions of the program. Now the tabs are at the top of the window
to the right of One Box. The idea is that this arrangement gives you more
room on the screen for viewing the web pages you want to visit. You can
change the position of the tabs, however, if you'd like to set up the page differently.

1. In the Internet Explorer 9 window,
   right-click the area at the top of
   the browser window.

2. Click Show Tabs on a Separate
   Row.

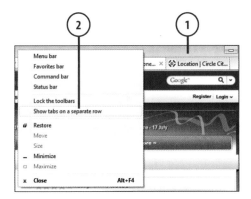

Beam Me Back, Scotty

Unfortunately, after you pop a tab
out into its own browser session,
there's no going back to the tab
row. This means that the web
pages continue to be displayed in
their respective browser windows
for the duration of your session—
which means you may have to
use Alt+Tab to switch among the
open browser windows.

Displaying Colorful Tabs

If you do a lot of browsing and like to have multiple tabs open at once, you may have noticed that moving among many tabs can be confusing and cumbersome. Internet Explorer 9 now color-codes tabs while keeping track and grouping the sites you're visiting depending on the links you follow.

For example, if you're browsing on one page and you create a new tab from that tab, both the original page and the new one are displayed in the same color. Those tabs are grouped and appear in the same color to help you see at a glance which tabs are related.

1. In the Internet Explorer 9 window, display a web page with content you're interested in (such as tennis).

2. Click the New Tab to the right of that web page window.

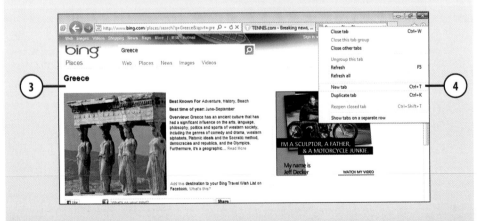

3. Display a page with different content (say, Greece).

4. When the page is displayed, right-click the tab for the web page and click New Tab.

⑤

5. Display another page about the second topic (Greece). Internet Explorer 9 displays the second set of tabs in another color to help you differentiate them from the first browsing session.

Working with Tab Groups

If you right-click the first tab (about Tennis) and select New Tab, the tab you create is part of the first tab group. If you click a tab about Green and select New Tab, the new tab belongs to the second group. You can close entire groups together by right-clicking the group you want to close and clicking Close This Tab Group. You can also ungroup tabs so they each function as their own standalone pages by right-clicking a tab in the group and clicking Ungroup This Tab.

Pinning a Site to the Taskbar

When you visit a particular site often, you can easily pin it to the taskbar so that you can open it quickly with a click of the mouse. You might do this, for example, if you have sites you like to check in the middle of the day—perhaps a particular news site or your favorite social media site. This way, you don't need to set a particular page to be one of your Home pages, but you can still access it easily when you want to.

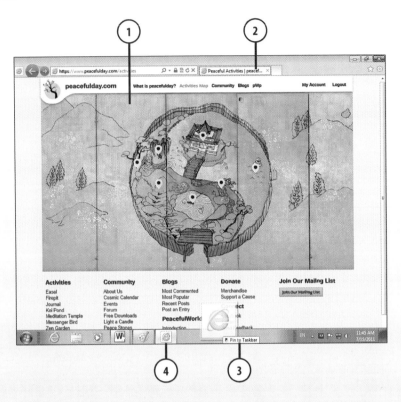

1. Display the site you want to pin to the taskbar.

2. Click the tab of the web page.

3. Drag the tab to the taskbar. The icon says Pin to Taskbar to indicate the action.

4. Release the mouse button. The icon is added to the taskbar automatically, and you are able to open the page by clicking that icon whenever you like.

Removing Pinned Pages

You can remove a pinned page from the taskbar at any time by right-clicking the taskbar icon and choosing Unpin This Program from Taskbar.

CHOOSING MORE SITES TO PIN

Internet Explorer 9 offers a gallery of sites that have been pinned to other users' taskbars, and they think you might like to add one or two to your own Windows 7 experience. To visit the gallery, click the Tools icon in the far-right side of the IE9 window and click Go to Pinned Sites. In the IE9 Gallery, you can search for specific sites or drag the site's icon to your taskbar to add it to your own pinned sites.

If you don't want too many website icons cluttering up your taskbar, another quick-look area you can add to the website is the Start menu. Simply display the website you want to add, click the Tools icon in the top-right area of the IE9 window, point to File, and click Add Site to Start Menu.

It's Not All Good

This may seem like a minor point, but for some reason when you pin a site to your taskbar, the Home icon in the upper-right corner of the IE9 window disappears. And the Home icon isn't gone only for that site, but for any new tabs you add during that session. Odd.

I have no idea what the functional reason behind this might be; whether you're visiting a favorite site or not, going to the page you identified as Home seems like a good feature to offer users. To get your Home icon to show up again, click the Internet Explorer 9 link (*not* a pinned site) to open your next browsing session.

Working with IE9 Tools

The new streamlined look of Internet Explorer 9 may leave you wondering where all the tools on the toolbar went. Now the menus you may be looking for are tucked away in the Tools menu, off to the right side of the Internet Explorer window. You can display the tools by clicking the Tools icon.

Previewing and Printing Web Content

Some pages have their own print tools directly on the page. For example, when you're looking at a news site, chances are you'll see an option that allows you to print the story without all the ads and video boxes and whatnot that are also present on the page. When you want to print the contents of what you see in your web browser (or the page doesn't provide its own print option), IE9 gives you the tools to do that.

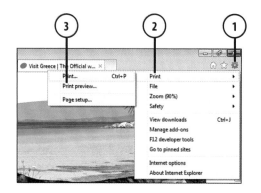

1. With the page that you want to print open in your browser, click Tools.

2. Point to Print.

3. Click Print Preview to see how the page will look when printed.

4. Change the orientation of the page from portrait (8.5 × 11) to landscape (11 × 8.5) if you like.

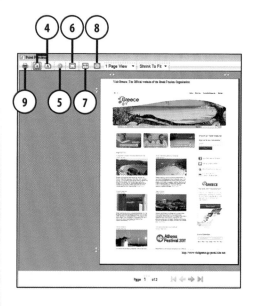

5. Display the Page Setup dialog box to change paper size; choose whether background images are printed; and modify the headers, footers, and margins.

6. Click to turn the headers on and off for the page that will be printed.

7. Zoom in to see the page displayed full width in the preview window.

8. Zoom out to display the full page in the preview window.

9. When you're ready, click Print.

Go Directly to Print, Do Not Collect $200

If you just want to print the fastest way possible, bypassing Print Preview, you can click the Tools icon, and click Print and then Print. Choose the printer you want to use and click Print. Or, even faster yet, press Ctrl+P, enter your printer options, and click Print. Super-fast.

10. Click the printer you want to use.

11. Leave All selected if you want to print all pages required to print this web page; otherwise, click Pages and enter the page or page range you want to print.

12. Enter the number of copies you want to print.

13. Click Print.

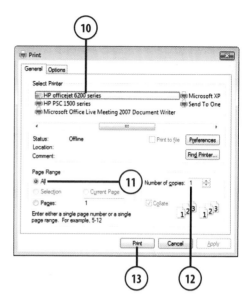

SETTING UP YOUR PAGE BEFORE PRINTING

If you want to control just what gets printed—so that you don't print a bunch of images you don't want, for example—you can set up the page and exclude background images. Here's how.

Click the Tools icon and point to Print. Click Page Setup. In the Page Setup dialog box, click to clear the check mark from Print Background Colors and Images, and then click OK. When your page prints, any shades, colors, or images used on the background of the site are omitted and you see your printer on traditional white paper. Nice.

Changing Site Display

The way we like our web pages displayed—very large or ultra-small or anything in between—is largely a personal preference issue. Maybe you like page content to be as small as possible so you can fit other open windows on your desktop at the same time. Or maybe you want the text to be large enough that you can read it without your glasses. Whatever your preference, you can easily change the display to fit your comfort level in IE9.

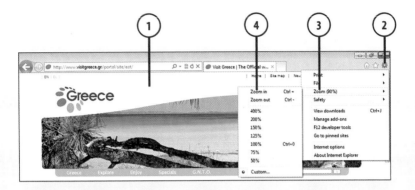

1. Open Internet Explorer 9 and display a page you want to see.

2. Click the Tools menu.

3. Point to Zoom.

4. Click a Zoom setting. You can click Zoom In or Zoom Out if you want to magnify or reduce the size of the page content by increments. If you want to change the display to a specific value, you can choose one of the Zoom options. You would use 400% only for situations in which you want to see something extremely magnified; most reading values are in the range of 75% to 150%.

Setting Your Own Zoom Value

If you want to set the zoom value to something not shown on the list, click Custom, and in the Custom Zoom dialog box, type the percentage of display you want to see. Click OK to save your settings.

Adding and Managing Favorites

The web is a big, big place. And it's getting bigger all the time. How will you ever remember the great site you found with discount travel packages? Or what about the funky blog with the great sense of humor you liked? Keeping all the websites organized so that you can find them again easily is the job of your IE9 favorites. You'll find favorites in the tools on the right side the Internet Explorer 9 window. Some of the more common tasks you may want to do with favorites include adding new favorites, using the favorites you've already saved, or organizing your favorites so that you can go right to the sites you want to see.

Working with the Favorites Bar

Earlier in this chapter, you discovered that you can display additional toolbars in IE9 if you don't mind them taking up onscreen browsing space. The Favorites bar is one of those toolbars worth the trade-off of space. The items you add to your Favorites bar are the sites you want to get to easily and often. The Favorites bar appears at the top of the browsing area where you can click your favorite sites easily.

1. Right-click the top of the IE9 browser window.

2. Click Favorites Bar. The Favorites bar appears at the top of the browsing area.

3. Click in One Box and type the web address of (or search for) the website you want to add as a favorite.

4. Drag the icon of the site—to the left of the web address—to the Favorites bar.

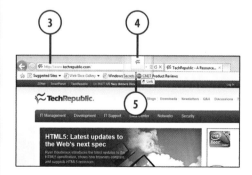

5. Use the black position marker to select the place on the bar where you want the favorite to appear. When the marker is in the place you want, release the mouse button and the favorite is added to the Favorites bar.

Adding Favorites Fast

Another quick way to add favorites to the Favorites bar is to use the Add Favorites button that appears on the far-left end of the bar. Firs, navigate to the page you want to add and then click Add to Favorites Bar. IE9 places the favorite in the first position on the bar. You can then click it and drag it to wherever on the bar you want it to appear.

Adding Favorites

The Favorites icon on the right side of the IE9 window contains a number of tools you can use to add and organize all the favorite websites you add to Internet Explorer 9.

Click to pin the Favorites Center open in the browser window

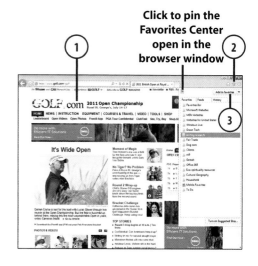

1. Display the web page you want to add to your favorites.

2. Click the Favorites tool in the upper-right area of the browser window.

3. Click Add to Favorites.

4. The name of the page is highlighted in the Name box. Type a new name if you like or leave it as is.

5. Click the Create In arrow and choose the folder in which you want to add the web link.

6. If necessary, click New Folder to create a new folder to store the favorite. Type a name for the folder and click OK.

7. Click Add to add the web link to the selected folder.

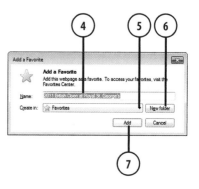

Accessing Your Favorites

When you want to display a website you've saved as one of your favorites, you can display the Favorites Center, open the folder in which the favorite is stored, and click it to display the page. Here are the steps:

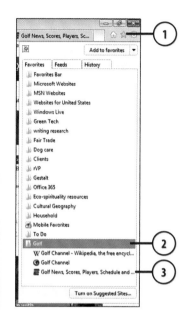

1. In the Internet Explorer 9 window, click the Favorites icon.

2. Click the folder containing the web page you want to view.

3. Click the web page you want to see. The page opens in the browser window.

IMPORTING AND EXPORTING FAVORITES

If you have a well-loved set of favorites, you can easily import them from another computer and export them from your existing one. Click the Favorites icon in the IE9 window and then click the arrow to the right of the Add to Favorites button. Click Import and Export.

In the Import/Export Settings dialog box, click either Import from a File or Export to a File, depending on which you want to do. (Importing allows you to add the favorites from a file into your IE9 Favorites Center; exporting enables you to create a file of your favorites currently in your IE9 Favorites Center.) Click Next, and choose whether you want to export or import Favorites, Feeds, and Cookies. Choose the folder where you want the file to be stored, enter a name for the file if you're exporting, or select the name of the file if you're importing. Finally, click Export or Import, and the operation is completed. Click Finish to close the dialog box.

Organizing Your Favorites

From time to time, you may decide you want to reorganize your favorites, moving some from one folder to another or deleting ones you no longer need. You can organize your favorites in the Favorites Center in Internet Explorer 9.

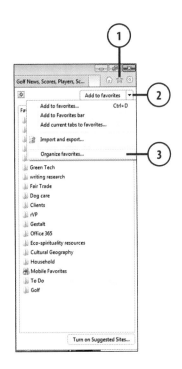

1. In Internet Explorer 9, click the Favorites icon.

2. Click the arrow to the right of the Add to Favorites button.

3. Click Organize Favorites.

4. In the Organize Favorites dialog box, click the folder that contains the links you want to move.

5. Drag the link to a new folder, or click the Move button and click a destination folder and click OK.

6. Click to rename the link. The link is highlighted, and you can type a new name and press Enter.

7. Click to delete an unneeded link. Be warned, however; IE9 doesn't ask you to confirm the deletion, so after you click Delete, the link is gone (and Ctrl+Z won't bring it back).

8. Click Close.

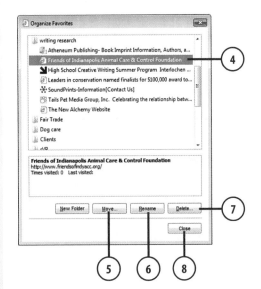

USING SUGGESTED SITES

Go Further >>>

Suggested Sites are sites that Internet Explorer 9 believes you would like to view, based on your past browsing and searching history. The Suggested Sites feature is turned off by default because tracking this information means that your browsing activities are sent to Microsoft. If you want to turn on Suggested Sites, click the Favorites icon in the IE9 window and click Turn On Suggested Sites at the bottom of the Favorites panel.

A message box asks you to confirm that you want to enable the feature. Click Yes to add Suggested Sites. A web page appears with a number of sites that you may like, given your past browsing history. You can also see more suggested sites at any time by clicking See Suggested Sites button at the bottom of the Favorites panel or by clicking the Suggested Sites arrow in the Favorites bar.

Viewing Your RSS Feeds

If you love keeping up on things—following news stories, keeping an eye on sports teams, researching your favorite hobbies—chances are you've already discovered RSS feeds. RSS stands for Really Simply Syndication, and it's a way to get updated content from sites you like to visit without having to go there and search for it. Instead of browsing to all these different sites, you can get the RSS feeds from those sites brought to you. Internet Explorer 9 makes it easy to view those RSS feeds in the Favorites Center.

1. In the Internet Explorer 9 window, click the Favorites icon.

2. Click the Feeds tab.

3. Click the RSS feed you'd like to view. The feed opens in the browser window.

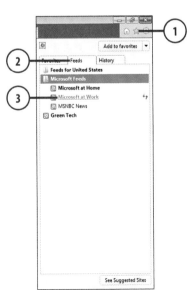

4. Click the link of the story you're like to see.

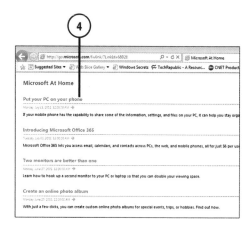

WHERE DO YOU FIND RSS FEEDS?

When you're browsing in IE9, you will notice a small, orange RSS icon you can click to sign up to a site's RSS feed. When you click the orange icon, a page of RSS entries appears, offering you the link: Subscribe to This Feed. Click the link, and when IE9 displays the Subscribe to This Feed dialog box, click Subscribe. The RSS feed is added to your Feeds tab so that you can get back to the content easily—and as often as you wish.

You can also use the Command bar to discover sites that have an RSS feed. Display the Command bar by right-clicking the top of the browser window and clicking Command Bar. When you browse to a page that offers RSS feeds, the View Feed on This Page tool becomes available. Click the tool and choose the RSS feed you want to add.

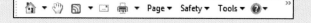

Displaying Your Browsing History

Have you ever had one of those moments when you wished you'd saved a website as a favorite—but you didn't—and now you're racking your brain trying to remember the name of the site so you can try to find it again? Luckily, Internet Explorer 9 has an antidote for that memory lapse: It's called the History tab, and it's conveniently located in the Favorites Center.

1. In the Internet Explorer 9 window, click the Favorites icon.

2. Click the History tab.

3. Click the day of the week you want to view.

4. Look through the list, click the site you want to see, and click the web page within the site. (Or, if necessary, click a different day and look through *those* links.)

5. When you click the page link, the web page appears in the browser window, and the Favorites Center closes.

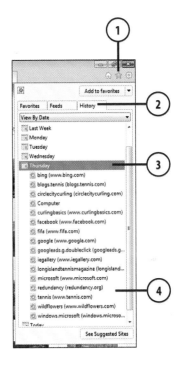

THINKING TRACKING PROTECTION

Sometimes there is more going on behind the scenes on a website than you may know. A company placing an ad on a site, for example, may also be tracking your browsing habits from site to site. Have you ever noticed that something you searched for—like a vacation destination or the best airfare rates—suddenly show up as ads on all kinds of sites? Suddenly, you're seeing ads everywhere for the item you recently searched. This happens because your browsing activity was picked up and is now being used to trigger the ads that are shown to you.

Internet Explorer 9 enables you to control this behavior if you like. You can make a choice about which sites can gather your browsing activity. Tools that help you stay in control of your information in this way are known as tracking protection tools. You can create a list to block content from any sites that you don't want to receive your information.

At the present time, Internet Explorer 9 doesn't have its own tracking protection feature, but you can download and use a number of add-ons. Go to the Internet Explorer gallery (http://iegallery.com/en/trackingprotectionlists/) to find out more.

Adding Web Slices

In addition to RSS feeds and website favorites, you can save web slices that deliver updated content from specific web parts on a page. For example, a web slice on an e-commerce site might show the latest shopping discounts. When you subscribe to the web slice, you can view the deals as they are updated, whether or not you actually go to the site.

When you are viewing a page that has web slices available (and not many pages do, yet), the Add Web Slices tool becomes available in the Command bar.

1. Browse to a page containing a
    web slice and click the Add Web
    Slices tool in the Command bar.

2. Click the name of the web slice
    you want to add.

3. A message box appears, giving
    you information about the slice.
    Click Add to Favorites Bar.

4. You can view the web slice at any
    time by clicking the slide on the
    Favorites bar. This way, you can
    get updated information without
    needing to go to the website to
    see it.

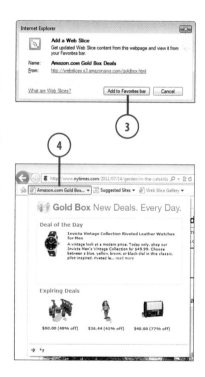

Securing Your Browsing Experience

Internet Explorer 9 is designed to give you the most secure web experience
possible. You can control which types of information sites gather about you,
which sites are allowed to download files to your computer, and which sites
are able to play animations or run other programs through ActiveX controls.

Blocking ActiveX Controls

ActiveX controls are common on websites these days, running an automated photo album, rotating banner ads, and more. In some cases, developers use these types of controls to track information about you and also to personalize the ad content displayed during your browsing experience. With Internet Explorer 9, you control whether or not ActiveX controls appear. You can turn off ActiveX controls so they are blocked for sites you are unfamiliar with, and then you can turn the controls back on when you are viewing a site you trust.

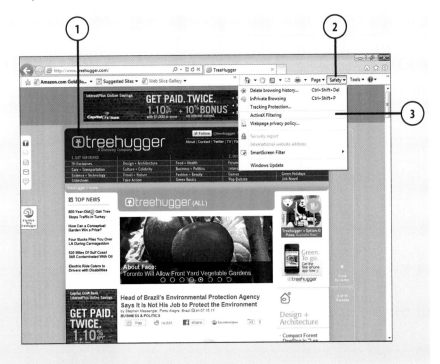

1. Open IE9 and display a web page you want to view.

2. Click Safety in the Command bar.

3. Click ActiveX Filtering.

Blocked ActiveX control

Blocked ActiveX control

4. The ActiveX controls on the page are blocked. You can redisplay the controls if you like by choosing Safety and clicking ActiveX Filtering a second time to clear the check mark.

Deleting Cookies

It's a good idea to regularly clean off the cookies that have accumulated on your computer, both to keep their drain on your computer's memory low and to weed out any potentially sneaky cookies that could be sending information back to the site that placed them.

1. In Internet Explorer 9, click Safety in the Command bar.

2. Click Delete Browsing History. The Delete Browsing History dialog box appears.

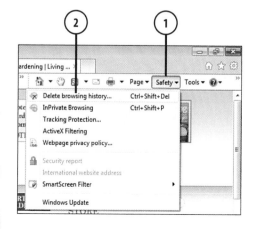

3. The first item in the dialog box, Preserve Favorites Website Data, retains information—cookies and all—related to sites that you have marked as Favorites. In most cases, you should leave this item selected.

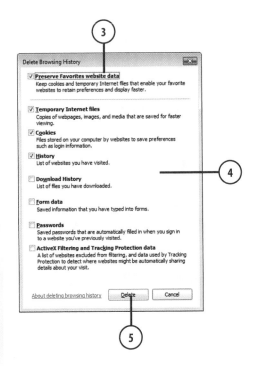

4. Review the list of checked and unchecked items. The checked items are deleted; the unchecked items are not. Change the items as needed to suit your preference. You may, for example, want to delete all the form data you have entered in online forms; if so, check the Form Data check box.

5. Click Delete to delete the cookies and other information you've selected.

SO WHAT ARE COOKIES, ANYWAY?

>>> Go Further

The websites you visit want you to come back (and buy something—from them or one of their advertisers), so they want you to have a personalized experience on their site. This means they want to make visiting their site a pleasant experience for you, so they save information about your time on the site—your preferences, your username and password, if you created them—in what's known as a *cookie*, and the cookie is stored on your computer. Then whenever you return to that site, your preferences are there to personalize your web experience with the items you said you like. Pretty clever, right?

But some cookies can do more than save your preferences. They may also track your web activities, and that borders on infringing upon your privacy. In Internet Explorer 9, you can control the cookies stored on your computer by deleting them, limiting them, or blocking all of them.

Set Privacy Options

Internet Explorer 9 enables you to set privacy options in a way that makes sense for the way you like to browse the web. You can choose from a range of settings that offer a low amount of protection to a high level of protection.

1. Click Tools in the IE 9 Command bar.

2. Click Internet Options. The Internet Options dialog box appears.

3. Click the Privacy tab. This tab enables you to set the level of privacy you want to have when browsing.

4. Drag the Settings slider up to increase the privacy protection or down to decrease the protection. You can choose from six settings: Allow All Cookies, Low, Medium, Medium High, High, and Block All Cookies.

5. Click Apply to apply your new settings.

6. Click OK to close the dialog box.

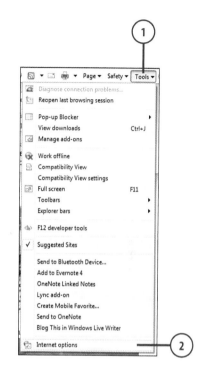

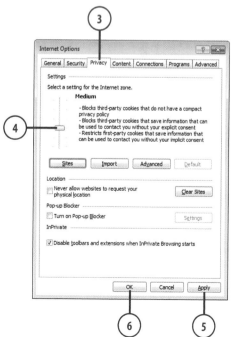

What Is IE9 Looking For?

When you increase the various privacy levels using the Privacy tab in the Internet Options dialog box, Internet Explorer 9 gradually increases the level of protection by blocking or restricting (1) sites that do not have a privacy policy and (2) sites that may save cookies to your computer that can be used to contact you without your consent. Some sites allow third-party sites to place cookies on your computer; for example, a magazine site might include an eBay ad and the eBay content might download the cookie on your computer; other sites include only their own cookies. With the Setting slides on the Privacy tab, you can control what you allow to be saved on your computer and what you don't.

>> Go Further

GETTING A PRIVACY REPORT

You can find out what's going on in relation to privacy issues on sites you visit by clicking Safety in the Command bar and choosing Webpage Privacy Policy. The Privacy Report dialog box appears, showing you all the cookies that are present on the site you're visiting. You can also see the current status of the cookies—whether or not they are accepted according to your privacy settings. You can click one of the links and click Summary to get an overview of the site's privacy policy as well as a summary of current information gathered. When you finish viewing the report, click Close.

Increasing Your Browsing Security

Other tools in the Internet Options dialog box that can help you have a secure browsing experience are in the Security tab. You can set the overall security level for Internet Explorer and also add the websites you visit frequently to your Trusted Sites list.

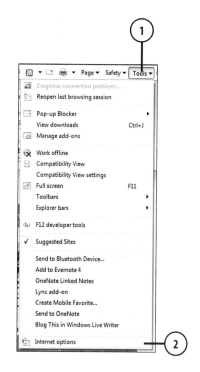

1. In the browser window, click Tools in the Command bar.

2. Click Internet Options. The Internet Options dialog box appears.

3. Click the Security tab. On this tab, you can choose the different zones, or types of sites you deal with, and choose the security level for each one. The different zones are Internet, Local Intranet, Trusted Sites, and Restricted Sites. Internet is chosen by default, and this setting influences all the browsing you do on the web.

4. Drag the slider up to increase the level of protection; drag the slider down to decrease protection. You can choose from three levels: High, Medium-High, and High. Medium-High is selected by default.

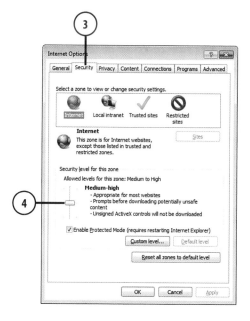

5. You can optionally click Trusted Sites and change the security level for sites you trust.

6. Click Sites to add the web addresses of sites you visit regularly and feel you can trust.

7. Click Apply to save your settings.

8. Click OK to close the dialog box.

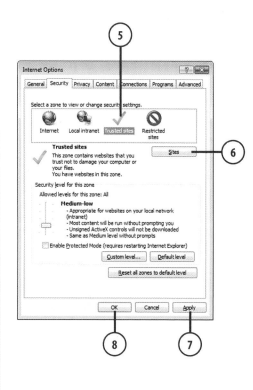

Doing Away with Pop-Ups

Do pop-ups annoy you? Yes, you and everybody else on the planet. You can do away with pop-ups easily in Internet Explorer 9. Click Tools in the Command bar and point to Pop-Up Blocker. Click Turn On Pop-Up Blocker. Now you can browse to your heart's content, and IE9 keeps any pop-ups from appearing without your consent. The notification bar lets you know when a pop-up has been blocked, giving you the option to view it if you like.

FINDING PHISHING WITH SMARTSCREEN FILTER

Internet Explorer also includes a feature called SmartScreen Filter that enables you to submit a site you may suspect as a phishing site to Microsoft for a closer look. Microsoft then compares the site to its database of phishing sites. If the site is located on the list, the site is blocked and you are given a warning about the site.

SmartScreen Filter also checks files you download against the list to make sure that the downloads aren't known to be unsafe. Again, if a problem is discovered, SmartScreen Filter blocks the download.

You can find out more about SmartScreen Filter by clicking Safety in the Command bar, pointing to SmartScreen Filter, and clicking Check This Website. Click the link How Does SmartScreen Filter Help Protect Me? to find out more about the utility.

Sending a Link by Email with Windows Live Mail

How often does it happen that you're browsing the web and suddenly you find something you want to share with somebody else? Internet Explorer 9 gives you direct access to your Windows Live mail account, a web-based mail account that you can access from your web browser or your phone. Windows Live Mail is similar to Hotmail—in fact, it's just a later incarnation of the original Hotmail program. Windows Live Mail is a full-featured program you can use to add contacts, send and receive email, work with your calendar, interact with Windows Live Messenger, and more.

Signing In to Windows Live Mail

Getting to your web-based mail is as simple as moving to the website where it's stored in Internet Explorer 9. And there's a command built into the program to take you directly there.

1. In the IE9 window, click Page in the Command bar.

2. Click E-Mail with Windows Live. The login page for Windows Live appears.

3. Enter your username (it may already be highlighted for you).

4. Type your password.

5. Click the Keep Me Signed In check box if you want Windows Live to remember your username and password.

6. Click Sign In.

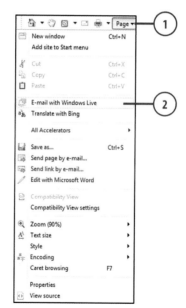

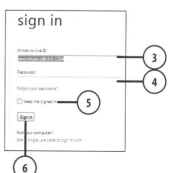

Simple Sign-In

You can click the Get a Single Use Code to Sign In With link if you want to have Windows Live text you a code you can use for a single login.

Sending Mail

The web page you were displaying when you chose E-mail with Windows Live Mail is inserted as a link in a new message after you log in to Windows Live Mail. You can enter the email address of the person you want to send the message, add a Subject line, expand the text in the content area, and click Send.

Click to open Contacts list

Add attachments

Format the text of the message

Display your calendar

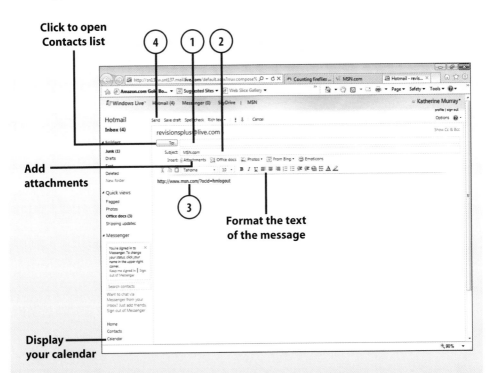

1. Click in the To line and type the email address of the person you want to receive the message.

2. Click in the Subject line and type a topic, such as **Take a look at this article!**

3. Click in the body area and write a note to the recipient.

4. Click Send to send the message.

Where's the Inbox?

You can display your Windows Live Mail Inbox at any time by clicking the Inbox selection in the left panel of the Windows Live Mail window.

Find Out More about Windows Live Mail

You can learn more about Windows Live Mail, and the other services avaliable in Windows Live, by reading *Using Microsoft Windows Live* (Que, 2011), available at www.quepublishing.com/store/product.aspx?isbn=0789743868.

Working with Your Calendar

While you're using Internet Explorer 9 to review and send mail in Windows Live Mail, you may also want to check your calendar and schedule appointments. The calendar is always available to you online, from wherever you have web access.

1. In the Windows Live Mail window, click Calendar.

2. Click the day on which you want to add an appointment.

3. Click Add. The Add Event pop-up box appears.

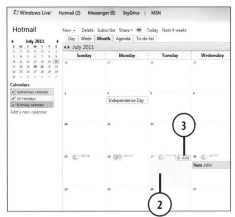

4. Click in the What box and type the title for the appointment.

5. Click in the Where box and enter the location.

6. Click the Calendar arrow if you want to assign the appointment to a different calendar.

7. Enter a Start day and time.

8. Enter an Ending day and time.

9. Click Save to save the appointment to your calendar.

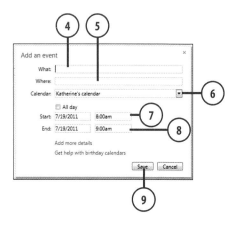

Where in the World Are You?

The first time you click Calendar in Windows Live Mail, the program prompts you to select your time zone so that the appointments you set appear in the right time frames. Click the arrow to display world time zones, click yours, and click Go to Your Calendar.

Sharing Your Calendar

You can easily share your calendar with others by clicking Share at the top of the Calendar window and selecting your calendar name from the list. In the Share Settings window, click Share This Calendar and click Save. Specify the people you want to share the calendar with by clicking the Add People button and choosing people from the Contacts list displayed in the pop-up message box. Click Add to add those you want to share with and click Save to save the sharing settings.

Talk about media! Windows 7 knows you want to watch shows, listen to music, and stream videos on your PC, and it includes a number of fun tools to help you do just that.

Play, watch, and stream media with Windows Media Player.

Windows Media Center enables you to watch Internet TV, videos, and more.

In this chapter, you learn how to make the most of media—Internet TV, songs, videos, and more—on your Windows 7 PC. You find out about doing these tasks:

→ Watching TV and movies on your PC
→ Enjoying media with Windows Media Player

Ready, Set, Media!

"This year, I'm giving up something different for Lent," a friend said to me not long ago. "Oh, really?" I asked. "What are you giving up?"

"Media," he said, looking at his feet. "And I'm really not sure I can live without it."

In one way or another, most of us feel somewhat similar. Media keeps us connected to our world. We learn the latest headlines. We discover far-away places. We laugh as we watch our favorite shows. Media picks us up, keeps us informed, prepares us for upcoming events. Where would be without our media?

And, of course, there's the all-important entertainment factor as well. When was the last time you watched a movie just because it was good? (If it's been too long, maybe you can use the techniques in this chapter to pick out a good show and watch it—just because.) This chapter shows you how to use two primary different tools in Windows 7 that can help you make the most of your media: Windows Media Center and Windows Media Player.

Watching TV and Movies on Your PC

Windows Media Center makes it possible—even easy!—for you to watch TV and movies on your Windows 7 PC by simply streaming it over the Internet. You can watch a number of Internet shows, for free, without a TV tuner. And if you want to invest in a PC TV tuner, you can set up Windows Media Center to stream live television to your PC. Sound too good to be true? Read on.

Launching Windows Media Center

We need to begin by starting Windows Media Center. Notice that the interface is much different from anything you've seen in Windows 7 before—beautiful, blue, and fluid.

1. On the Windows 7 desktop, click Start.

2. Click in the search box and type **Windows Media Center**.

3. Click Windows Media Center. The utility launches, and the opening screen appears on your desktop.

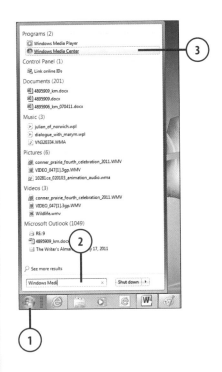

WHAT'S THE DIFFERENCE BETWEEN WINDOWS MEDIA CENTER AND WINDOWS MEDIA PLAYER?

Chances are that you've seen both Windows Media Center and Windows Media Player on your Windows 7 computer. Both programs are included with Home Premium, Professional, Ultimate, and Enterprise versions of Windows 7. Why do you need two different programs for working with your media? How do these two programs differ?

In general, Windows Media Center is a comprehensive, media-savvy program that enables you to catalogue, organize, watch, and enjoy media on your Windows PC and throughout your home—if you have created a home network and added Windows Media Extenders so that you can use Windows Media Center in various rooms. You can watch Internet TV, download videos, and more in Windows Media Center, and it will look great on your big screen TV in whatever room you choose to watch it.

Windows Media Player is designed so that you can listen to and watch media files resident on your computer, the web, or your mobile device. You can download and catalogue your files, burn CDs and DVDs, listen to Internet radio, and much more.

Looking Around the Windows Media Center Window

The Windows Media Center has a unique scrolling interface, much different in appearance from anything you've seen in Windows 7. Hover the mouse pointer over the list of options, and arrows appear. Click the arrows to scroll through your options and display additional choices on the screen. What's more, the words and images on the screen are oversized and bring a touch of design to the interface. As you will see, Windows Media Center is about much more than simply functional media viewing: You will hopefully be swept up in this new media world and enjoy all the entertainment options it offers.

On the Windows Media Center opening screen, you see the following elements:

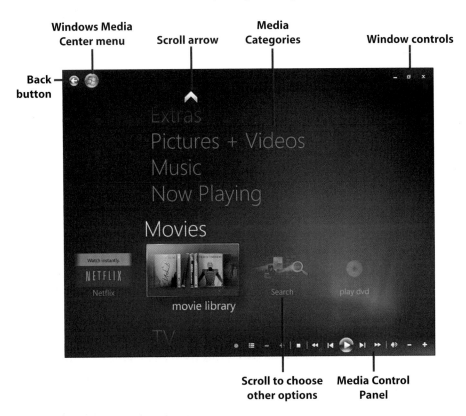

- **Windows Media Center menu.** Clicking this green button from any point in Media Center returns you to the home page display.

- **Scroll arrow.** Hover the mouse pointer above the list of options, and the scroll arrow appears. Click the arrow to scroll through additional choices.

- **Back button.** Click Back to move to the previous Windows Media Center window.

- **Media Categories.** Click one of the categories to see the media options it contains.

- **Scroll to choose other options.** When you click a media category, the options for that item appear to the right of the selected category.

- **Media Control Panel.** Use these controls to play, pause, and customize your media viewing.

- **Window controls.** Click one of the window controls to minimize, restore, or maximize the Windows Media Center window.

Extras You May Want to Get

Windows 7 comes with Windows Media Center and already includes everything you need to watch Internet TV on your PC. If you want to watch live TV shows, however, and record your favorite shows and movies to your computer, you need to purchase a TV tuner. A TV tuner is a simple device you connect to your computer through a USB port (if you're using an external tuner) and connect the other end to your cable line (or to a small digital antenna if your signal is airborne). PC Tuners range in price from $50 to $180, and just make sure you're getting one that works with Windows 7 and Windows Media Player. Installation is simple: Just plug in the device, install the software from the CD that comes in the package, and you're ready to watch live television on your PC!

Watching Internet TV on Your PC

You can choose from among dozens of Internet TV shows available in Windows Media Center, and you can watch the shows without needing a PC tuner, so your Windows 7 computer is ready to go just the way it is. The Internet TV shows you can watch are episodes of sitcoms, previews of reality shows, and other popular shows that have made their content available in Windows Media Center. The first time you click TV, you are asked to agree to the terms of service. After you click the check box and click Install Now, Internet TV is installed in Windows Media Center, and you can view the Guide and choose a show to watch.

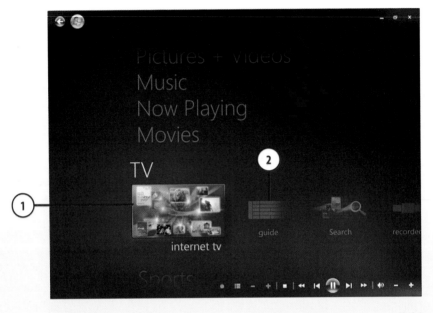

1. In Windows Media Center, click TV. The TV options become available.

2. Click the scroll arrow one time and click Guide.

3. Click the category of show you'd like to see.

4. Click a show in the grid to go directly to that show.

5. Scroll through the episodes until you find the one you want to view. Click the episode.

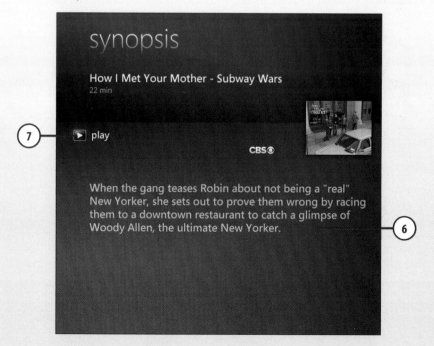

6. In the Synopsis screen, read through the description of the episode.

7. Click Play to begin viewing the show.

8. Use the Media Controls to pause, stop, or move ahead or back in the video. You can also adjust the volume by clicking the – and + tools at the far end of the tools row.

9. Drag the slider on the timeline to move to another point in the clip.

10. Click to reduce the full-screen window to a smaller window you can position alongside your other open applications if you like.

It's Not All Good

Well, the Internet isn't ad free by a long shot. Just like the soft drink ads you see now at the beginning of movies shown at the theater, commercials are part of your normal, Internet TV experience.

And unfortunately, even though you can skip around during the regular streaming shows—dragging the slider forward or back while viewing—when the commercials come on, the slider is disabled. Go figure.

There is one saving grace, however. Windows Media Center displays in the episode status bar small cross-point indicators that show you where the commercials are. So if they really bug you, you can drag the slider over the mark at just the right moment and continue on with the show without commercials.

Watching Live TV on Your PC

If you have added a TV tuner to your computer—like the PCTV HD stick or the Hauppage WinTV—you can watch live TV through Windows Media Center. Here's how to find the shows you want and get the ball rolling.

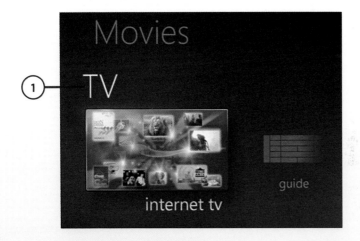

1. In Windows Media Center, click TV.

2. Scroll to the right to Live TV and click it.

3. The Live TV Setup utility asks whether you want to use the listings in your local area to determine what's available through your cable system. Click Yes.

4. When prompted to enter your ZIP Code, do so, so that Windows Media Center has access to the viewing guide that's right for your area.

5. You are then presented with a lengthy Electronic Programming Guide Terms of Service (a full version of the user agreement is available at http://go.microsoft.com/fwlink/?Linkid=8430). If you want to continue, click I Agree and click Next.

6. You are next asked to read and agree to the Microsoft PlayReady PC Runtime user agreement, which covers the Internet-based service Microsoft is providing when you use Windows Media Center to watch live TV. Again, click I Agree and click Next. Microsoft PlayReady begins installing.

7. After the installations are complete, Windows Media Center checks your cable provider and finds your set-top box. If you are using an adapter and not a set-top box, you can click Manual Install to answer questions individually.

8. When all is said and done, Windows Media Center downloads the channel guide to your PC. Don't be alarmed if the whole process takes 30 minutes or more, and you may need to—as I did—reboot during the middle because the scan stopped midstream. At the end, though, you should have a wonderfully functioning live TV stream coming right into your computer, ready for you to record whenever you feel like it!

It's Not All Good

The Not-So-Happy Ending

There are a number of different sources for live TV—antenna, cable, and satellite. And there are many different types of PC tuners, not all of which work with Windows Media Center or Windows 7. And even if you have a PC tuner that reportedly works with Windows Media Center, you may have a number of wrinkles to work out in the process that are related to your particular cable provider or the way in which your cable is set up.

On some Windows Media Center configurations, the tuner doesn't configure properly and Windows Media Player prompts you for an IR control cable to be plugged into your cable set-top box. The IR cable is for the remote control—when the IR cable is in place, the Windows Media Center remote control can communicate with your set-top box. But—and this is a big but—not all TV tuners come with Windows Media Center remote controls. So before you purchase a TV tuner, and before you spend your entire evening trying to figure out why live TV isn't working on your computer, make sure you have the right equipment for your particular setup and be prepared to experiment with different methods to get Live TV to work. (I finally resorted to using the antennae option and started picking up Live TV stations.) Also be sure that you know how to get to the TV Tuner Troubleshooter in case you get stuck halfway through. (To start the TV Tuner Troubleshooter, click Start, type *troubleshooter* in the Search box, click View All in the left panel, and click Set Up TV Tuner.

Recording a Series or a Show

Did you know that you can also record shows using Windows Media Center? All you need is a TV tuner and functioning Live TV (see the previous section), and you can watch, schedule, and record shows to your heart's content.

1. In Windows Media Center, display the Guide.

2. When the Guide appears, select the series you want to record.

3. Click the Record button (the small red circle) in the left end of the viewing controls. A prompt at the bottom of the screen says "This show will be recorded." If you want to record the entire series and not just the current show, double-click the Record button, and it changes to show three overlapping red icons—this lets you know you've told Windows Media Center to record multiple shows.

Canceling a Series

If you decide you'd rather not record an entire series after all, you can right-click above the timing status bar to display Program Info, and then click the information that appears to display the show Synopsis window. Click Cancel Series to tell Windows Media Player not to continue recording the shows you've selected. Click Yes when Windows Media Center asks whether you want to cancel the series.

4. As you watch the show, the small "recording" red icon appears to the left of the show information. You can record to the end of the show, or right-click to display the show synopsis and click Stop Recording.

5. Click Yes when Windows Media Center asks you to confirm that you want to stop recording. You can then click Watch in the show synopsis screen to watch what you've recorded or select the show later by clicking TV in Windows Media Player and choosing Recorded TV.

Wondering Where Your Media Went?

Windows Media Player stores all recorded shows to the location you enter in the Recorder Storage screen. Display that setting by clicking Tasks on the home page and clicking Settings. Next, choose TV, Recorder, and Recorder Storage. Click + in Record on Drive setting to choose the device and folder where you want Windows Media Center to store your recordings.

Setting Recording Options

Sometimes you see a show you want to watch, click Record, and it's all over but the viewing. But occasionally your favorite shows may come on when you have other plans, and Windows Media Center can help you with that problem. You can set your recording options and schedule recording in advance so it happens automatically when your favorite show comes on.

1. In Windows Media Center, scroll down to Tasks.

2. Click Settings.

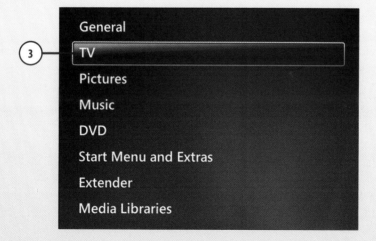

3. In the Settings screen, click TV.

4. Click Recorder.

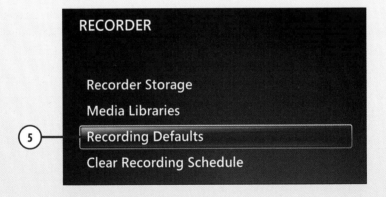

5. In the Recorder Settings screen, click Recording Defaults. The next screen provides you with a number of choices for the way in which your shows are recorded and saved.

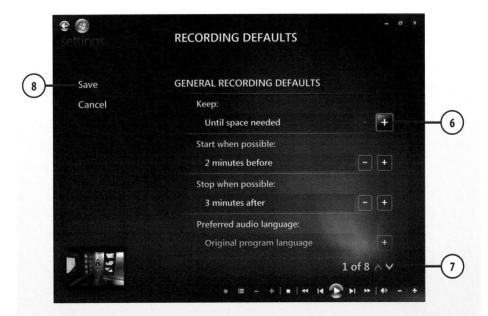

6. In Recording Defaults, click the + button beside each option to see additional choices. When the option you want is displayed, move on to the next option.

7. Click the down arrow to see additional Recording Defaults and set those options. You can choose how long you want to keep recorded shows, when you want to begin and end recording, and how you want series to be recorded in Windows Media Center.

8. Click Save to save your settings.

How Much Storage Do You Need?

The Recorder Storage option on the Recorder screen gives you what you need to know about allocating space on your hard drive for storing shows and movies. You can choose any storage device attached to your computer, which means if you have an external hard drive with a whopping amount of available space, you can use that for your media storage. Windows Media Center calculates the amount of space available and lets you know approximately how many hours of media viewing can be recorded in that space.

Sharing Media on Your Phone

Another way to enjoy your media is to take it on the road with you. With today's smartphones—including the Windows Phone 7, which is great for media—you can watch video, listen to music, and view photo albums on your phone anytime you have a few minutes' wait. But you don't need a Windows 7 Phone to watch media on your device—any smartphone with the necessary memory will do. The examples that follow show Windows Media Center syncing with a Windows Mobile 6.5 phone.

Mobile Media Trouble
If you're having trouble syncing your phone with Windows Media Center, consult your phone manual or manufacturer website for specific instructions on getting your model to work seamlessly with Windows Media Center.

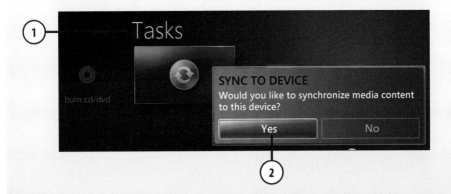

1. In the Windows Media Center home page, scroll down to Tasks and click the scroll arrow on the right.

2. Click Sync. Instead, Windows Media Center may automatically sense your device and ask whether you'd like to sync your media. Click Yes to continue.

3. Windows Media Center shows you how much room is available for storage on your device at the top of the window. Click the up and down arrows to prioritize the media you'd like to sync.

4. Click X to remove items from the list.

5. Click the scroll arrow to display additional screens of media selections.

6. Click Start Sync to sync the files with your device.

7. When the sync is complete, Windows Media Center lets you know. Click Done.

Maxing Your Phone Memory

Even though today's smartphones generally have quite a bit of memory, you also do a lot with your phone—send and receive email, get and send texts, take pictures, and more. Be aware that the media Windows Media Center syncs to your phone isn't being compressed, and you'll need some of that memory for other things. So you might want to choose the must-have albums or shows you need, a few at a time to keep your resource use as lean as possible.

EXTENDING MEDIA TO YOUR XBOX 360

If you have a wireless network and an Xbox 360 with Kinect (or a wireless adapter), you can set up the console as an extender for Windows Media Center. This means that you can stream movies, music, pictures, and more from your primary PC to the room where the Xbox 360 is located. Setting up your Xbox 360 as an extender is a simple process. Here's what you do.

In Windows Media Center, click Tasks and scroll right to Add Extender.

Click Next on the introductory page. Now go to your Xbox 360 and display the Xbox startup page. Press the right arrow to choose Windows Media Center. The Xbox gives you an eight-digit setup key. Write down the key and bring it back to your Windows 7 PC. Type the eight digits in the two boxes provided and click Next. Follow the additional instruction provided and click Finish. There—your Xbox 360 is now a Windows Media Center extension!

Enjoying Media with Windows Media Player

Windows 7 also includes Windows Media Player, the trusty media-play-all utility that has been included with several versions of Microsoft Windows. The latest and greatest version of Windows Media Player enables you to listen to and watch media files, rip music from CD to your Windows Media Player libraries, create playlists, burn media files to DVD, stream content live from the Internet, and much more. Although Windows Media Center seems more geared toward television and movies—but works well with all media—Windows Media Player seems geared more specifically toward your music files and video clips. What's more, you can easily sync Windows Media Player with your portable device so you can take your tunes on the road.

Exploring the Windows Media Player Window

The first thing you might notice about Windows Media Player is that it has a much different interface from Windows Media Center. This is a totally different animal, one that is more like a conventional Windows app. These windows are built more for functionality and speed and work well on your smaller display where you're perched just inches from the screen, as opposed to the sweeping entertainment effect available in Windows Media Center.

Display the Windows Media Player by clicking Start, clicking All Programs, and clicking Windows Media Player. The player will open and you'll discover the following tools and elements in the player window.

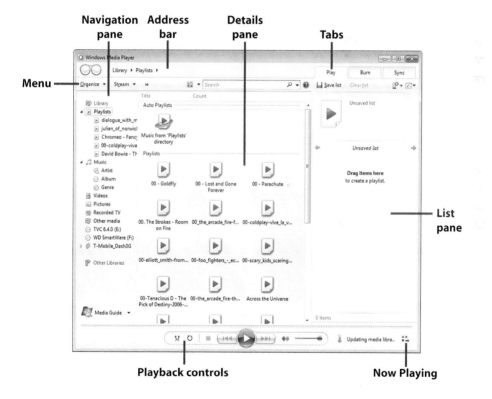

- **Navigation pane.** You use the Navigation pane to choose the artists, playlists, and media you want to listen to or watch.

- **Menu.** Choose to organize your files or stream media to other computers in your household or remotely.

- **Address bar.** The address bar shows you the currently selected folder.

- **Details pane.** The Details pane lists all the media files in the currently selected folder. You can display the files in a number of different ways—in Icons, Tile, and Details view.

- **Tabs.** The Play, Burn, and Sync tabs give you a way to choose what you want to do with the files you've added to the List pane.

- **List pane.** Drag the files you want to play, burn, or sync to this tab, and Windows Media Player knows these are the selected files.

- **Playback controls.** The Playback controls at the bottom of the Windows Media Player window enable you to play, pause, stop, shuffle, repeat, or navigate through your selected media files. You can also increase and decrease the volume of the player.

- **Now Playing.** Clicking Now Playing displays Windows Media Player in a reduced mode.

Keeping Your Workspace Clear

If you're just interested in listening to a few tunes while you work and don't want the big Windows Media Player window open on your desktop, click Now Playing in the lower-right corner of the screen. This reduces the player to a small window that you can minimize while you do your work.

Playing Tunes in Windows Media Player

When you're ready to play a song in Windows Media Player, the task is a simple one. Just find the file you want to play, drag it to the List pane, and click Play at the bottom of the window. All things in life should be so easy.

1. In Windows Media Player, click a song you'd like to listen to.

2. Drag the song to the List pane.

3. Release the mouse button, and the song is placed in the top of the List pane and begins to play automatically.

4. Pause the song if you like by clicking Pause in the playback controls.

5. Adjust the volume by moving the Volume slider.

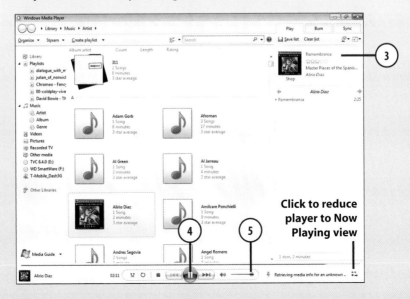

Multiple Media

You aren't limited to playing one song at a time. You can select multiple songs and drag them all at once to the List pane, or you can choose an album (or several albums) or double-click a playlist to add it to the List pane.

Rating Media

Beside the album cover at the top of the List pane is a rating tool you can use to indicate how much you enjoyed the recording. This information is saved with the media file so that you can easily see at a glance which are your favorite tunes and which aren't.

>> Go Further

CONTROLLING YOUR MEDIA FROM THE TASKBAR

If you have added a whole list of songs to the List pane and you know they'll be playing for a while, you can minimize Windows Media Player and get back to what you wanted to do—browse online, email your friends, play games, shop for new furniture.

You can manage the songs playing in Windows Media Player without opening the player window. Simply hover your mouse pointer over the taskbar and point to the Windows Media Player icon. The name of the current song appears, and you can pause playback or move to other tracks.

Finding the Media You Want

When you first begin listening to songs and watching video clips, you might not think you have much media to manage. But over time, you'll be amazed to see how your libraries can grow. Finding what you need and organizing them in a way you can access them easily becomes an important part of keeping track of your favorite media files.

View displays all music listed in alphabetical order

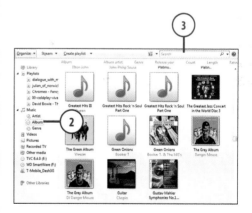

1. In Windows Media Player, click Music in the Navigation pane. Scroll through the list and find any music on your current system displayed by album or artist.

2. To further narrow the search, click Album. This view displays the albums you have added to your music collection in alphabetical order by album title. You can also click Artist and Genre to see how the files appear sorted in these different ways.

3. If you want to find a specific album, artist, or song, click in the search box and type a word or phrase to identify what you're looking for.

Where Do the Album Covers Come From?

Microsoft updates information in Windows Media Player regularly, and album covers and information—like artist, recording date, and studio—are added to your files. Additionally, when you rip files from one of your favorite albums to Windows Media Player, identifying information is included with the album files that provide that information to Windows Media Player.

Works for Other Media Too

You can use this technique with other folders in the Navigation pane to locate video files, pictures, recorded television shows, and other media you may have on any of the devices connected to your Windows PC.

Changing Playback Order

As you go through your list and decide on the various songs you want to listen to or videos you want to watch, they are added to the List pane in the order you select them. But what if you want to change the order and listen to your favorite artist first? Here's how to do that.

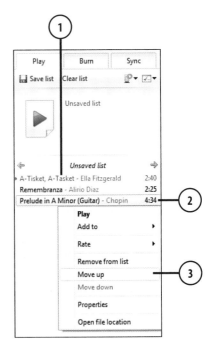

1. Add the media you want to listen to so the files appear in the List pane.

2. Right-click the media file you want to move.

3. Click Move Up. You may need to do this more than once, depending on where in the list you want the media file to appear. You can also drag the song from one position to another, which is a better technique if you plan to move the file farther up or down a list.

Other Right-Click Choices

You can also do a number of different things using the right-click list in the List pane. When you right-click a media file, you can choose to play it on the spot, add it to a playlist, rate it by clicking the number of stars you want to assign to it, move it up or down the list, or open the location where the file is stored.

Creating a Playlist

In Windows Media Player, you can easily create a playlist of your favorite songs. After you create and name the playlist, you can listen to it whenever you want, sync it with your mobile devices, or burn it to a disc.

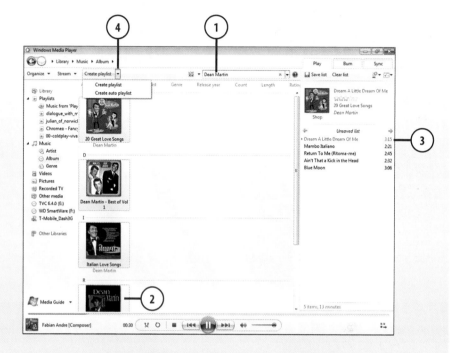

1. In Windows Media Player, click in the search box and enter the artist's name you want to include in the playlist.

2. Select the albums or songs you want to include.

3. Drag the selection to the List pane.

4. Click the Create Playlist arrow and choose Create Playlist. Windows Media Player adds a new playlist in the Playlists area of the Navigation pane and selects the name so that you can type a new one.

5. Type a name for your new playlist and press Enter.

6. Select the songs in the List area (click the first one, press Shift, and click the last one in the list).

7. Drag the selection to the new playlist.

8. Click the new playlist to see the songs that are included.

9. Click Play to listen to your playlist.

Adding Songs to Your Playlist

You can easily add songs to a playlist you've created by dragging them to the List pane, selecting the lot, and then right-clicking. Point to Add To and then click the name of the playlist to which you want to add the songs. If you don't see your playlist listed, click Additional Playlists and, in the Additional Playlists dialog box, scroll to the playlist you want, select it, and click OK.

Creating Media CDs

When you're ready to create a CD of your media files, you can complete the task easily. It's almost as simple as drag-drop-click.

1. In Windows Media Player, click the Burn tab.

2. Add the files you want to copy to the CD to the List pane. You can do this by dragging and dropping a playlist, selecting files or albums, or searching for the files you want and adding them to the list.

3. Insert a blank CD or DVD in the CD-RW drive and click Start Burn.

4. Windows Media Player lets you know about the status of the burn operation. If you want to cancel midstream, click Cancel Burn.

5. After the burn operation is complete, click Clear List.

It's Not All Good

One annoying little trait about the way media discs work is the fact that you always have to burn to a blank CD or DVD. If you just added a number of songs to a disc and then saw a few more you forgot, you're out of luck—for that disc, anyway. Windows Media Player asks you to insert a blank CD if you try to add songs to the previously recorded CD.

So to keep your frustration level low, do a thorough search and make sure you've gathered up all the songs you want before you click that Start Burn button.

Streaming Your Media

Windows Media Player makes it possible for you to share your media with other computers on your home network, or even with your laptop remotely as you travel around and work at various points in the city. You can also play these great playlists you've created on other computers in your house or on devices connected to your Windows PC. Seems incredible, I know! But if you love your eclectic taste in music—more than you do the song lists on popular radio stations—it's worth trying.

Do You Have What You Need to Stream Media?

You can access your home media files over the Internet with all Windows 7 versions except Windows 7 Starter or Windows 7 Home Basic. All other versions—from Home Premium on up—support streaming.

1. In Windows Media Player, click the Stream arrow.

2. Click All Internet Access to Home Media. The Internet Home Media Access dialog box appears.

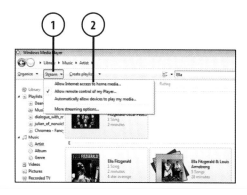

3. Click Link an Online ID. This links your Windows Live ID to your home media access so that you can use it to access your media files remotely.

4. Click Link Online ID.

5. Sign in to your Windows Live ID by entering your username and password.

6. Click Sign In.

7. Back in the Internet Home Media Access dialog box, click Allow Internet Access to Home Media.

8. Windows Media Player lets you know streaming has been set up, and you can click OK to return to Library view.

Want to Set Up a Home Network?

Before you can stream media in Windows Media Player, you need to have created either a wired or wireless network. If you don't yet have a home network but would like to create one, check out Chapter 12, "Networking—at Home and on the Road."

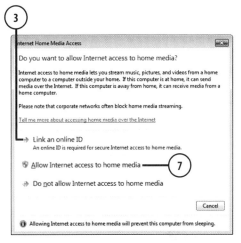

>>> Go Further

GETTING YOUR OTHER COMPUTERS READY FOR STREAMING

You can prepare other Windows computers on your home network to stream music from Windows Media Player by clicking Stream and choosing Turn on Media Streaming. In the Choose Media Streaming Options for Computers and Devices, choose your Windows 7 PC (as the source of streaming) and select Allowed. Click OK to save your settings. Now you are able to access the media libraries on your Windows 7 PC from that computer as well. You can repeat this process for other computers and devices—including your Xbox 360—on your home network.

Syncing a Media Device with Windows Media Player

Everything today that works with media needs to take mobile devices into consideration, and Windows Media Player is no exception. You can easily sync your favorite media files with your MP3 player, smartphone, or other compatible portable device. Begin by connecting your device—your phone, MP3 player, or other portable device—to your computer.

1. In Windows Media Player, choose the media you want to sync to your device.

2. Click the Sync tab.

3. Click Start Sync. Windows Media Player lets you know the status of the sync, and when all is said and done and the files are copied, you can disconnect your device from your Windows 7 PC.

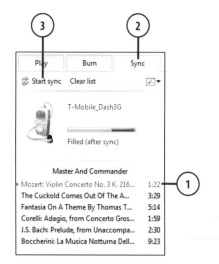

Relief for a Full Device

If you find that after you add the media to your phone or device you've taken up so much room that you need to delete a few files, you can use the Windows Explorer to select your device and delete any files you don't want. That saves you some room on the device and enables you to weed out any files you no longer need. You can also manage files from Devices and Printers in the Control Panel or by using the Windows Mobile Device Center or the phone management utility that came with your model of mobile phone.

It's Not All Good

Missing Out on Windows Media Player Goodness

Unfortunately, not all popular devices work with Windows Media Player. The iPhone and the iPod are two examples of those that can't sync and listen to media using Windows 7. Of course, those devices have iTunes for the same purpose. If you're wondering whether your device will work with Windows Media Player, check out the Windows 7 Compatibility Center (www.microsoft.com/windows/compatibility/windows-7/).

Viewing the Media Guide

The Media Guide in Windows Media Player displays what's hot in the world of media entertainment, provided for you by Microsoft. You can find music, movies, TV, games, and Internet radio—some for purchase or subscription, some for free. Take a look around and listen to or watch a few clips to sample what's there.

1. In Windows Media Player, click Media Guide in the lower-left corner of the player.

2. The Media Guide appears in the Details area of Windows Media Player. Click the links at the top of the Media Guide to access the types of media you want: Music, Movies, TV, Games, and Internet Radio.

3. Click the category (in this case, of Internet radio) you want to hear.

4. Click the station you want to listen to.

Different Topics, Different Choices

The choices you have available to you vary depending on the type of media you select in the Media Guide. But all clips and samples have a similar goal: to give you access to a great (almost unlimited!) store of media selections so that you can sample the different styles and choose the ones you like.

It's Not All Good

One of the not-so-great things about all the variety in Media Guide—in the Internet Radio section anyway—is that there isn't a common use of the playback controls in Windows Media Player.

Some stations enable the use of the Playback controls, so you can pause the music and click a different station; others disable the controls so that you can't do anything but click another icon to stop the music. Even clicking a different category in Media Guide (Movies or TV, for example) doesn't stop the music feed. Your only recourse is to click a different music sample that *does* make use of the controls and click Stop when you're ready to turn off the music.

Windows 7 makes it fun and easy for you to add, manage, edit, and share all those photos you love.

View, manage, edit, and share your favorite pictures in Windows 7.

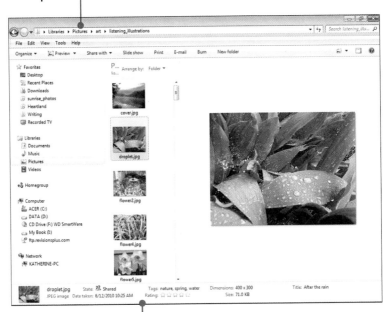

Add file properties to your pictures so you can find them easily later in a search.

In this chapter, you learn how to download your pictures from your camera to your Windows 7 PC and then work with them in a variety of ways:

→ Adding pictures to your PC

→ Scanning pictures with Windows Fax and Scan

→ Viewing photos in the Pictures library

→ Managing your pictures

→ Sharing your photos

→ Printing pictures

Cataloging and Fine-Tuning Your Photos

So, do you love to take pictures? Photos of your kids, the dog, the house, the garden; photos of events—family gatherings, trips to the beach, picnics in the park, beautiful sunsets? No matter what kinds of photos you take—or whether or not you consider yourself a photographer—Windows 7 makes it easy for you to collect, organize, view, edit, and share the pictures that mean something to you.

Collecting the files from your camera, phone, or scanner is a simple process, and when the files are on your computer, you can use Windows Explorer in Windows 7 to organize, view, categorize, tag, rename, and manage the files so that you can find them easily later and use them in anything you want. Sounds fun, right? Let's get started.

Adding Pictures to Your PC

The way in which you like to take pictures determines what you need to do to get them on your PC. If you use a digital camera, you can connect your camera to your Windows 7 PC using a USB cable and then copy or move the photos to the folder where you want them to be stored. If you take photos on your phone, you can sync the phone with Windows 7, which will likely copy the photos to the folder you specify. And if you want to digitize photos you have in your albums or photos you've had produced at a photo processing center, you can easily scan them and turn them into electronic files using Windows Fax and Scan, a utility available as part of Windows 7.

Connecting Your Camera and Downloading Pictures

Different digital cameras may have slightly different procedures for the way you download photos to your computer. Kodak cameras, for example, come with their own software that takes over the download process and stores files in Kodak. When you transfer photos to your PC—either through a USB cable or by inserting the memory card or stick from your camera into the memory card port on your PC—the action automatically activates the AutoPlay dialog box so that you can choose what you want to do next. Begin by inserting your memory card or stick or connecting your camera to your USB port. The Windows Explorer icon appears highlighted, indicating that there's an action you should take.

1. Click the Windows Explorer icon in the taskbar. The AutoPlay window appears.

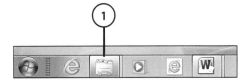

Downloading Automatically

Some cameras may download any new pictures to your computer automatically. If you want to change this automatic setting, look for an Options link or menu item you can click to find out how to turn off the automatic download settings. You can also search the camera manufacturer's website to find out more about customizing the settings on your particular device.

2. Click Import Pictures and Videos.

3. In the Import Pictures and Videos dialog box, type a tag you want to assign to the pictures.

4. Alternatively, you can click the arrow and choose a tag that you've entered previously.

5. Click the Import Settings link to choose where to put your pictures and what file naming convention to use.

6. In Import Images To, click Browse and choose the folder where you want the pictures to be stored.

7. In Folder Name, click the arrow and choose the way you want the folder to be named for the important photos. For example, a folder with the Date Imported + Tag naming option will appear as 2011-08-11 Nature.

8. Click the import options you want to apply. For example, you can have Windows 7 prompt you for a tag for the files, erase the files from your camera after the images are imported, rotate pictures as needed, and open Windows Explorer after the pictures are importer.

9. Click OK. If you made changes, Windows 7 will tell you that Import Pictures and Videos will restart. Click OK.

10. Back in the Import Pictures and Videos dialog box, click Import to add the pictures.

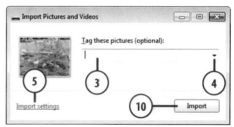

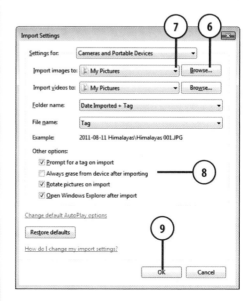

Always Do This with Pictures

If you know that you'll always want to open the folder whenever you're working with pictures in Windows 7, you can click the Always Do This for Pictures check box at the top of the AutoPlay dialog box to tell Windows 7 to open Windows Explorer directly next time instead of displaying the AutoPlay dialog box.

Adding and Viewing Pictures from Your Phone

If you like to take pictures on your mobile phone, you can sync the pictures to your favorite folder by connecting your phone to your Windows 7 PC via the USB cable and allowing your phone to synchronize the way it normally does. If you've previously specified a folder for your pictures, the images are stored in that folder automatically. If you haven't specified a folder, the default may be used.

Viewing Photos on Windows Phone 7

If you are using Windows Phone 7, Zune software will launch automatically when you connect your phone to your computer. If you're using another type of phone, the software designed for that phone will probably launch automatically when you connect the phone. (If not, you can choose the software from the All Programs list to start the program.)

1. Click the icon in the lower-left corner of the Zune window to check your phone sync status. Zune automatically detects any additional media files—pictures, videos, or music—and syncs the new files with the appropriate subfolder in your Collections folder.

2. Click Go to Your Collection.

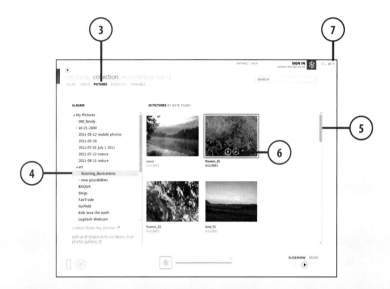

3. Click Pictures.

4. Click the folder containing the pictures you want to view.

5. Scroll through the details pane to view the pictures you want to see.

6. Hover the mouse over an image to display image tools. You can click Play to begin a slide show with the selected image; click Edit to edit the image in Windows Live Photo Gallery.

7. Click the close box to exit Zune when you finish syncing your pictures.

Copying Pictures to Your Phone

If you want to copy some of your favorite pictures from your PC to your phone, you can display the Zune software, click Collection at the top of the window, and click Pictures. Then simply drag and drop the pictures you want to copy to the phone icon in the lower-left corner of the window.

Picture Import Options on Your Phone

So what kinds of choices can you make in relation to the way Windows 7 imports pictures from your phone? Your choices involve choosing the directory to which you want to import the pictures, choosing a folder name, and deciding whether you want to keep the original filenames. You can also set import options, like whether you want the files to be removed from your phone. You can also have the import process prompt you to add tags to the photos (so you can find them in a search easily), rotate pictures if necessary, and automatically open Windows Explorer so that you can review the imported photos. You can set import options in the Zune software by clicking Settings.

Scanning Pictures with Windows Fax and Scan

When you have old photos you want to preserve digitally, or you have copies of pictures others have shared that you want to be able to show online, you can easily scan pictures and save them on your computer. (Assuming you have a scanner, of course.) Begin by placing the photo you want to scan face down on your scanner.

1. Click Start.

2. In the Search box, type **Windows Fax.**

3. Click Windows Fax and Scan. The Windows Fax and Scan window opens.

4. Click New Scan. The New Scan dialog box appears.

5. Click Preview. The scanner scans the image quickly and shows you how it will look when scanned.

6. Drag the scanning handle to frame the area you want to save in the scanned file.

7. Click Scan. Windows Fax and Scan scans the image and displays the image in the Windows Fax and Scan window.

8. Click Save Scan to display the Save As dialog box.

9. Choose the folder where you want to save the file.

10. Enter a filename for the scan.

11. Click Save.

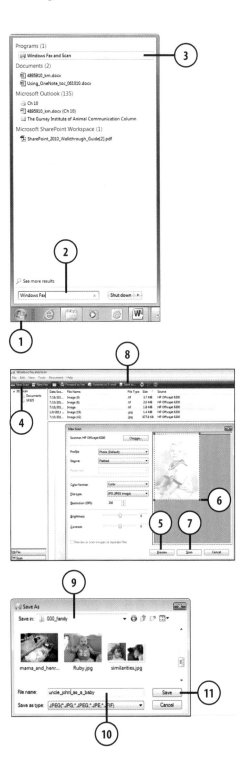

Viewing Photos in the Pictures Library

As you learned in Chapter 7, "Organizing Files and Folders," the Library folders in Windows 7 aren't really *folders* in their own right; rather, they are indexes of all similar files stored in folders throughout your PC. This means that the Pictures library you see in Windows 7 isn't actually a specific place on your hard drive where all the pictures are stored; it's a library of links to various folders where you've stored your images. The great thing about the Pictures library is its convenience—you can see everything together at once which is a great help when you're searching for something specific.

Looking Around the Pictures Library

You can display the Pictures library by selecting Pictures in the Start menu or by clicking Pictures in the Library area of the Windows Explorer window. A number of tools available in the Pictures library window can help you work with your photos the way you'd like.

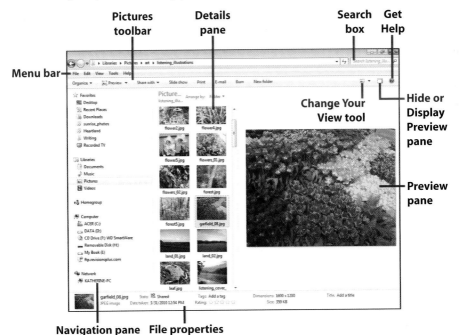

- The Navigation pane enables you to choose the folder in which you want to store pictures.

- The Details area shows thumbnail images of pictures in the selected folder.

- The Preview pane shows a larger version of the selected image.

- File properties give you information about the selected file and enable you to add tags, specify a title, or rate the image.

- The Pictures toolbar offers the tools you can use to work with the selected picture.

- The menu bar provides additional commands for working with pictures.

- The Change Your View tool enables you to change the display of picture files in the current folder.

- The search box makes it easy for you to locate the files you want (especially if you've previously tagged the images).

Viewing Pictures in the Picture Library

When you're paging through photos and looking for something specific, reducing the size of the images may be helpful so that you can quickly scan a bunch at a time. Or maybe you prefer a walk down memory lane with your photos displayed as large as possible. Either way—or at an increment in between—you can set the size so that you can review and select the files you want easily.

1. In the Pictures library window, click the More Options button to the right of the Change Your View tool.

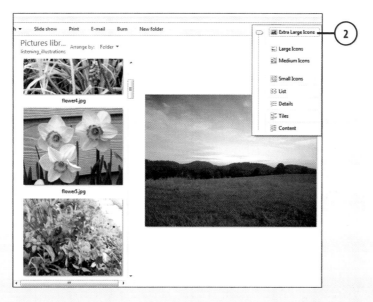

2. Click Extra Large Icons. The images in the Details pane enlarge and take up more room in the center of the window.

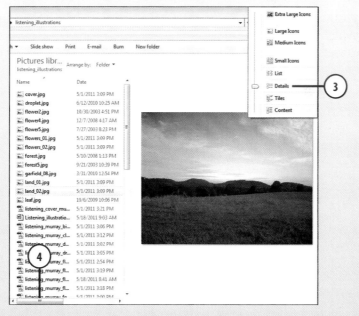

3. Click More Options a second time and click Details. The display shows the filename and dates the file was last modified.

4. Drag the scrollbar to the right to show additional properties, including Tags, Size, and Rating.

Windows 7 Picture Views

You can display eight different views for your photos in the Pictures library. You can choose Extra Large Icons to Large, Medium, and Small Icons, which all show the image in various sized. There's also List view, which displays only the file-name and a small icon; Details view, which shows a range of file properties with the small icon and filename; Tiles view, which shows a thumbnail and gives the filename, size, and file type; and Content, which shows a thumbnail image, along with the filename and any tags you've assigned. An easy way to change views using the mouse is to click and rotate the mouse wheel as you change the view.

Using the Windows Photo Viewer

While you're working in the Pictures library, you can open a picture in the Windows Photo Viewer and work with it in many different ways. You can order prints of the picture, print it, share it with others through email, or burn it to a CD or DVD.

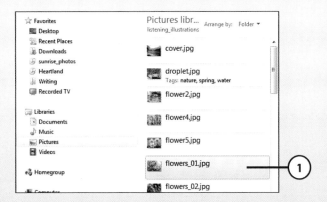

1. In the Pictures library window, double-click the picture you want to view in the Windows Photo Viewer.

2. In the Windows Photo View window, click the Change Size tool to modify the size of the image.

3. Click Actual Size to return the image to normal size.

4. Click the right-pointing arrow to display the next picture in the folder.

5. Click the left-pointing arrow to display the previous picture in the folder.

6. Click the red X to delete the file. Windows Photo Viewer displays a message box asking you to confirm that you want to delete the file.

Go Further

ORDERING PRINTS ONLINE

You can order prints of your photos from within Windows Photo Viewer. Display the photo for which you want to order prints and click the Print menu at the top of the Windows Photo Viewer window. Click Order Prints and choose a printing company from the Order Prints dialog box. Click Send Pictures, and Windows Photo Viewer leads you through a set of screens that enable you to make your choices and complete your order.

Displaying a Picture Slide Show

You can display an ongoing slide show of a specific folder in your Pictures library if you want to display your images one at a time in full-screen view.

1. Click to display the folder containing the photos you'd like to see.

2. Click Slide Show in the Pictures toolbar. The slide show begins, filling your screen.

3. Right-click one of the slide show images to see the slide show options.

4. Click whether you want the images to be shuffled (displayed in a random order) or looped (shown in a repeating sequence).

5. Change the speed of the presentation by clicking Slow, Medium, or Fast.

6. Click to Exit the slide show. You can also stop the slide show by pressing Esc.

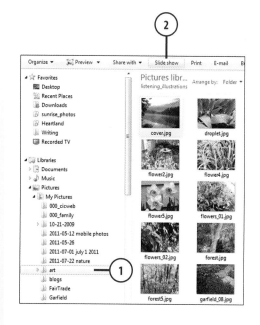

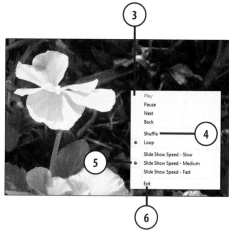

Navigating a Slide Show

If you want to move quickly through some of the images to get to the ones you really want to see, you can use the right-arrow and left-arrow keys to move through the files in the folder. When you're ready to return to Windows Explorer, press Esc.

Starting a Slide Show from Windows Photo Viewer

You can also display a slide show while you're using Windows Photo Viewer by clicking the center of the navigation tools in the tools row. This begins the display of a slide show in full-screen view. You can stop the slide show by pressing Esc.

Managing Your Pictures

You can easily organize the pictures you collect by dividing them into folders where you can find them easily. You can also rename them, copy and move them around, rotate them, and tag them so that you can locate them easily in future searches. You can manage pictures in the Pictures library or in the individual folders where your pictures are stored.

Creating a New Folder

You can create as many folders as you'd like within your My Pictures folder; in fact, you can create subfolders of subfolders of subfolders if you choose. Think through how you'd like to organize your images. Some people organize pictures by category: Vacations, Kids Sports, Family, and so on. Others organize their images by the dates (or months) in which they were created. The way in which you organize your photos depends on how you will want to find them later. When you're ready to add folders, it's a simple matter in Windows Explorer.

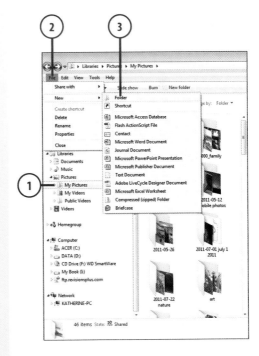

1. In the Navigation pane of the Pictures library, click the folder within which you want to create a new folder. If you want to create a folder within your My Pictures folder, for example, click My Pictures.

2. Click File to open the File menu.

3. Point to New and click Folder. The new folder appears in the Navigation pane.

4. The name of the folder is already highlighted. Type a new name for the folder and press Enter.

Moving a Folder

If you accidentally create the folder in the wrong place or you decide that you'd rather put it in another place, you can easily move the folder by clicking it and dragging it to the new location in the Navigation pane. A black bar shows you as you drag the folder where it will be placed when you release the mouse button.

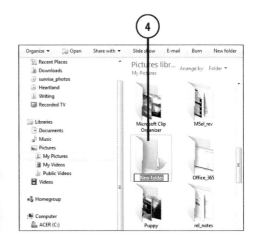

For More Folder Info

The same folder tasks you learned about in Chapter 7 apply here, so if you need a refresher on folder operations, be sure to review that chapter.

Rotating Pictures

Depending on the subject of your photo and the way you were holding your camera or your phone when you captured it, you may need to rotate it in the Picture library. You can rotate an image to the right or left.

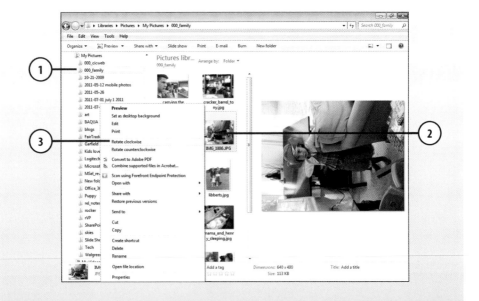

1. Navigate to the folder containing the image you want to rotate.

2. Right-click the photo.

3. Click Rotate Clockwise or Rotate Counterclockwise, depending on the direction you want to rotate the image.

Did You Rotate the Wrong Way?

No biggie. Just press Ctrl+Z to undo your action and then choose the correct choice, or select Rotate again to continue to rotate the picture until it looks the way you want it to look.

Copying and Moving Pictures

Part of organizing your images the way you want them requires that you move pictures from folder to folder. You can do this easily using a simple drag-and-drop technique. If you drag a photo from one folder to another, the photo is moved by default. If you want to copy the photo (leaving the original in the original folder), press Ctrl while you drag the photo. You can also use menu selections to complete the process as well as to move large volumes of pictures from one place to another.

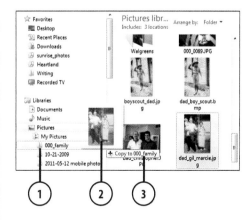

1. In the Pictures library, select the folder with the files you want to copy.

2. Click a photo.

3. Press Ctrl and drag the photo to a new folder. The ToolTip tells you that you are copying files and shows you the number of files involved in the copy operation. When the files are positioned over the folder, release the mouse button.

4. To move multiple photos, begin by selecting the photos you want to move. If the files are side by side, click the first file, hold the Shift key, and press the last file you want to move. If the files aren't side by side, click the first photo and then hold Ctrl while clicking subsequent files.

5. Click Edit to open the Edit menu.

6. Click Move to Folder. The Move Items dialog box appears.

7. Click the destination folder for the files.

8. Click Move.

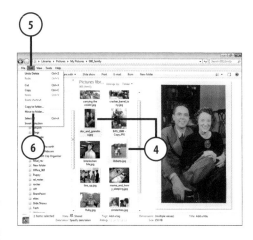

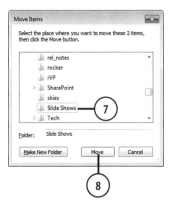

Creating a New Folder in the Move Items Dialog Box

If you don't see a folder you want to move the files to, you can click the New Folder button in the Move Items dialog box, type a name for the new folder, and press Enter. Click Move, and the photos are added to the new destination you just added.

Editing Your Photos

Although the Pictures library in
Windows Explorer doesn't offer its
own true editing tools—for example,
that would enable you to change the
contrast in a photo, remove red-eye,
or change color tone—it does give
you access to all the programs on
your computer that can do those
tasks. You can also set a default editing program so that when you
choose to edit an image in the
future, the program you want is used
by default.

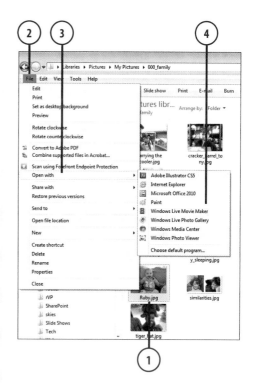

1. Select the photo you want to edit.

2. Click the File menu.

3. Point to Open With.

4. Click the name of the program
   you want to use to edit the
   image. When the program opens,
   you can edit the photo as you'd
   like and then save the image and
   return to Windows Explorer.

>>> Go Further

SETTING A DEFAULT PICTURE EDITOR

You can choose the program you want to use by default when you select a picture for editing by clicking the File menu, pointing to Open With, and choosing Choose Default Program. In the Open With dialog box, click the program you want to use as a default editor for your pictures, and click OK.

Tagging Pictures

Tagging your pictures is an important part of identifying them with specific themes or topics that you can find easily in a search later. You might have tagged photos earlier when you imported your photos (if your import options are set to prompt you for tags). But, you may also want to add tags later after you've saved the photos to your computer. You can add tags easily by clicking Tags in the status area of the picture window for the selected image. You can add multiple tags, separating them with commas, and change the tags any time you like.

1. Click the picture you want to tag in the Explorer window.

2. Click in the Tags area at the bottom of the window.

3. Type one or more tags, separating multiple tags with commas.

4. Click Save.

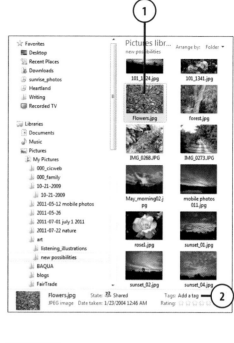

KEEP TRACK OF TAGS

Keeping track of the tags you use in identifying your photos is optional—but a good idea—especially if you plan on tagging other files on your hard drive as well. For example, suppose you're planning for your parent's 50th wedding anniversary, which is coming up next spring. You can add an *anniversary* tag to all photos you want to use in the scrapbook, on the invitations on the web page. And you can add a tag to the file properties for the Excel worksheet you use to keep track of the budget and the Word document in which you collect anniversary stories. Then when you click the Start button and type **anniversary** in the search box, all the files you've been working on for the anniversary event will appear so that you can click the one you want.

Setting File Properties

While you're setting tags in the status area of the Pictures library window, you may also want to set other file properties. For example, you can add a title to the picture or rate the image so that it stands out as one of your favorites in a list. If you want to change a greater number of properties, you can right-click the image and click Properties to add your changes in the Properties dialog box.

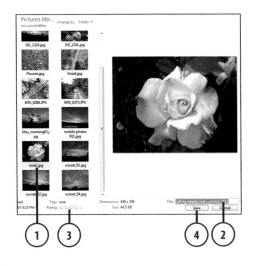

1. Click the photo for which you want to change properties.

2. Click in the Title area of the status bar and type a title for the photo.

3. Click the rating you want to assign to the picture, if you like.

4. Click Save.

5. To display the Properties dialog box, right-click an image you want to change properties for.

6. Click Properties.

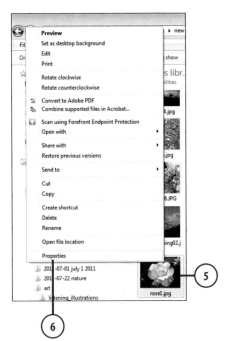

7. In the Properties dialog box, click the Details tab.

8. Hover the mouse pointer over an item you want to change, and the text box appears. Click and type your changes. You may want to add the author's name, add comments, or scroll down the list and add information about the camera and lens you were using when you took the photo.

9. Click OK to save your changes.

PROTECTING YOUR PRIVACY BY REMOVING PROPERTIES

Adding various file properties to your photos will help you find them easily in a search later, and you will also be able to share information about the file with others you choose to share your pictures with. But if you plan on posting your photos on the Internet or making them publically available on a website, for your own privacy you should remove any identifying properties that might give others more information about you than they need to know.

You can remove properties by displaying the Properties dialog box (right-click the picture in Pictures library and click Properties) and clicking the Details tab again. This time, click the Remove Properties and Personal Information link at the bottom of the dialog box. The Remove Properties dialog box appears so that you can choose whether you want to create a copy of the image with the properties removed or you want to remove the properties you select from the existing file. Make your choices and click OK.

Go Further
>>>

Sharing Your Pictures

It's natural to want to share photos that you love—especially when they are fun pictures of family trips, funny images of loved ones, or beautiful pictures you're sure others will enjoy. You can share photos with your HomeGroup or with other users of your computer, email the pictures to friends and family, or burn the photos to a CD you can share with others.

Sharing Files and Folders

The sharing, emailing, and burning techniques in this section apply whether you want to share a single photo or a whole folder full of photos. Simply click the file or folder you want to use and then follow the steps given here to complete the task.

Sharing Your Photos

When you're ready to share your photos, you can share them with individual people or with a whole list of folks. Additionally, you can share the files with others in your HomeGroup, if you've created one.

No HomeGroup...Yet?

No worries! We get to that topic in Chapter 12, "Networking—at Home and on the Road."

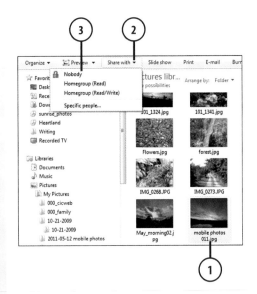

1. Click the photo or photos you want to share.

2. Click the Share With arrow in the Picture toolbar.

3. Click your choice for sharing. If you have set up a HomeGroup and want others to be able only to view the photo, click HomeGroup (read). If you want to allow others to edit the images, click HomeGroup (read/write). To share the photos with individuals, click Specific People.

4. Click the arrow on the far end of the list box and click the name of the person you want to share the photos with. The users that appear in the list are those who have user accounts on your Windows 7 PC.

5. Click Add.

6. Click Share.

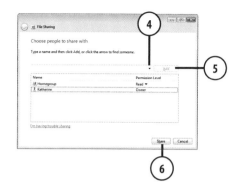

Emailing Pictures

You can email images directly from the Pictures library by simply choosing the picture you want to send, clicking E-mail, and choosing the size you want to use when sending the photo. This helps you keep the size of the attachments low so that you can send multiple photos with one message if you choose.

1. Click the photo you want to send.

2. Click E-mail.

3. In the Attach Files dialog box, click the arrow and choose the size you want the file to be when you send it. You can choose from the smallest size (640×480) to the largest size (1280×1024). The dialog box shows the size of the file selection you've made.

4. Click Attach. A new email message window opens, and you can enter the recipient's email address in the To line, add a Subject line, type a comment, and click Send to send the photo.

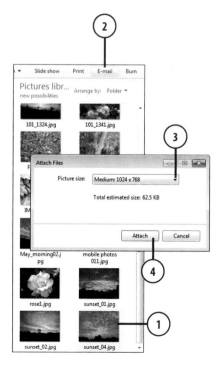

Burning Pictures to a Disc

You can easily prepare a photo disc full of your favorite images to share with others—perhaps for a Mother's Day or Father's Day present or simply a nice surprise for a relative who hasn't seen your family in a while. Adding photos to a disc is super simple. Begin by inserting a disc in your CD-RW or DVD drive.

1. Click the photo you want to add to the CD.

2. Click Burn.

3. Windows Explorer displays the copying status. You can click More Details if you'd like to see additional information about the copy. This info might be helpful if you are copying a number of files and want to see how far you have to go, but for one or two files, the copy process is very short.

4. Click Cancel if you'd like to stop the procedure. Otherwise, Windows Explorer completes the copy, and you can view the photos on the CD by clicking the drive number in the Navigation pane and reviewing the CD contents.

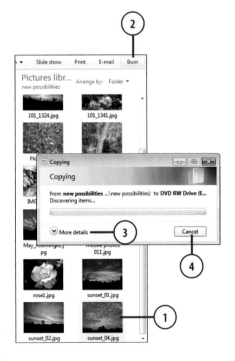

Printing Pictures

Another way you may choose to preserve and share your favorite photos involves printing them. You might want to use them on scrapbook pages or print them on photo paper and frame them.

Printing Your Photos

You can find the tool for printing your photos in the Pictures toolbar, and all you need to do to prepare to print is to select the photos you want to print. You can print one or many; the Print Pictures dialog box enables you to page through the selected photos and set the options for them one at a time. Insert the photo paper you plan to use for your photos.

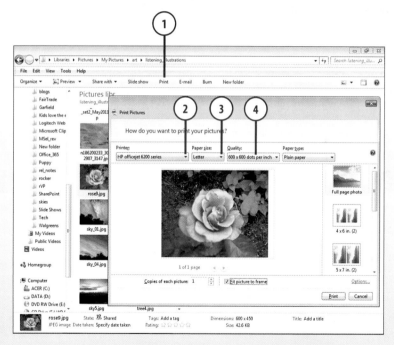

1. With the photos you want to print selected, click Print in the Pictures toolbar.

2. In the Print Pictures dialog box, click the arrow and select the printer on which you want to print the photos.

3. Click the Paper Size arrow and choose the size of your photo paper.

4. Click the Quality arrow and choose the resolution you want.

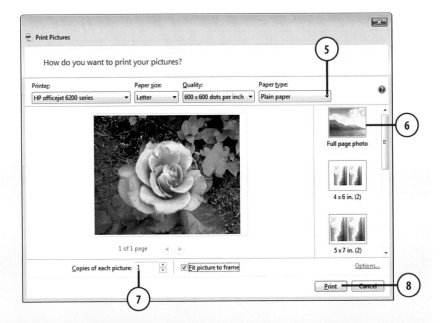

5. In Paper Type, click the arrow and choose the type of paper you will use to print the photos.

6. Click the layout style for the photos you will print.

7. Click to specify the number of copies you want to print.

8. Click Print.

Choosing a Photo Size

You can click the paper size you want for the photos you are printing. Bear in mind that oversized photos that you print at a size larger than their original file size may be less clear than photos printed at their original size or smaller. Among the Paper Size options are borderless print sizes 4×6 and 5×7. Click the size you want and click the layout style on the far-right side of the dialog box before proceeding.

Fit Picture to Frame

The Fit Picture to Frame check box is selected by default. This option stretches the image to fill the picture frame so that you have printing photos of uniform size. The problem with this is that if you have irregularly sized photos—perhaps because you cropped the original photo—the photo may be resized and less clear than an image that hasn't been stretched. Try viewing the photo with the check box selected and without to see whether there's a noticeable difference in picture quality.

After you use Windows 7, you may have some ideas about ways you want tweak the program if you could. Well, here's your chance! You can personalize the Windows 7 display and change some of the ways in which the program operates.

You can make your desktop
fanciful or functional—or both.

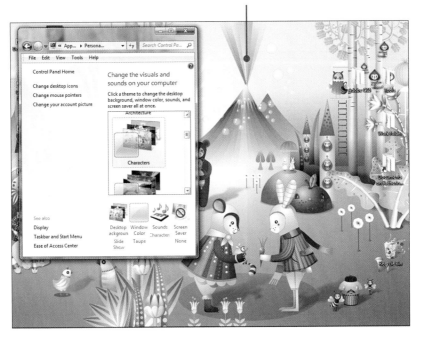

Would you love to put your own touches on Windows 7? In this chapter, you learn to personalize your Windows 7 experience by performing the following tasks:

→ Changing your desktop
→ Adjusting the look of Windows 7
→ Adjusting mouse behavior
→ Changing system sounds

Personalizing Windows 7

You know, you probably spend a lot of time with your computer. You're browsing, composing, viewing, shopping, and more. Being comfortable while you're computing is an important part of enjoying your computing experience—and that means being able to set up things the way you like them.

Think of it this way: If your mouse isn't functioning properly— perhaps the mouse pointer moves too fast or too slow across the screen—you probably feel frustrated when you try to point to an option or click a button. And over time, that kind of low-grade frustration can grow. So this chapter is an exercise in "have it your way" as you learn how to customize a number of Windows 7 settings so you can get things working just the way you like them to work.

Changing Your Desktop

The first thing you're likely to notice about Windows 7 is the desktop background. Depending on the type of computer you purchased and the choices of the manufacturer, you could have a different customized desktop (for example, showing your computer manufacturer's logo in addition to the traditional Windows color scheme). You can modify the background—and choose some great new looks—with other themes and backgrounds available in Windows 7.

Choosing a New Background

Windows 7 offers you a number of different choices for your background image. You can select a single image or multiple images, which display at increments you set, like a slide show.

1. Click Start.

2. Click Control Panel.

3. Click Change Desktop Background. The Choose Your Desktop window Background appears.

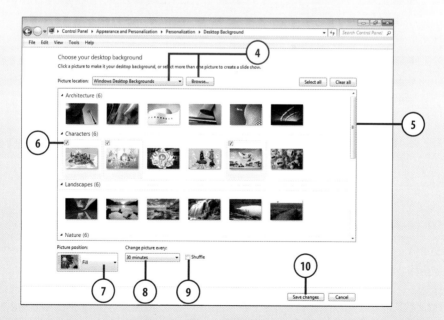

4. Click the Picture Location arrow to choose the choices for backgrounds displayed in the Background window. If you choose Pictures Library, you can click Browse to choose the folder containing the images you want to use.

5. Drag the scrollbar to view all the choices in the display window.

6. Click at least three background images by clicking the check box in the upper-left corner of the image.

7. Click the Picture Position arrow and choose whether you want the image to fill the screen, fit the screen width, stretch, tile, or center.

8. Click the Change Picture Every arrow and choose how often you want pictures to change on the desktop. Your choices range from changing every 10 seconds (which is fast!) to changing once a day.

9. Click the Shuffle check box if you want the order of the images to be shuffled so they appear in different orders.

10. Click Save Changes.

Choosing a Desktop Theme

A theme in Windows 7 is like a set of preferences that control the desktop background, color scheme, sounds, and screen saver. The settings for those items are all coordinated and are set automatically when you choose a Windows 7 theme.

You can choose from a number of Windows 7 themes, ranging from beautiful imagery that cycles through like a slide show to simple high-contrast displays that make it easy for you to read the screen.

1. In the Control Panel, click Change the Theme.

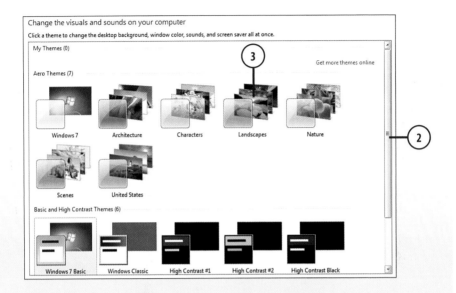

2. Scroll through the list to see all available themes.

3. Click an Aero theme if you want to personalize the look with high-quality graphic images; click Basic and High Contrast Themes if you are concerned about the performance of your computer and want to keep things running as quickly as possible. The new theme is applied to your desktop.

What's Aero?

Aero is the name of the interface theme that Microsoft introduced in Windows Vista and is also available in Windows 7. Aero, which requires a modern graphics processor, offers what the developers hope is a more aesthetically pleasing design for users, offering live thumbnails, transparency, and more.

View	▶
Sort by	▶
Refresh	
Paste	
Paste shortcut	
Undo Move	Ctrl+Z
NVIDIA Control Panel	
Shared Folder Synchronization	▶
Next desktop background	
New	▶
Screen resolution	
Gadgets	
Personalize	

4. You can easily change the theme or further personalize your desktop by
right-clicking an open space on the desktop and clicking Personalize. This
takes you back to the Themes window, where you can make another
choice.

GET MORE THEMES

If you want to browse through some fun, beautiful, and creative themes you
might want to adopt for your own desktop, click the Get More Themes Online
link in the Themes window of the Personalization page in the Control Panel.

Click the different theme categories—new themes, animals, art, automo-
tive, branded themes, games, holidays and seasons, movies, nature, and
places and landscapes—to view a collection of different themes related to
the various topics. To find out more about a specific theme, click the Details
link. To download a theme you like, click the Download link just beneath it
and click Open in the notification bar that appears at the bottom of the
screen. The theme is stored in your My Themes area of the Personalization
window in the Control Panel.

>>> Go Further

Changing Desktop Icons

It's easy to get a cluttered desktop.
First, you save a file there just
because you don't want to lose it in a
folder somewhere. Then, before you
know it, you've littered your desktop
with lots of folders and programs
you never use. You can let Windows 7
help you keep your desktop clean
(so you can see that fabulous new
theme you just added to the background) by making choices about
your desktop icons.

1. Click Start.

2. Click in the search box and type
   desktop icon.

3. Click Show or Hide Common
   Icons on the Desktop.

4. Click the check boxes of items
   you want to appear on the desktop. Click to clear the check boxes
   of items you don't want to
   appear.

5. Click Change Icon if you want to
   choose a different symbol used
   for a particular icon.

6. Leave the Allow Themes to
   Change Desktop Icons check box
   selected if you want the desktop
   icons to take on the style of the
   selected theme. (This can undo
   changes made to icons.)

7. Click OK to save your changes.

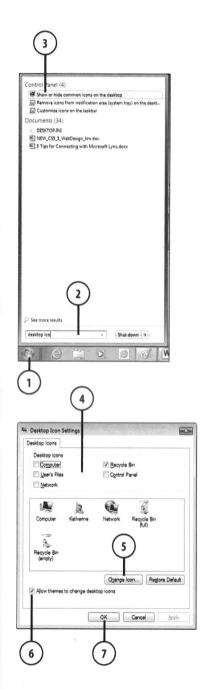

Returning to Normal

If you make changes to the desktop icons and then wish you hadn't, you can return the icons to their default display by clicking Restore Default in the Desktop Icon Settings dialog box. Click OK to save the settings.

Adjusting the Look of Windows 7

In the preceding section, you learned how to personalize the desktop by changing the background images and also by changing your choice of Aero themes—those high-color, artsy, and sometimes fun desktop themes—to give your computer a new look. There are other functional ways you can alter the look of Windows 7 to enhance your computing experience. You may want to choose a different Windows color scheme, adjust the size of the text you're reading, or change the date and time to reflect your place in the world.

Not with Aero Themes, You Don't

When you apply a Windows 7 Aero theme to your computing experience, the theme comes with desktop backgrounds, a color scheme, sounds, and in some cases, a screen saver. This means that depending on the theme you've selected, you may or may not be able to set color scheme, sounds, and screen savers independently. If you want to be able to customize individual elements, choose a Basic or High-Contrast theme before changing the additional settings.

Choosing a Color Scheme

If you selected one of the Windows Basic themes as your desktop background of choice, you also can change the color scheme used throughout your Windows 7 experience. Begin by displaying the Personalization window in the Control Panel (to do that, click Start, Control Panel, Appearance and Personalization, and Personalization).

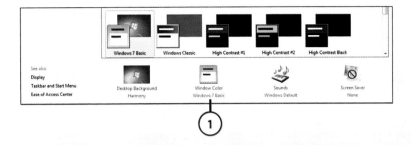

1. Click Window Color at the bottom of the Personalization window. The Window Color and Appearance dialog box appears.

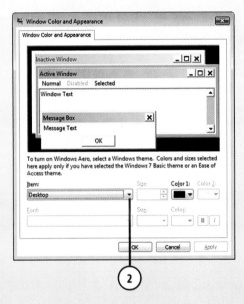

2. Click the Item arrow to display a list of choices and choose the item you want to modify. There are a total of 21 items you can select, from message boxes to active windows to scrollbars. Some of the items enable you to change a variety of settings—Colors 1 and 2, for example, as well as font changes.

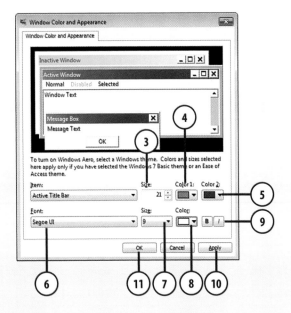

3. Click to increase the size of the item you selected.

4. Click to choose the first color (in this case, the color on the left side of the window title bar).

5. Click to choose the second color (the color on the right side of the window title bar). Not all items allow you to choose colors.

6. Click to change the font used in the item. Choose from the list that appears when you click the arrow.

7. Click to choose the size of the font.

8. Choose the color for the font.

9. Apply Bold or Italic to the font.

10. Click Apply to save your settings.

11. Click OK to close the Window Color and Appearance dialog box.

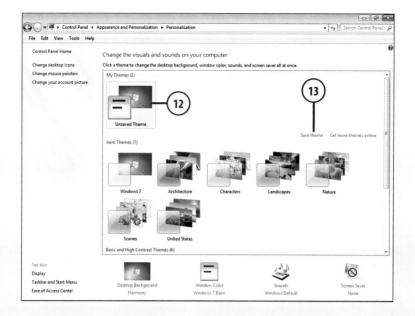

12. Back in the Personalization window, Windows 7 displays your new Unsaved Theme in the My Themes area at the top of the window.

13. Click Save Theme.

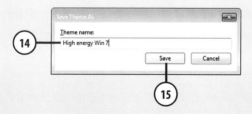

14. In the Save Theme As message box, type a name for the new theme.

15. Click Save. You can now choose the theme by clicking it in the My Themes area of the Personalization window to add it to your Windows 7 experience.

Quick Save

You can also save your theme quickly by right-clicking the theme and clicking Save Theme.

IT'S NOT ALL GOOD

Experimenting with color combinations in the Window Color and Appearance dialog box is pretty fun. The preview window shows you how the colors change based on the selections you make. After you save the theme and return to the desktop, however, it may be hard to find the changes you made. Some may appear and othersЄnot so much.

The trick is to experiment with the various items in the Items list and try different colors to make the changes really stand out. Also, remember to use only the Windows 7 Basic theme as the starting point; other themes block the display of your modified color choices.

Changing the Font Size

There are a number of ways to change the size of the font you're working with in Windows 7. The easiest way involves changing the size by default so that all text appears automatically at a size that's comfortable for you to read. Whether this is large or small, you can adjust the Display setting once and know it will be in effect for all the programs you use.

1. Click Start.

2. Click Control Panel.

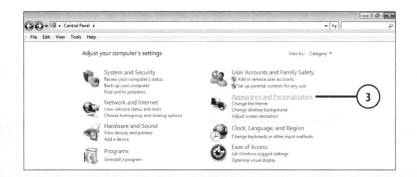

3. In the Control Panel, click Appearance and Personalization.

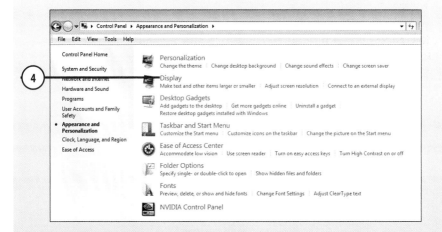

4. Click Display.

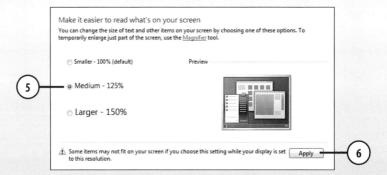

5. Click the percentage of display you want to use. Medium magnifies the screen to 125%, and Large magnifies it to 150%.

6. Click Apply to change the size of the text displayed.

Want to Do It Another Way?

You can also change the size of text on your display by changing the screen resolution you are using. And luckily, that's the subject of the next section.

Changing Screen Resolution

You can easily change the screen resolution—that is, the resolution at which Windows 7 and all your programs appear on your monitor. You can set the resolution to the highest your monitor is capable of displaying, such as 1280×1024 or 1024×768, or you can set the display to a lower resolution, which shows a smaller screen display and also magnifies what you see on the screen.

1. In the Control Panel, click Adjust Screen Resolution.

2. In the Change the Appearance of
Your Display window, click the
Resolution arrow and click your
choice.

3. Click Apply. Windows 7 shows you
a preview of the resolution and
displays a message box asking
whether you want to keep the
change.

4. Click Keep Changes to keep the
new resolution or click Revert (or
do nothing) to return to the previous setting.

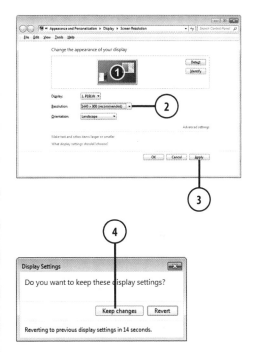

Magnifying Screen Size

Most of the application programs
you will use are likely to have a
zoom tool or a way to magnify
the screen, so if you're concerned
about being able to read the
numbers and text, you can
increase the size of the document
without changing the screen resolution. For example, in Microsoft
Word and Microsoft Excel, you
can use the view controls in the
lower-right corner of the program
window to control the size of the
window contents.

Changing the Date and Time

You can let Windows 7 know where you are so that the data and time are correct on your computer no matter who you're chatting with online and where in the world they may be. Having the date and time set to your local time is also helpful when you are scheduling calls and online meetings with others who may be in different time zones; Windows Live Mail automatically translates the time changes for you.

1. In the Control Panel, click Clock, Language, and Region.

2. In the Date and Time area, click Set the Time and Date.

3. Click Change Data and Time and select the day and time in the Date and Time dialog box.

4. Click Change Time Zone and choose your time zone from the Time Zone Settings dialog box.

5. Click OK to save your changes.

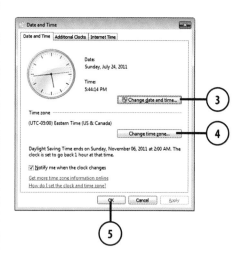

Adding Other Clocks

You can keep your eye on clocks from other areas by clicking the Additional Clocks tab in the Date and Time dialog box, clicking Show This Clock, and adding another time zone and clock name. When you hover the mouse pointer over your clock in the system tray of Windows 7 (on the bottom far-right corner of your screen), you are able to see the new clock time as well.

Selecting a Screen Saver

Windows 7 comes with several screen savers you can use, or you can create one on the fly by pointing the screen saver to a folder full of photos you want to use. Begin by displaying the Control Panel and clicking Appearance and Personalization.

1. Click Change Screen Saver. The Screen Saver Settings dialog box appears.

2. Click the Screen Saver arrow and click a screen saver you'd like to use.

3. Specify the number of minutes of inactivity you want to allow before the screen saver begins.

4. Click Apply to save your settings.

5. Click OK to close the dialog box.

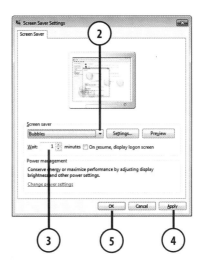

Back to the Logon Screen

If you want the screen saver by default to display the Windows 7 logon screen—perhaps so you can change user accounts or enter your password—click the On Resume, Display Logon Screen check box in the Screen Saver Settings dialog box before you click OK.

>> Go Further

SETTING SCREEN SAVER OPTIONS

Not all of the screen savers you select in Windows 7 have options that you can set, but some do. For example, the 3D Text screen saver lets you enter your own custom text (of course), and Photos lets you choose the folder containing the pictures you want to use, as well as the speed at which the photos are displayed. You can choose the screen saver options in the Screen Saver Settings dialog box.

Click Settings, and if the screen saver you selected doesn't have any options available, Windows 7 displays a message box telling you that there are no options available; simply click OK to close the message box. If the screen saver does have options, a dialog box listing your choices appears. Make your choices (for example, for the Photos screen saver, choose the folder containing the images you want to use and select the speed at which you want them displayed); then click Save and OK.

Adjusting the Mouse

In an ideal world, you could just plug in your mouse and go. The mouse buttons would feel comfortable; double-clicking would be intuitive; and the pointer would be just the right speed as it moves across the screen. But the mouse may need a little tweaking to feel just right to you—and that tweaking might involve changing the click speed or response times, modifying the mouse buttons, or changing the pointer you use onscreen while you work.

Changing Mouse Pointers

The mouse pointers that appear when you're using your mouse with Windows 7 are actually controlled by the theme you have selected. You can change the theme and the pointers, and even substitute different pointers if you like, to help your mouse experience feel more intuitive.

1. Click Start.

2. Click in the search box and type **mouse**.

3. Click Mouse, the first item in the results list. The Mouse Properties dialog box appears.

4. Click the Pointers tab.

5. Click the Scheme arrow and choose the Scheme you want to change pointers for.

6. Double-click the pointer you want to customize. The Browse dialog box appears.

7. Click the filename of the icon you want to use.

8. Click Open.

9. Click OK.

Themes and Pointers

By default, Windows 7 allows the theme changes to change the pointer style as well. You can veto this action if you like, by clicking to clear the check mark in the Allow Themes to Change Mouse Pointers check box in the Pointers tab of the Mouse Properties dialog box.

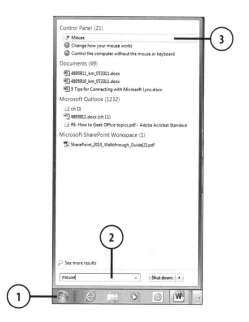

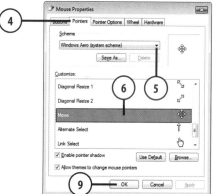

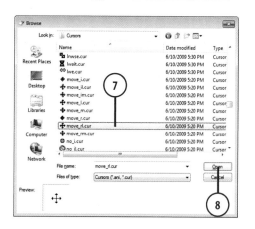

Setting Pointer and Click Speed

You might think that having a slow mouse—where the pointer lags behind where you're pointing as you drag it across the screen—would drive you batty, but in reality, having a too-fast mouse can have the same effect. For the best possible results, we would like our mouse to move like a seamless extension of our hand as we move the mouse across the mouse pad. Any lagging or jerky behavior is going to throw you off and interrupt your computing experience.

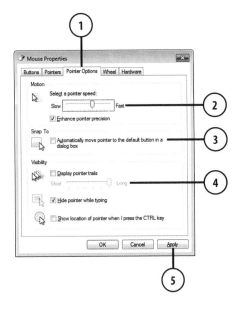

1. In the Mouse Properties dialog box (refer to "Changing Mouse Pointers"), click the Pointer Options tab.

2. Adjust the slider in the Motion area to slow the movement of the pointer or increase the speed. For best results, leave the Enhance Pointer Precision check box selected.

3. If you want Windows 7 to automatically position the pointer on a default setting in a dialog box, click this check box.

4. If you like to see the "trails" of the pointer—or a series of pointers in a trail as you move the mouse— click Display Pointer Trails. You can also choose whether you want the trail to be Short or Long (or any point between the two).

5. Click Apply to save your changes.

6. Click the Buttons tab.

7. Drag the slider in the Double-Click Speed area toward Slow or Fast, depending on whether you want to increase the speed of the double-click or decrease it. If you decrease the speed, you can double-click more slowly, and Windows 7 still recognizes it as a double-click.

8. Click OK to save your settings.

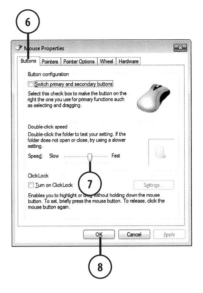

Hiding and Displaying the Pointer

By default, Windows 7 hides the mouse pointer when you are typing on the keyboard. If you don't want to suppress the display of the pointer, click to clear the Hide Pointer While Typing check box in the Pointer Options tab of the Mouse Properties dialog box. If you opt to leave the pointer hidden while you type, you may want to click Show Location of Pointer When I Press the CTRL Key so that you can just press Ctrl to display the pointer quickly on the screen.

Changing the Way Your Mouse Buttons Work

Generally speaking, you click the left mouse button when you want to select something or execute a command, and you click the right-mouse button when you want to see a list of options about the object at the pointer position. Windows 7 enables you to change the function of the mouse buttons, however, so you can tailor them to fit the way you want to work.

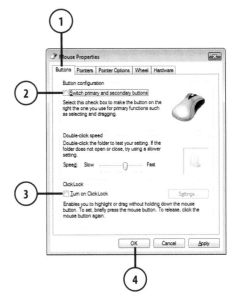

1. In the Mouse Properties dialog box (refer to "Changing Mouse Pointers"), click the Buttons tab.

2. Click the Switch Primary and Secondary Buttons in the Button Configuration area. The picture of the mouse on the right side of the dialog box shows the primary selection button in blue.

3. If you want to be able to highlight and drag without holding down the mouse button, click the Turn on ClickLock check box.

4. Click OK to close the Mouse Properties dialog box.

CONTROLLING THE MOUSE WHEEL

If you have a mouse that includes a mouse wheel between the mouse buttons (typically located toward the top of the mouse where you click the button), you can change the settings that control the way the wheel works.

Click Start and choose Control Panel; then click Hardware and Sound. Click
Mouse in the Devices and Printers area at the top of the screen. In the Mouse
Properties dialog box, click the Wheel tab. You can then change the number
of lines the wheel will scroll when you move it vertically, and the number of
characters that will scroll when you are horizontally scrolling. Change your
settings, click Apply, and then click OK to put your new settings into effect.

Changing System Sounds

You've no doubt heard the Windows 7 startup chime by now, and if you've
used other programs, like Windows Live Messenger, you've probably noticed
the alerts and dings you hear when the program wants to let you know that
something new has just occurred. In Windows 7, you can choose another
sound theme to apply new sounds to system events, and you can even save
your own custom sound theme if you like.

Choosing a New Sound Scheme

Windows 7 actually offers you 15 different sound schemes (one of which
is No Sound) that you can use to
coordinate the system sounds while
you work.

1. Click Start.

2. Click in the search box and type
   sound.

3. Click Sound in the results list.

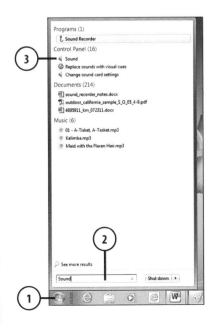

4. Click the Sounds tab in the Sound dialog box.

5. Click the Sound Scheme arrow and choose the scheme you want to use.

6. Alternatively, click Save As and enter a name for a new sound scheme you want to create. Click OK.

7. Click a Program Event for which you want to change the sound.

8. Click the Sounds arrow to display all available sounds.

9. Click Test to hear the sound.

10. Click Apply when you find the sound you like. Continue setting sounds by clicking the event, choosing a sound, and clicking Apply.

11. When you're done setting sounds, click OK.

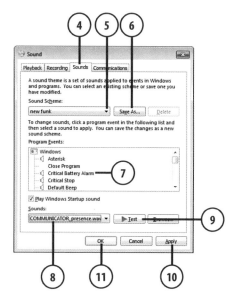

Turn That Down, Will You?

When you use the phone through Windows 7—perhaps using Microsoft Lync Online or Windows Live Messenger to make a call—Windows 7 reduces the volume of system sounds so that you can hear what's going on in your call. Display the Sound dialog box and click the Communications tab to review and perhaps change your settings. Click Apply and then OK to save your changes.

With Windows 7, you can easily create a home network to connect all your computers and devices and make it easy to share music, media, and other resources along the way.

Create a HomeGroup and share files with all computers in your home.

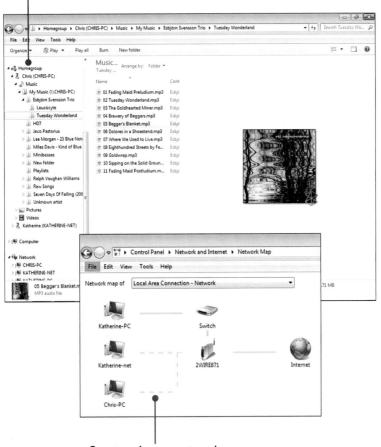

Create a home network simply and easily.

In this chapter, you learn how to set up and work with networks on your home system. The following tasks help you set up your own home network and then create a HomeGroup that enables you to share files, media, and more among your home computers and devices:

12

→ Setting up your wireless network
→ Getting started with a HomeGroup
→ Using your HomeGroup

Networking—at Home and on the Road

In this day and age, connecting to a network is an important part of what we do with our PCs. Whether you are logging in to a computer at work, getting web access at a coffee shop, or creating a home network so that all the computers in your house can share resources like your printer, music, and pictures, knowing something about networking is important.

Setting up a home network used to be a task reserved for high-tech enthusiasts who knew how to get all the necessary equipment and set up confusing and cryptic configurations. Today the whole process is simple, thanks to improvements in personal computers in general and, more specifically, with Windows 7. Now with Windows 7, you can create a HomeGroup of recognized PCs that can easily share files, music, media, and more throughout your home network. Thanks to Windows 7's network discovery feature, you can find new networks in your area when you're at the coffee shop or in the office and connect to those (if you have the permissions you need) so that you can continue your connection to the web no matter where you are.

Setting Up a Home Network

Setting up a home network enables you to easily share files, printers, and more—and connect all the computers in your house so that you can access your files from any network location. This is something you can do easily—in just a few minutes—when you have the equipment you need.

Gathering Your Equipment

To set up a wireless network, you just need a wireless router and wireless adapters for each of the computers you plan to connect to your home network. Most laptops and netbooks sold today have wireless adapters built in to their systems; you may need to purchase wireless adapters for the other PCs you want to add to your network. If your computer is in close proximity to your router, you can also connect a wired PC by cable to a port on your router, which generally supplies a faster, more reliable connection. Here's a quick introduction to the equipment you need to set up your network:

- A wireless router enables you to connect wired or wirelessly with other computers in your home. Many manufacturers offer routers designed for different needs; for example, some routers are built for the fastest access possible, whereas others are meant to support a lot of activity at once (for example, while you're browsing online and both your kids are playing online games). Research router types online and be sure to find one that is Windows 7 compatible.

- If you want or need to use a wireless connection, but your system lacks built-in wireless support, you can purchase a wireless network adapter. Many of these adapters come in the form of simple USB sticks you can plug into an open port on your PC. The adapters come with a CD that contains the software the adapter needs to be able to work. Insert the CD in your drive, and the driver should install automatically. When Windows 7 sees the new device (thanks to Plug and Play), you should be ready to connect your home network.

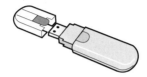

And, of Course, the ISP...

In Chapter 2, "Preparing Your Windows 7 PC," you learned how to set up your Internet connection, which requires an account with an Internet service provider, so hopefully you already have this piece of the networking puzzle in place. If you haven't yet set up an account with an ISP, you need one to be able to connect to the Internet for web browsing and email.

Establishing Your Network

Begin the process by setting up your router as directed in the installation instructions that came with the router. The router may simply be plug-and-play, which means that you can connect it and Windows 7 does the rest. Depending on the router you have, you may be a CD of software you need to run to get the necessary drivers installed for Windows 7. If so, insert the CD into your drive and follow the instructions on the screen to install the software.

1. Click Start and click Control Panel.

2. Click Network and Internet.

3. Click Network and Sharing Center.

4. Click Set Up a Connection or Network.

5. Click Set Up a New Network.

6. Click Next. A wizard walks you through the rest of the process. Follow the instructions provided by the wizard, and click Finish when the process is complete.

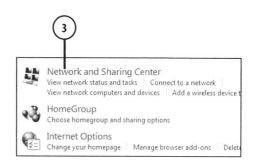

Wireless and More

Windows 7 enables you to set up other types of networks as well, including Ethernet (conventional wired), HomePNA, and Powerline networks. To find out more about setting up those additional types of networks, visit www.windows.microsoft.com and search for **network technologies**.

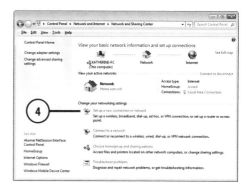

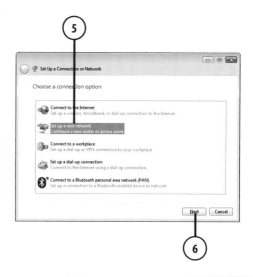

Adding Other Computers to Your Home Network

After you add the wireless adapters to the other systems in your house and run the installation software that comes with the adapters, your computers should be able to recognize the wireless connection available with your wireless router. You can discover this and connect to the network by clicking the Connect to Network tool in the system tray, on the right end of the Windows 7 status bar.

1. Click the Connect to Network icon in the system tray.

2. Click the name of your wireless network.

3. Click Connect. Windows 7 accesses the network. If it's secured, you'll need to enter a password to log on to the network; the Connect to a Network dialog box appears.

4. Type the password you've been given for the network.

5. Click OK. The connection is made and you're ready to surf!

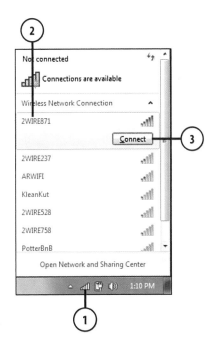

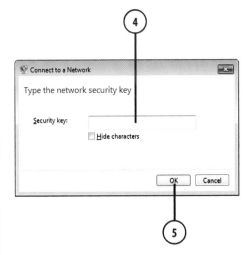

Checking Network Status

You can use the Network and Sharing Center to check the status of your network and make sure everything is working properly. Here's how to see what your connection looks like and check the connection of other computers to your home network.

1. Click Start, click in the search box, and type **network and sharing**.

2. Click Network and Sharing Center.

3. Review your network status. Clear lines indicate that you are connected to your network and to the Internet.

4. View all the computers added to your network by clicking See Full Map.

5. The unbroken lines show your wired connections.

6. The broken lines indicate your wireless connections. Close the window when you're done looking at this information.

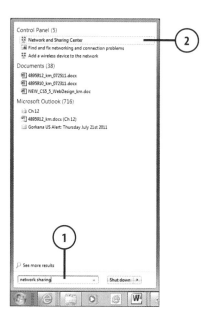

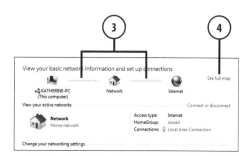

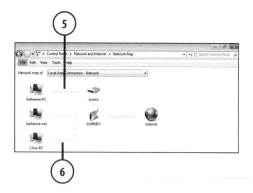

A MULTIWINDOWS NETWORK

As you learn in the next section, if all the computers on your home network use Windows 7, you can create a HomeGroup to share files, music, videos, and more. That's the easiest way to set up file and printer sharing in Windows 7.

But HomeGroups aren't available if you have a variety of computers running a variety of Windows operating systems. For example, if you have one computer running Windows XP, one running Windows Vista, and one running Windows 7, you need to create a workgroup so your computers can all find and access each other on the network.

To find the workgroup name on your computers, click Start and right-click Computer (or My Computer in Windows XP). Click Properties, click the Computer Name tab, and click Change to change the workgroup name. Make sure that all your computers have the same workgroup name.

Next, make sure that you have the same type of network set up in Windows 7 and Windows Vista. The correct setting for your home network is Home (surprise, surprise). Adjust password protection as needed, and, when all is said and done, you should be able to see and access the other computers in the Network area of Windows Explorer.

Getting Started with a HomeGroup

When you have your home network set up, you can create a HomeGroup to take care of everything else. A HomeGroup makes it easy for you to share music, media, and other libraries on your Windows 7 PC with other computers in your home. This means someone using the living room PC can watch a video clip that is on your computer in your office upstairs; your Xbox can play music and slide shows from another computer; and you can share printers and other resources that you set up as part of your HomeGroup.

Creating and Setting Up a HomeGroup

Creating a HomeGroup is a simple matter of opening your Network and
Sharing Center and seeing what Windows 7 has already created for you! Yes,
it's really that easy. By default, Windows 7 sets up a new HomeGroup automatically for your home network. You can then go to the other computers in
your home and add them (which is covered in the next section, "Joining a
HomeGroup"). To view the HomeGroup that Windows 7 has already set up,
follow these steps.

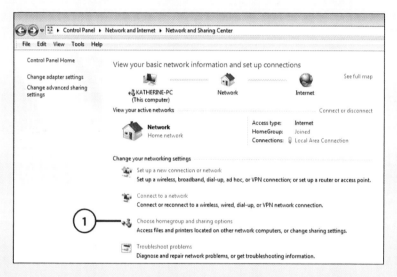

1. In the Network and Sharing Center, click Choose HomeGroup and
    Sharing Options.

2. In the Change HomeGroup Settings window, click the check boxes of any
    libraries and printers you want to share.

3. Choose whether you want to stream media on your home network.

4. Click View or Print the HomeGroup Password.

5. Review or write down the password. By default, Windows 7 assigns this
    password to your HomeGroup, and you use this password to add other
    computers to your HomeGroup.

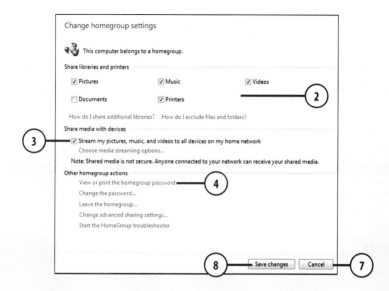

6. Alternatively, click Print This Page to print a copy of the password. Click Print in the Print dialog box.

7. Click Cancel.

8. Click Save Changes.

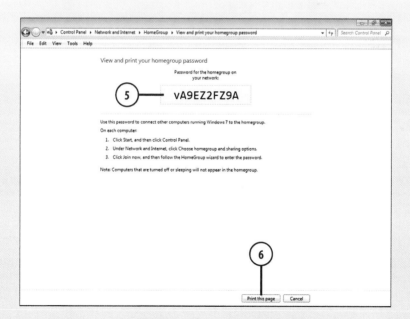

It's Not All Good

HomeGroup is a feature that is available only to Windows 7, which may not seem like a big deal because you obviously have a Windows 7 PC—or you wouldn't be reading this book. The challenge comes when you consider the other computers you may have in your house. If you have a Windows Vista system, a Windows XP system, and maybe a Mac, those computers aren't able to join your HomeGroup because it's for Windows 7 machines only.

Only computers running Windows 7 Home Premium or higher versions can create and manage HomeGroups. If you are using Windows 7 Starter or Windows Home Basic, you can still *join* a HomeGroup that somebody else creates.

New Files in Shared Libraries

When you indicate the libraries you want to share, this means that all files—present and future—that are part of those libraries will be shared. So if you add files to the libraries later, others in your HomeGroup will also be able to access those new files.

Joining a HomeGroup

After you set up the HomeGroup that has been created on your home network, you can easily add other computers to the group. You need the password you noted or printed in the preceding section as you set up the other computers on the HomeGroup. Use the following steps to add your other computers to your HomeGroup:

1. In the Network and Sharing Center of the other computer, click Choose HomeGroup and Sharing Options. The Share with Other Home Computers Running Windows 7 window appears.

2. Click the Join Now button.

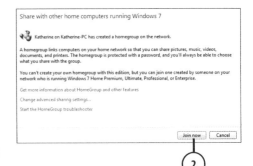

3. Click the check boxes of items you want to share with other computers in your HomeGroup or clear the check boxes of items you don't want to share.

4. Click Next.

5. Type the password you wrote down or printed when you set the options for the original HomeGroup computer.

6. Click Next. Windows 7 lets you know that you have joined the HomeGroup. Click Finish to complete the process.

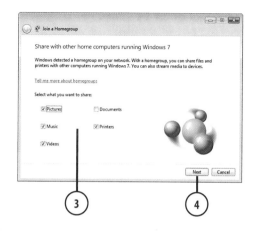

Synchronize Your Watches

Because all computers in a HomeGroup must have synchronized clocks, make sure that all your computers are set to use Internet time so you can be sure the time is accurate. You can set the time to Internet time by clicking Date and Time in the Control Panel and clicking the Internet Time tab, choosing the necessary option, and clicking OK.

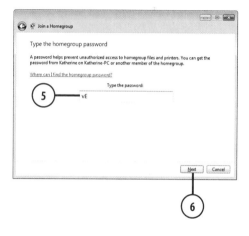

UNIQUELY NAMED

Another item that can get in the way of joining a HomeGroup is duplicate names. If you have a primary computer that you named one way (for example, my PC is Katherine-PC), be sure to give other computers on your network unique names. Don't name your netbook Katherine-PC, for example, or when Windows 7 goes to join the HomeGroup, a conflict will occur and you won't be able to join.

To rename your computer, click Start, right-click Computer on the right side of the Start menu, and click Change Settings in the Computer Name, Domain, and Workgroups Settings area. In the System Properties dialog box, click the Change button and type a new name for your computer in the Computer Name box. Click OK twice, and Windows 7 prompts you that the system needs to be restarted before the name change will take effect.

Using Your HomeGroup

When you get all the computers in your house set up in the HomeGroup, you can easily find, access, work with, and share music, pictures, videos, and documents. The actual content you can access depends on what each user chooses to share when setting up or joining the workgroup, however. If one user decides not to share her music, for example, the other computers in the HomeGroup aren't able to access the music on that particular PC.

Viewing Your HomeGroup

You can easily access the various computers in your HomeGroup by using Windows Explorer. The HomeGroup appears in the navigation pane on the left side of the screen, just below your libraries.

1. Click the Windows Explorer icon in the taskbar. Windows Explorer launches.

2. Click HomeGroup in the left pane.
    The computers in your HomeGroup
    appear in the Details pane.

Visible HomeGroup Computers

Note that the HomeGroup computers you
can see when you're viewing the
HomeGroup in Windows Explorer do not
include the one you're using. Instead,
Windows Explorer shows you the *other*
HomeGroup computers on your network.
This enables you to view and choose files
on those computers through the Home-
Group, while still accessing the files on
your own computer using the traditional
route—clicking your own Documents,
Music, Pictures, or Videos libraries.

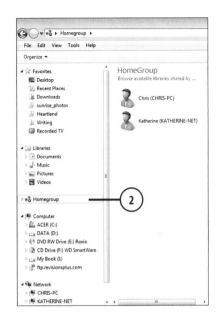

Accessing Files on Shared Computers

Now that you know how to view and
navigate the folders on other computers
in your HomeGroup, accessing the files is
a simple matter—and most likely, one
you've done dozens (if not hundreds!) of
times already.

1. In Windows Explorer, click
    HomeGroup in the left pane.

2. Click the library you want to view.

3. Click the arrow of the folder and
    subfolders.

4. In the Details pane, click the file
    you want to view or play.

5. Click the tool in the toolbar at the
    top of the Windows Explorer win-
    dow that matches the action
    you'd like to take.

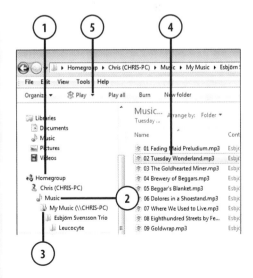

Changing Your Mind About Sharing

If you decide after the fact that you would rather not share some of the libraries you've shared with your HomeGroup, you can turn off sharing of those folders. Click Start, click in the search text box, and type **homegroup**. Click the HomeGroup choice that appears in the results list. This takes you to the Change HomeGroup Settings window, where you can remove the folders you don't want to share by clicking the box to remove the check mark. After you make your changes, click Save Changes.

SHARING A PRINTER ON THE HOMEGROUP

Go Further

If you have a wireless printer, you are now able to print from any computer in your HomeGroup. If you are using a traditional printer connected to one of the computers by a printer cable, all is not lost.

You can still log in to the computer the printer is attached to, access the document using the HomeGroup shared files, and print from the computer with printer access. Neat, huh?

Getting regular updates, running troubleshooters as needed, and using System Tools to clean up your hard drive are good practices for a healthy PC.

Choose how you want Windows 7 to download and install updates.

Remove files you no longer need.

Clean up your hard disk so programs run more efficiently.

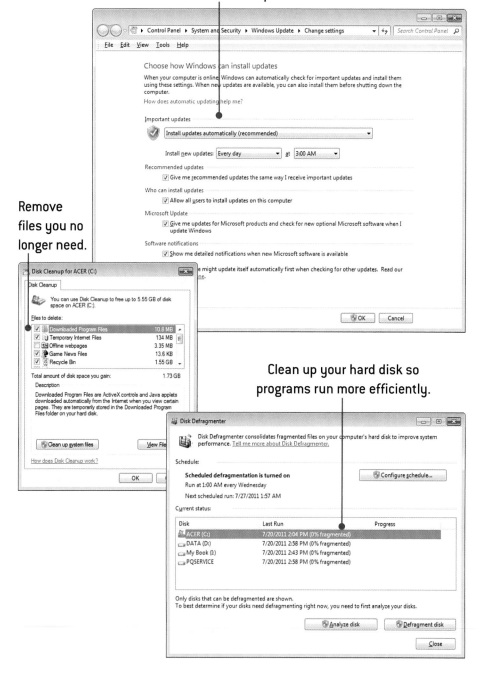

In this chapter, you learn how to care for your Windows 7 PC and troubleshoot problems when they arise by learning about these tasks:

→ Upgrading Windows 7
→ Backing up and restoring your files
→ Using System Tools
→ Solving compatibility issues with Windows 7

Windows 7 Care, Feeding, and Troubleshooting

Taking care of your Windows 7 PC is a fairly simple matter, but like everything else in life, it needs a bit of your attention on a regular basis. One regular maintenance task—which Windows 7 can do automatically for you when you set it up—is check periodically for Windows Updates. Another thing you can do is back up your files to make sure you have saved copies of everything that's important to you.

Beyond the regular maintenance, you can give your PC periodic checkups using the various tools in the Windows 7 System Tools folder. And if you ever really get into trouble, you can use one of the many troubleshooters in Windows 7 to save the day.

Updating Windows 7

One of the most important things you can do for your Windows 7 PC is sign up for automatic updates with Windows 7. Updates can provide new security features, bug fixes, and more, so they are important for keeping your computer as up to date as possible. You can choose how you want Windows 7 to check for and install any available program updates. When you let your computer update automatically, it downloads any new updates and installs them at a time you set, preferably when you're away from your computer and don't need it.

Turning On Automatic Updates

Your first step in setting up automatic updates involves telling Windows 7 how you want to handle the checking-and-installing process. You can have Windows 7 do everything for you automatically at the time you specify, or you can have it let you know when updates are available so that you can download and install them when you choose.

1. Click Start and click in the Search box and type **automatic updates**.

2. Click Turn Automatic Updating On or Off.

3. Click the Important Updates arrow and click the setting of your choice. Install Updates Automatically is selected by default; this causes Windows 7 to download and install all updates without any action from you. Your other choices are Download Updates but Let Me Choose Whether to Install Them, Check for Updates but Let Me Choose Whether to Download and Install Them, and Never Check for Updates.

4. Click the arrows to choose when you want Windows 7 to check for updates (providing you selected one of the automatic features in step 3).

5. Click to clear the Recommended Updates check box if you want to limit the updates you receive to only those that are considered important for the functioning of the software or your PC security.

6. Click to clear the Allow All Users to Install Updates on This Computer check box if you want to limit who is able to install updates on your computer (for example, if you want to do it all yourself, click the check box).

7. Click to clear the Give Me Updates for Microsoft Products… check box if you don't want to receive updates for other Microsoft products and check for new software when your updates are downloaded.

8. Click to clear the Show Me Detailed Notifications… check box if you would rather not receive notifications about new Microsoft software.

9. Click OK to save your changes.

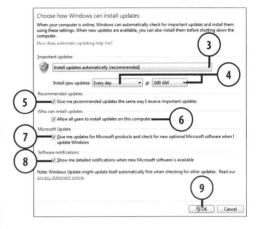

Best-Practice Updating

Microsoft recommends that you set your update schedule so that you're receiving updates at least once every week. When important updates are released, they typically arrive on the second or fourth Tuesday of the month. There are intermittent releases, however, so checking more frequently than every two weeks is a good idea.

Checking for Updates Manually

You can also check manually for updates instead of relying solely on the automatic updating system. You might do this, for example, when you have heard that there's a new patch available for a specific feature or you have been waiting for a coming upgrade that will impact some features you care about in Windows 7.

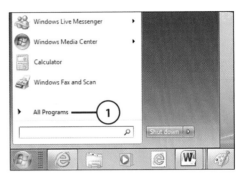

1. Click Start and click All Programs.

2. Click Windows Update in the All Programs list.

3. Click Check for Updates in the left panel of the Windows Update window. Windows 7 displays a Checking for Updates status box while checks are being performed. Any updates that are found then appear in the Windows Update window.

4. Click Install Updates to update your version of Windows 7.

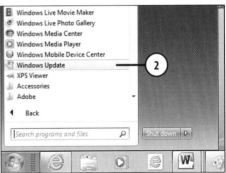

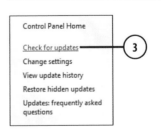

REVIEWING UPDATE HISTORY

If you're wondering what kinds of updates Windows 7 has *already* performed without your knowledge, you can check out the update history to see the full list. In the Windows Update window, click View Update History. A large list of updates appears, and you can get more information about individual updates that were performed by double-clicking the update name.

When you finish reviewing updates, click OK to close the Review Your Update History window.

Backing Up and Restoring Your Files

You might already be making copies of important files and tucking them away someplace safe—like copying them to an external hard disk, burning them to DVD, or saving them on a flash drive. If not, you should be. Making regular backups of your files helps you feel secure knowing that your files are protected and that you have an extra copy, just in case something happens. You can make these simple file backups yourself by using Windows Explorer to copy the files to the folder or device where you want to store the backup files.

Windows 7 also provides a backup utility you can use to back up everything on your hard disk. You should do this larger backup regularly—once every month or so. This ensures that your files have been saved so that if something unexpected happens to your computer—for example, you wind up with a virus that damages important files—you can restore the files from your backup and go on as usual.

Backing Up Your Files

The first step in backing up your files involves setting up the backup utility. When you do this, you tell Windows 7 where you want to save the backup files and when you want to do the backup. You can change those settings at any time, of course; but Windows 7 will take care of the backup for you automatically from here on out on the day and time you specify.

1. Click Start and type Backup in the search box.

2. Click Backup and Restore.

3. In the Back Up or Restore Your Files window, click Set Up Backup.

4. In the Set Up Backup dialog box, click the drive or device where you want to save your backup.

5. Click Save On a Network if you want to back up your computer to another folder on your network.

6. Click Next.

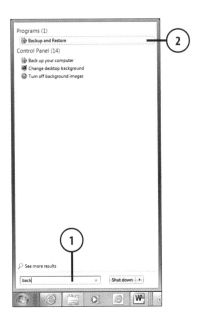

Accepting Recommendations

Windows 7 will let you know which destination is the recommended one for your backup, and in most cases that's the way to go. Windows 7 looks for the spot with the most space, and the fact that the backup location is external to your current hard drive is key. You wouldn't want to create a backup on your same hard drive, for example, and then experience your hard drive failing (heaven forbid!). Then, you would lose your files *and* your backups at once. Better to save your backup to a place that is outside your everyday hard disk, like an external drive or another device.

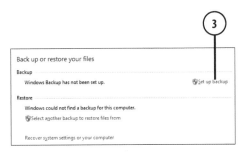

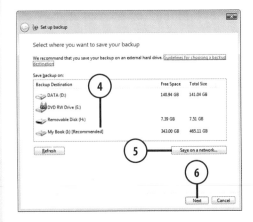

7. In the What Do You Want to Back Up? Window, choose whether you want Windows 7 to choose the files to be backed up for you, or you want to choose the files yourself. In most cases, leaving the default selection is best.

8. Click Next.

9. Review your backup settings.

10. Click Change Schedule to choose when Windows 7 runs the backup utility.

11. Click the How Often, What Day, and What Time arrows and choose the frequency, day, and time you want the backup to be completed.

Scheduling Backups

When you click Change Schedule in the Set Up Backup dialog box, the Run Backup on a Schedule checkbox should automatically be checked. If not, click it so that the checkmark appears. This tells Windows 7 that you want an automatic backup to be performed regularly, and the backup will be done according to the schedule you set in the How Often Do You Want to Back Up? window.

12. Click OK.

13. Back in the Set Up Backup dialog box, click Save Settings and Run Backup. Windows 7 displays the Back Up or Restore Your Files window and shows you that the backup is in progress.

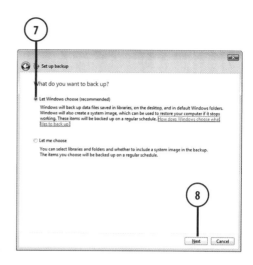

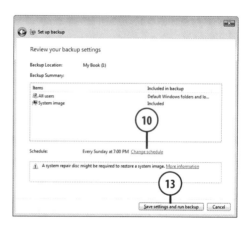

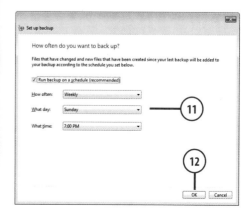

Backing Up...Impatiently

If you are curious about what's taking so long to complete your backup or you're just wondering what's being included in the backup process, click View Details in the Back Up or Restore Your Files window, and a Windows Backup dialog box appears, showing you the status of the backup and listing the files that are being copied. Be sure when you close this dialog box to click the Close box and not the Stop Backup button, unless you really want to cancel the backup mid-stream.

Restoring Files

It might happen that at some point you need to restore the files you've saved in a backup. Perhaps you accidentally deleted an important folder. Or maybe you had a computer problem and had to clean off your files, and now you're ready to put the files back. Whatever the situation, Windows 7 can easily restore your most recently backed-up files.

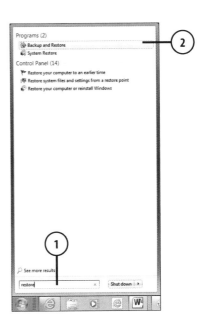

1. Click Start and type *restore* in the search box.

2. Click Backup and Restore. The Back Up or Restore Your Files window appears.

3. Click Restore My Files.

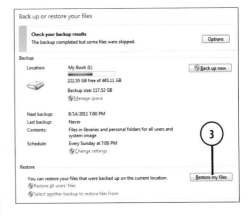

4. In the Restore Files dialog box, click Search if you want to locate specific files to restore; Browse for Files if you want to select multiple files; or Browse for Folders if you want to restore entire folders.

5. In the Browse the Backup for Folders or Drives dialog box, navigate to the folder or files you want to restore.

6. Click the button to add the folder or files. If you clicked Browse for Folders in step 4, the button you click will be named Add Folder. If you selected Browse for Files, the button will say Add Files.

7. After you add the files or folders, they appear in the list in the Restore Files dialog box. Click Next.

8. Restore Files asks where you want to restore the files, and if you want the files to be placed in their original location, leave the first option selected. You can click In the Following Location and click Browse to choose the folder where you want to store the files if you have rearranged your folders or want to store the files in a new location so that you can compare their contents.

9. Click Restore. Windows 7 restores the files. If you have copies of the files in the original location, the Copy File dialog box will prompt you to choose whether you want to copy and replace the files, skip the copy operation, or copy, but keep both files. Click your choice and the restore continues.

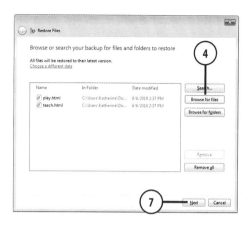

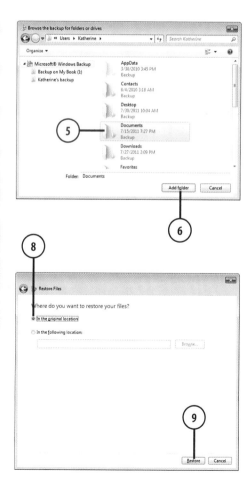

10. The final window tells you that your files have been restored and you can now click Finish to complete the operation.

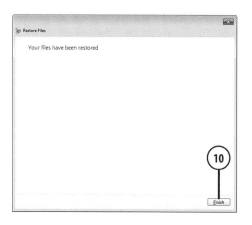

Searching for Files to Restore
If you click Search in the Restore Files dialog box, the Search for Files to Restore dialog box opens so that you can enter a portion of a filename or folder name and then click Search. Windows 7 displays all the files and folders that match your criteria in the results box, and you can click the files or folders you want to restore and click OK.

Using System Tools

Windows 7 System Tools folder—available in the Accessories folder in the All Programs list—contains two special utilities that can help you clean up your hard disk and make sure it is running as efficiently as possible: Disk Cleanup and Disk Defragmenter.

Disk Cleanup

Disk Cleanup is a utility first made available for Windows XP, and it can help speed up your computer by finding and deleting files you no longer need. Don't worry—these aren't application files like the letter to Aunt Martha you're not quite finished writing; these are files like temporary Internet files, leftover files from programs you downloaded and don't need anymore, files in your Recycling Bin, and so on. When you start Disk Cleanup, the utility scans the drive you specify and then reports back, suggesting items for deletion. You can always opt out and decide *not* to delete the files Windows 7 suggests, but using Disk Cleanup once in a while can help you keep your computer as clean as possible.

1. Click Start, All Programs, and click the Accessories folder.

2. Click the System Tools folder.

3. Click Disk Cleanup. The Disk Cleanup dialog box appears.

4. Click the arrow and choose the disk or device you want Disk Cleanup to check.

5. Click OK to begin checking your disk. The Disk Cleanup message box appears, showing you the status of the check. You can stop the process at any time by clicking Cancel.

6. In the Disk Cleanup dialog box, enable the check box of any files you want to delete. Clicking an item displays a description of the files in the center of the dialog box so that you can easily see what you're deleting.

7. You can view the files, if you like, before deleting them by clicking the View Files button.

8. If you want Disk Cleanup to also take a look at your Windows 7 system files and determine whether any unnecessary files can be deleted there, click Clean Up System Files.

9. Click OK to delete the selected files.

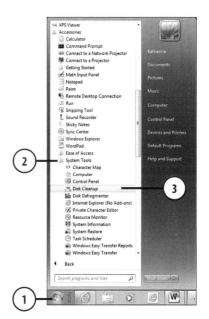

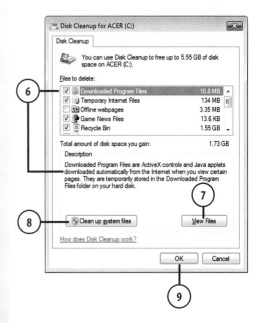

Disk Defragmenter

During the normal course of opening, modifying, and saving files, your computer saves new information in different places on your hard drive. When you look at the folders in Windows Explorer, everything looks nice and neat, a kind of sequential line-up of your files. But the way your computer is actually storing the data isn't quite that linear. Oh, the computer knows where everything is, but over time, bits and pieces of files can be saved in various places all over the drive. And to present the file to you as a complete whole so you can work with it as usual, your computer has to do some behind-the-scenes processing. The Disk Defragmenter utility can clean up your hard drive by consolidating those bits of files and putting them back together in one place again.

Disk Defragmenter might already be turned on for your Windows 7 PC, but it's a good idea to know where to find the tool so that you can run it yourself if need be (or you can turn on the feature if it's not already enabled.) Disk Defragmenter can free up some additional space on your hard drive and also increase the processing speed of your computer because there won't be so much knitting-together going on as you open, work on, and close files.

1. Display the System Tools folder as discussed in the "Disk Cleanup" section and click Disk Defragmenter. The Disk Defragmenter dialog box appears.

2. Click the disk you want to defragment.

3. Click Analyze Disk. This process
   tells you whether the selected
   disk needs to be defragmented.

4. Click Defragment Disk to start the
   operation.

5. After the process is finished, click
   Close.

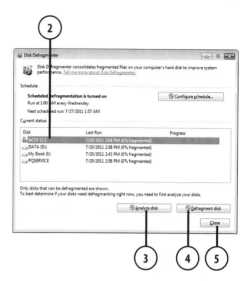

SCHEDULING REGULAR DEFRAGMENTING

You can put your PC on a steady defrag diet by having the system automatically defragment your hard drive at a specific time of the week or month.
Click Configure Schedule in the Disk Defragmenter dialog box. In the Disk
Defragmenter: Modify Schedule dialog box, click the Run on a Schedule
check box and click the Frequency, Day, Time, and Disks arrows to make
your choices. Click OK to save your settings, and Disk Defragmenter will run
automatically on the day and time you specified to keep your files as com-
pact as possible.

Compatibility with Windows 7

Sure, *you* have a Windows 7 PC, but chances are you need to trade files and
perhaps work with programs that were created long before Windows 7 came
on the scene. A number of users face challenges in using software and hardware that weren't made to work with Windows 7. How can you get the programs and hardware working together to complete the tasks you need to get
done? This section offers some resources that can help you resolve compatibility issues.

Using the Windows Compatibility Center

Microsoft recognizes that helping users know how to use their computers and programs together—no matter which Windows version they may be using—is an important part of supporting its product. For that reason, Microsoft has created the Windows Compatibility Center, which offers a wide range of software and hardware you can check for compatibility with Windows 7.

1. Click the Internet Explorer icon in the taskbar.

2. Click in One Box and type **Windows 7 Compatibility Center**. In the search results that appear, click the first link, Windows 7 Compatibility Center.

Click to see compatible hardware.

Click to use the Windows Upgrade Advisor, which helps you determine when to upgrade your version of Windows 7.

Click to view other Windows products.

3. In the Software tab, click the area in which you'd like to find a program compatible with Windows 7.

What's the Windows Upgrade Advisor?

Windows Upgrade Advisor was originally designed to help users who were considering upgrading to Windows 7 determine whether their system was compatible with the new operating system. If you already have Windows 7, you can run the advisor to see which upgrade might best fit your computer—for example, upgrading from Home Basic to Home Premium will offer you additional features, as will upgrading from Windows 7 Professional to Windows 7 Ultimate.

Using Older Programs with Windows 7

Not all older programs work well in Windows 7. Most of these programs—sometimes called *legacy* programs—run without a hitch, but others may function incorrectly or hang up completely. If you're having trouble with an older program, you can run the Windows 7 Program Compatibility troubleshooter to try to fix whatever's causing the problem.

1. Right-click the icon of the program you want to check.

2. Click Troubleshoot Compatibility. The Program Compatibility dialog box shows you the status of the check.

3. Click Try Recommended Settings to run the program with the settings Windows 7 suggests for it.

4. Test the new settings for the program by clicking Start the Program. Work with the program by opening menus and trying a few common practices to see whether it is working properly. Close the program.

5. Back in the Program Compatibility dialog box, click Next.

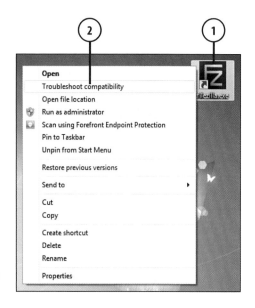

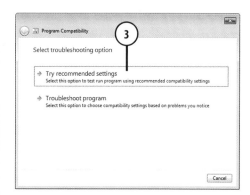

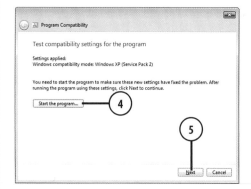

6. In the final screen of the troubleshooter, Windows 7 asks you whether the problem is fixed. Click Yes to save the new settings; No to try again; or No to report the problem to Microsoft.

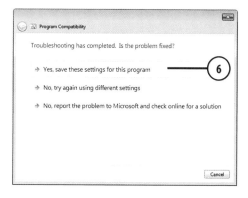

WINDOWS ONLINE TROUBLESHOOTING SERVICE

>>> Go Further

Windows 7 includes a number of troubleshooters you can use to resolve issues you may be having with your PC or software. You can find out more about the different troubleshooters available by clicking Start and typing **troubleshooting** in the search box. Click Troubleshooting, and the Troubleshooting Computer Problems window appears.

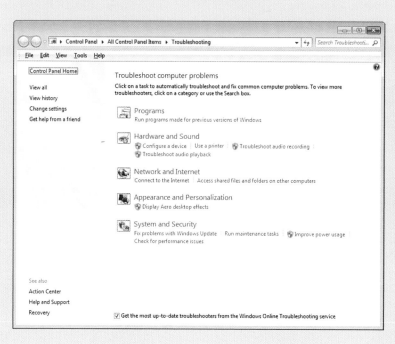

You can find troubleshooters similar to the one in this section that help you sleuth out problems with programs, hardware, sound, your network, your Internet connection, the appearance of Windows 7, your personalized settings, and your Windows 7 PC system and security.

What's more, you can go online to find further help, request help from a friend, or see a history of troubleshooters you've used in the past. Help is only a click away—thank goodness—in Windows 7.

Index

A

X-Y-Z

My Microsoft® Windows® 7 PC

Katherine Murray

FREE Online Edition

Your purchase of **My Microsoft® Windows® 7 PC** includes access to a free online edition for 45 days through the Safari Books Online subscription service. Nearly every Que book is available online through Safari Books Online, along with more than 5,000 other technical books and videos from publishers such as Addison-Wesley Professional, Cisco Press, Exam Cram, IBM Press, O'Reilly, Prentice Hall, and Sams.

SAFARI BOOKS ONLINE allows you to search for a specific answer, cut and paste code, download chapters, and stay current with emerging technologies.

Activate your FREE Online Edition at www.informit.com/safarifree

> **STEP 1:** Enter the coupon code: WBKBOVH.

> **STEP 2:** New Safari users, complete the brief registration form.
> Safari subscribers, just log in.

If you have difficulty registering on Safari or accessing the online edition, please e-mail customer-service@safaribooksonline.com